You can't botox your ass

You can't botox your ass

Divorce and Hell to Wild and Free

EMMA RIVERS

Paperback ISBN 978-0-473-50737-4 Amazon edition
Published by New Horizons 2019 Limited

Also available on Amazon as Kindle ebook ISBN 978-0-473-45941-3

Although based on actual events, the names and physical descriptions of all characters, companies, institutions, professionals, dates, and locations have been changed to protect the anonymity of the individuals and entities concerned.

Thank you to all copyright holders for permission to include their work as quotations and poems. Every effort has been made to contact the copyright holders with respect to seeking approval to feature their work. If we have been unable to contact you, please accept our apologies and get in touch.

All poems not credited in the text have been written by the author.

Contact: info@emmarivers.world

Emma Rivers
www.emmarivers.world
Instagram: emmarivers1971
www.facebook.com/EmmaRivers1971

Cover Artwork
Free Me by Emma Rivers

For love

and the
bravest of
souls are
those who
choose love
over and over

e corona

Contents

Prologue

'Oh, Jesus,' I hissed, as my quads and glutes strained under the weight of the 120-kilogram leg press. With teeth clenched, my razor eyes were fixed, glaring straight ahead. My reddened face grimaced in pain. Sweat glistened and poured from my tiny frame.

'Come on, Emms. Give me three more,' Courtney smirked and casually leaned against a weight machine within arm's reach of me. Courtney was my professional bikini bodybuilding coach. I wanted to smack that bitch.

She took me through the weight training programme she had devised. By the end of our session, I struggled to walk. Still, I wasn't complaining. I was thriving on the challenges of the sport and the insight into Courtney's world. I had also made a new friend. 'You've got this, Emms,' she said.

I didn't always work out with Courtney – most of my training was done at the local gym out west on the outskirts of Auckland. With earplugs in and Spotify on, I pumped weights on my own and escaped this world. My mind wandered with the rhythm of the music. I considered the demise of my marriage and where my life was heading.

I had worked honestly and ethically to get to where I was with my businesses. I threw the same level of commitment into my marriage. I was faithful to my husband for the near-ten years we had been together and yet, in mid-2012, I felt the cruel, vice-like crush of betrayal.

Divorce was, and is, a cold, bleak, dark empty cesspit called hell. When my husband left me, I felt blinded. Frozen in fear. I had no idea what day it was, let alone which direction to turn. The very person who was supposed to love and support me had deceived me in the worst imaginable way. Within a heartbeat, I was taken from a position of security to abandonment and confusion. My businesses had been dissolved, and I had the responsibility of raising a preschool child on my own. Poverty was a confronting and very real possibility for me. I could feel myself teetering on a precipice as my marriage, and my life's work, lay in ruins at the bottom of a cliff.

In the weights room, as I struggled with glute cable kickbacks and smith machine sumo squats, my mind threw me back to the early months of 2012. I was no "Stepford Wife", and yet I was fulfilling the defined role of wife and mother. I gently hustled for my own independence within the confines of marriage.

At the time, I was under the illusion my life was loosely mapped out. Our three-year-old daughter was delightful, my husband Tim was successful, and we lived in a beautiful home. I owned several businesses, was self-made and proud of it. My family was fit and healthy and we travelled internationally for business and pleasure. I had wonderful supportive friends. To anyone looking in from the outside, I appeared to have it all.

And then, with almost no warning, Tim accepted a position working as Head of Securities for an investment bank in Sydney. He left New Zealand to commence his new job within a matter of weeks. I was instructed to stay behind with our daughter to facilitate the sale of our properties and to dissolve my businesses. Bella and I would be free to join him in Sydney after that. We were all to start a new life together there, as a family.

I was somewhat alarmed with his bold announcement; he had accepted the position in Australia without consulting me. He left me no choice but to fall in line with his demands. What other option was there? Stay in New Zealand and get a divorce?

I lacked the strength and conviction to confront him. Instead, I remember ruminating over my options at the time, thinking perhaps I was ready for a change. Never before had I imagined relinquishing my self-determination and financial independence to become a full-time mother. I channelled my thoughts to make the best of the situation and convinced myself I was looking forward to the change.

And yet I felt uneasy. Something just didn't feel right.

Lingering chest infections and asthma plagued me. My husband's barbaric verbal jibes had escalated over the preceding couple of years to full-blown verbal and emotional abuse. Random outbursts of anger and demonic screaming from him became the norm. I remembered the sharp pain in my back as he pushed me into walls and door frames. I became compliant for fear of being punched in the face.

In January 2012, we consulted our family doctor over his abusive behaviour. I thought he may have been depressed, but she didn't share my view. My husband was an angry man, and I had no idea what he was angry about.

Once he left for Australia and abandoned our marriage and our daughter, the veil of Tim's duplicitous double life was lifted. Our lives were changed forever.

It took me considerable time to realise the enormity of his deception and to process my initial shock and trauma. I had no choice but to rediscover who I was as a solo parent. Could I find the strength to adapt to a world that had evolved and transformed while I had been isolated within the confines of my marriage?

In July 2012, Tim threatened me with court action. When it became apparent he was intent on taking all our combined wealth with him to Australia, I had to make a decision. Would I settle for my life in ruins? Or would I fight for the future our daughter Bella and I had earned and deserved?

I chose to fight.

With the realisation that our future was dependent on my ability to keep my mind and body in balance, I formulated a survival plan which focused on health, fitness, fun and well-being. Physical fitness would prevent a physical and/or mental breakdown. I had to keep my head clear to work tirelessly, to formulate strategy, and to make the best decisions I could, despite my vulnerability and paralysing self-doubt.

Through the winter of 2015, I was fixated on a goal, a very big goal. I had entered a bodybuilding competition. What the hell was I doing? I had never lifted a weight before mid-April that year. Suddenly, I had precisely four months to build as much muscle and drain as much fat from my already minuscule frame as I could. Whether I was ready or not, I would be competing at the Auckland Regional Champs in August 2015. As I was over 44 years of age at the time, in the minds of some people, I was an idiot.

Listening to gritty rock ballads and artsy pop as I pumped iron on the weights room floor allowed me to escape my nightmarish hell. I licked sweat from my thirsty lips. The sweat stung my eyes and made me squint. I took deep breaths and exhaled as my body bore the full load of the machines. My muscles rippled with satisfaction and ached with fatigue as I struggled to complete my training programme. Three lots of ten reps of 120 kilograms on the leg press was a lot for a woman weighing in at 56 kilograms. I was giving it everything I had.

For four months from mid-April 2015, I spent three hours every day training at my local gym and loved every second of it. As I thrashed out kilometre after kilometre on the treadmill, I relaxed to the beat of my own feet. My brisk, daily 10-kilometre walk became a meditation. I was in my happy place, escaping the chaos circling around me. I was gently resting in the eye of a tornado.

I daydreamed in the weights room of the gym as I soldiered on with daily routines of lateral pulldowns, bicep curls, tricep dips, and cable rows. I reflected on some of the men I had recently spent time with: the Builder, the Gangster, and the Player. I smiled as I recognised how these men had distracted me from my pain and reignited my sexual desires – they had brought me back to life.

I was conscious of the life I led on two levels – the confident and capable woman named Emma, who carried herself with ease in public, versus the subservient and often anxious woman who hid her insecurities behind closed doors. A lifetime of shame and fear had shackled me, despite my talents and success. It was time to peel back the layers of hurt and grief. I needed to confront my past, for my past had created my present. This was *my* chance to change *my* future.

PART ONE

CATASTROPHE AND BEWILDERMENT

one

Success is a mindset

Grit *(n.)* courage and resolve; strength of character.

Success is a mindset, a way of looking at situations. Do we see doors that close? Or do we see doors as openings and opportunities for change? Do closing doors signal defeat? Or do we need a change of approach to find new doors or new means of opening the very doors that have slammed shut in our face? It is up to us to decide how much we want something. Do we possess enough grit to see a task through to the end? What are we prepared to do to achieve our goals?

I pursued a career in a highly competitive industry, realising from the beginning that if I wanted to be fulfilled and to reach my financial goals, I had to be firm and dogged in my resolve to carry on. Whatever hurdle I came across, I vowed I would deal with it and learn from my experiences, good and bad.

I worked as an architect for twenty years, and owned and operated retail stores for eighteen. The importing and distribution company I launched in 2002 from my kitchen table now supplies in excess of 130 retail stores across New Zealand with homeware and gift lines.

Completing my work to a high standard is something I have always striven to achieve. The architectural projects I have been involved with have been acknowledged at both national and international levels. I am proud to have clients who are consistently delighted with my work, and many of them have become dear friends.

I woke each day with excitement for the tasks I was due to undertake, and, for the most part, I was content with my life.

I work in the industry I have chosen because of the passion I have for art and design. I have applied my artistic skills to make a living; nothing more than that.

The architectural and retail industry may seem frivolous and materialistic; however my chosen vocation does not make me a frivolous or materialistic person. I understand the importance of placing value on people over possessions.

I grew up in a family where the majority of individuals were self-employed. I was taught from a young age if you want to achieve in life, you must think and act honestly and ethically – not just once or twice, but every day. Always work hard and always try your best. I was taught to learn to love the word *no*, because over time a *no* will usually turn into a *yes*. If you never hear *no*, you will never hear *yes* either.

My first start-up business flourished when I was fifteen years of age. I made greeting cards and potpourri which I sold to florists and gift shops all over Christchurch. The drive I developed came from my desire to create beautiful objects. Selling my wares and making money was a challenge and a necessity; I needed to fund future projects. I wondered who would want to buy my treasures. Could I make some money? Then it was how much money could I make? Could I scale my home enterprise and make more money? It was all a bit of a game. Without even realising it, I was developing grit, which was founded on passion and the thrill of the chase.

I spent four years at university as a full-time student. Outside of my study I played interclub and representative tennis through the summer and was a regular gymgoer throughout the year. I had a busy social life and also managed to hold down several part-time jobs.

Through my fourth and final year at university I started a business hand painting terracotta pots. I sold thousands of pots to retail stores all over New Zealand. At the completion of my study, I had built up some useful sales skills and stashed a small nest egg in the bank. I had no debt, and I had been on many mini-adventures across New Zealand as I travelled to sell my wares to customers.

After graduating with a science degree and a postgraduate diploma in commerce, I worked for an international pharmaceutical company for a year. The job required constant travel and cold-call sales work to hardened professionals. The loneliness and harassment I endured had a detrimental effect on me. I lost respect for myself over my decision to quit my job. It was necessary, nonetheless. I was battling a raft of issues around that time, my job being only part of the equation. I had some family issues I was running away from, and I had broken up with my boyfriend of five years.

As a 23-year-old dealing with stress, I drowned my sorrows at the bottom of a beer bottle and a cocktail of other alcoholic beverages. I moved to Queenstown, took a number of part-time jobs, and lost myself to outrageously amazing sex with a blond, dreadlocked rafting guide named Steve. At the time, Steve blew my mind.

After six months in Queenstown, I packed my bags and headed for London to study architecture. I wanted to pursue a career that combined my passion for the arts with intellectual challenges. It was hard saying goodbye to Steve as he had been kind to me.

Living in London was a struggle for me. Money was tight, so I took on a female roommate to keep the rent to a minimum. I cleaned the shared bathroom for all four flats in the building. That saved me twenty pounds a week. I walked to work rather than pay for the tube and distinctly recall making a choice between buying a winter coat and buying food. My meagre earnings allowed for one, not both. I went hungry for two days but I was warm.

I had to work while I studied. I was constantly at war with my need to earn money to live, and with my need to allow enough time to complete assignments. I had one day off a week – always a Monday. Each Monday I immersed myself in the splendour of London culture and art; the vibe of the people, the architecture, the galleries, the monuments, and the history. Retail stores such as Harrods and Harvey Nichols fascinated me. I was captivated with the capability of exceptional interior design to transform space and influence buyer behaviour.

While all my New Zealand friends who worked in London took regular weekend breaks in Europe, I was unable to afford holidays. It bothered me a little to have to stand back and watch them enjoy themselves but not enough to change my behaviour. I wasn't about to sacrifice my dream. Day by day, I quietly worked towards my qualification as an architect. I would have my holidays later.

I took a few temp jobs when I first arrived in London. One position had its offices in St James's Street, Mayfair. I would exit the Green Park tube station and wander past The Ritz on my way to work. The infamous club, Quaglino's, was just down the road – I was taken there on dates a number of times.

Another temp placement was as receptionist at the bustling City of London office of a US-based multinational IT company. My role involved greeting businesspeople, receiving documents and parcels, and redirecting over a thousand telephone calls each day. I was required to remember the extensions of over one hundred key staff, and I was warned if I made a mistake, I ran the risk of instant dismissal.

One day a finely dressed young man wandered up to reception where my co-worker Lara and I sat. In his east-coast American accent, he politely introduced himself to me.

'Hello, Emma. My name is Ethan. I was wondering whether I might be able to …' he said as he was abruptly interrupted by a couple of couriers who ran between us and slapped several parcels down on the desk in front of me.

I stood and politely said in response, 'Oh, I'm sorry, Ethan. We're just a little busy here at the moment. If you don't mind, could you please take a seat and wait for a few minutes while I deal with these guys. I'll be free to speak to you soon.'

As I turned, I felt a sharp jab in my back from Lara's clenched fist. 'Emma, are you freaking crazy? Don't you realise who Ethan is?'

As I signed for the parcels I shrugged my shoulders. 'Ah, that would be a no, Lara. I don't know who Ethan is. He's just a guy who works upstairs, right?'

'No, Emma. Ethan's not just some dude from upstairs. He's the eldest son of the family who own this joint. As in the "whole joint", Emma. The "whole worldwide joint", Emma. Got it now? Jeez, you Kiwis!' Lara shook her head and laughed.

I dated Ethan for a few months. When he asked me to accompany him to one of his family's holiday homes in Costa Rica I nodded my head and politely said, 'Oh yes, thank you, Ethan, that sounds wonderful.' I had no idea where Costa Rica was.

Ethan lived in a superbly furnished stand-alone townhouse two blocks from Kensington High Street. Walking through his front door was like stepping into another world. His home was magnificent. He treated me to evenings out at exquisite restaurants and took me on some wonderful day trips to Stonehenge, Kew Gardens, Brighton, and Hampton Court Palace.

Despite his life of immense privilege, Ethan was a young man who struggled with his confidence and the expectations placed on him by his family.

As a woman, to live within elite, "monied" circles, you are generally either born into it or you marry into it. My education enabled me to hold my own in these circles, to a degree. Perhaps I was perceived as a novelty with my cute Kiwi accent. But something just didn't feel right in my relationship with Ethan. I couldn't see myself falling in love with him, so I ended it.

I never did get to Costa Rica, and to this day, I'm still not entirely sure where it is.

I was awarded a Distinction Pass at the architectural college. The awards ceremony was held at the Houses of Parliament on 5 November 1996. We ate canapés and sipped wine on the terrace overlooking the Thames. Barges floated past and let off fireworks to commemorate the anniversary of Guy Fawkes. One of the members of parliament took our small group of graduates on a guided tour of some of the buildings. We were shown through the Parliamentary Debating Chamber of the House of Commons. I gazed up to the rafters of Westminster Hall and saw where King Charles II had left Oliver Cromwell's head on a 20-foot spike to rot, as a deterrent to traitors. The significance of the evening was not lost on me.

I worked as an architectural drafting assistant for a company in the predominantly Jewish neighbourhood of Swiss Cottage during my last nine months in London. The company had some well-known clients, some of whom had connections to royalty.

London taught me a lot about myself. I got to see, first-hand, the extremes of vast wealth and the personal suffering of others. If there had ever been a chance that I would sacrifice my goals and dreams for a life of wealth as a kept woman, it would have happened in London. I had several opportunities to be with wealthy men, but I walked away from that life. I wanted self-determination – to live on my own terms. I always assumed I would find true love.

Towards the end of 1996, I travelled home to New Zealand for family reasons – my sole remaining grandparent, my Nana, was very ill.

In 1998 I ventured into sole practice as an architect and opened my first retail store selling homeware and gifts in October 2000. In 2002, I launched my importing business.

I met my future husband, Tim Rivers, in February 2003, and we were married within a year.

Later that year, Tim and I bought a two-storeyed, four-bedroom villa, set in one hectare in rural West Auckland. In 2007, we purchased an old flour mill (the Mill) and embarked on a nine-month renovation of the building. In September 2008, I opened my third retail store within the Mill.

Our daughter Isabella (Bella) was born in March 2008. I project-managed the renovation of the Mill and other architectural projects while I was pregnant with her.

Through 2005, 2006 and 2007 the collective annual turnover for my businesses was between $1.1 and $1.3 million per annum. I was able to achieve these levels of sales for three consecutive years. The economy was booming, and

I was blessed with youth and endless amounts of enthusiasm, creativity, and ambition. It was a busy and exhilarating time.

Between 2004 and 2008, Tim and I travelled to the United States, Fiji, Australia, Hong Kong and China, Tokyo, Sydney, France, Ireland, Rarotonga, and a few big domestic trips around New Zealand. My businesses paid for most of our travel.

The global financial crisis (GFC) of 2008 decimated the turnover of my businesses right at the time I opened my new shop in the Mill. In order to survive financially, I made immediate and sweeping changes to staffing levels and business overheads. I took on the role of National Sales Manager for my importing business, on top of running the retail store and the work I did as an architect. I was also a wife, and mother to our infant daughter. Being separated from Bella was difficult as I missed her.

People with business experience will be aware how challenging it is for a woman to forge a successful career as an entrepreneur. Running businesses was never easy, even when the economy was flourishing – let alone when the GFC hit with full effect.

I have seen bountiful years, and I have faced massive challenges. It is not in my nature to surrender to defeat. Rather, I will evaluate the situation, strategise, plan, and implement a path to move forward.

Tim told me he was moving to Australia to further his career in Sydney towards the end of February 2012. In mid-March, as I sat on our bed, Tim instructed me: 'I want you to sell our home, close down your businesses, close your retail store, and sell the Mill. I'm leaving for Sydney in two days. I don't want a long-distance relationship. If you and Bella are not in Sydney with me within six months, then I'll take it you don't want to be with me. We'll get divorced.'

The word *divorced* rolled off his tongue as though he had just asked me to run down to the corner store to buy some milk. All I could manage was to sit and stare at him in disbelief.

Despite the historical success of the businesses, Tim knew in the economic environment of 2012 that my businesses were worth very little. A sole practising architect cannot easily 'sell' their client base, and retail stores and importing businesses are sold with minimal goodwill. He knew the fastest way to access cash from the businesses was to liquidate them. I felt I was being forced into making the decision to close down my businesses. Tim had made his intentions clear; if I did not comply with his instructions and follow him to Sydney, he would divorce me.

I understood with the closure of the businesses, it would take considerable effort to re-establish myself in the future. A move to Sydney meant I would have no income, no independent financial means, no job, no networks of suppliers and customers, or prospective employers who knew me personally or professionally. I would have no friends, and no family around me.

Despite my silent concerns, I visited my wholesale customers across New Zealand and told them I was winding the businesses down. I advertised a closing-down sale at my shop. I told all my architecture clients, my suppliers, and customers that I was moving to Sydney.

I was being forced into choosing between my marriage and my financial independence.

I chose my marriage – for my child.

two

Timing is everything; being played

On the final day of my retail store closing down sale, Tim rang me. With no apparent reason, he screamed at me down the telephone. ‘Everything’s all about you. I came back from Australia to go to marriage counselling. I’ve tried to save our marriage but there’s no point. I’m sick of you. I want a divorce.’

It happened to be Sunday, 13 May 2012 – Mother’s Day. Once again, Tim had chosen to time the delivery of hurtful news to maximise the impact and injury his attack would bring.

I more or less glossed over his abusive behaviour while we were married, in an attempt to keep our relationship together. I thought he was depressed or frustrated with his job so I gave him space to diffuse. I didn’t see the point in challenging him and escalating the situation.

I was kind to Tim because I loved him. I was good to his friends and his family. I wasn’t ugly, lazy, depressed, or untidy. I took care of myself physically, I barely drank alcohol, and I didn’t take drugs. I didn’t gamble, and I hadn’t had an affair. I wasn’t a burden on him, financially or otherwise. It seemed being capable and loving my husband was not enough.

I had given Tim the best years of my life – my child-bearing years. As a woman, that is a big deal. I had always thought I would have more children. But when my husband had a vasectomy shortly after our only child was born, then declared he was leaving me when I was 41 years of age, I knew that would never happen. I was always conscious of how lucky I was to have the precious gift of Bella.

With the closure of my businesses, I was immediately vulnerable to Tim's demands. He had successfully manoeuvred me into a position where all of a sudden I had no income. Our family home had been sold so I had no choice but to move Bella and me into the Mill property.

The Mill was owned by a trust, of which Tim and I were joint trustees. When Tim refused to contribute to the financial obligations of the trust, as a joint trustee, I had to pay.

I was left to service the $570,000 mortgage at the Mill property, pay the council rates and insurance, and meet all our trust tax obligations on my own. Monthly mortgage principal and interest repayments were set at $ 5,400 and were locked in for a further two years. Tim would not allow the $430,000 equity in cash from the sale of our family home to be offset against the mortgage at the Mill, and he refused to assist me in meeting any of our joint financial responsibilities.

I realised if I couldn't access cash immediately, whether it be from alternative paid employment, starting new businesses, or a gift or loan from my parents, I would be forced to sell the Mill. Bella and I would be rendered homeless. If we were to move from the Mill, I would be unable to independently secure a mortgage on my own as I had no official income at the time. My days of home ownership would have been over, in that case. I had to find a way of paying the mortgage at the Mill, at all costs, if I was to stay on the property ladder over the long term.

There was a further $85,000 debt to the bank, which had been borrowed through my businesses to complete the renovation of the Mill. I was required to service that debt on my own as well. Tim simply didn't want to know about it.

Tim threatened me; he told me unless I did exactly what he wanted, he would take me to court and destroy me. He demanded I sell the Mill. He made it clear that I was the one who would have to facilitate the sale as he was living in Australia, after all. He would only consider offers over $1 million, plus GST, and I was to pass over all proceeds from the sale to him.

I was also instructed to agree to his demand of handing him the $430,000 that was sitting in a lawyer's trust account from the sale of our family home. He had already taken a marital asset of $82,000 in cash from the superannuation payout from his last job in New Zealand. At that stage, I was unaware of other marital cash assets that he had cleverly hidden from me and had taken to Australia.

He told me he would leave me with my businesses plus the $85,000 business debt, in exchange for $1,112,000 in cash, being the proceeds from the sale of our family home, the Mill property, and his superannuation.

But the businesses had all been wound down. All the stock had been sold and creditors paid. The businesses were effectively worthless.

Despite us having significant cash assets held in trust from the sale of our family home, Tim denied me access to those funds. Both our signatures were required for the funds to be released. He simply refused to sign the papers.

I was forced to ask my father for financial assistance. Without his help, I knew I would be unable to afford the costs of a legal defence whilst paying a mortgage on my own. If I chose not to defend myself against his attacks, Tim would certainly walk away with everything and I would be left penniless with a preschool child to care for.

It was a big deal for me to ask my father for help. I had barely spoken to him in years. There was a real risk he would simply say: "No, Emma, you're on your own."

Fortunately for Bella and me, my father came to our aid.

When you wake one day and realise you are looking down the barrel of a loaded gun, what do you do? Do you give up? Or do you pull yourself together, swallow your pride, and stand tall? Do you search for strength deep in your gut? Do you strategise and take charge of the situation yourself? Hell, yes, you pull yourself together! You formulate a path moving forward and you fight. Because if you didn't, it would mean financial annihilation and emotional devastation.

In mid-2012, I waited. I thought. I strategised. I thought some more. I played out scenarios on paper. What would happen if Tim did this? What if he did that? How would I react? Could I cope financially? Would I be able to hold down a full-time job, given I was suffering from stress and was a solo parent? How long would it take for Tim and me to resolve our issues? Would I have the mental and physical strength, and access to the financial resources it would take, to sustain a long-term legal attack? What support networks would I need? How would I stay fit and healthy in the meantime? How was I going to survive?

I instructed my father to incorporate three new companies. It was my intention to keep any business earnings, post separation, clear of any businesses which had operated during our marriage. I was under the assumption that businesses operating under my father's name and ownership after the separation would not be viewed as relationship property. I was to discover the court viewed these matters differently. It treated my father's companies as though they were half owned by Tim.

My father was the shareholder and director of the three new companies. He invested money to fund the purchase of stock and employed me as an office administrator. My job description allowed for me to be paid for twenty hours labour a week at the minimum wage of $15.25 per hour. I was receiving income of $249 per week after tax. Providing I could survive financially, I believed my frugal means might prove useful should the matter end up in court.

Launching new companies with my father's ownership and capital was the only way we would have any chance of meeting debt repayments of the original companies, mortgage repayments, and household bills. If I was to try to earn a living from any other form of paid employment, the mortgage and household expenses would have been paid from after-tax earnings. I simply couldn't earn enough from a wage or salaried position working for another firm to cover my outgoings without the assistance of my father's companies.

My father phoned me in October 2012. 'Emma, what are you doing about your settlement with Tim? I haven't heard anything about it since he turned your offer down in July. What's going on? Why aren't you doing anything?' He was always direct with me.

'Don't confuse *inaction* with *non-action*, Dad. It's a strategy. I'm merely waiting to see what Tim will do. He's a snake in the grass. He'll be aching to attack me. Give him another month or so, and he'll show his cards,' I said.

'Oh, I see,' said my father.

'Look, Dad, when Tim attacks me he will lose his advantage over me; he'll reveal his game plan. If I act first, I lose. And I will never allow that to happen. We don't have long to wait – he won't be able to help himself. Trust me on this.'

'OK, then. I hope you're right,' Dad responded.

From October 2012, I quietly made changes to my lifestyle. I had all but stopped drinking alcohol and I cleaned up my diet. Not that I was much of a drinker or indulged in eating junk food anyway.

I renewed my gym membership and increased my cardiovascular fitness by attending aerobic classes – my subconscious was gently guiding me with my lifestyle choices. Somehow I knew I was in for one hell of a battle with Tim. Physical fitness was going to be essential if I was to cope with the demands of working and caring for Bella on my own. I was determined I would not be a victim.

The stress of the separation and my changing circumstances saw me lose weight between May and December that year. I went from a healthy 60 kilograms to a very fragile 53 kilograms. If I failed to get fit, build muscle, and increase my appetite, I knew I would end up in hospital.

I swung upon a pendulum of grief and disbelief for months. I couldn't sleep and found it difficult to concentrate. My mind wrestled with understanding how Tim had lured me into the position I was now in. How was he able to deceive me with such callous intent? I thought he loved me.

But why had he done this to me?

How had it all gone so horribly wrong?

Through 2010 and 2011, Tim and I had agreed to apply for an expansion visa so I could expand my growing importing and distribution company into the United States. We had always enjoyed our holidays there and we felt, as a family, we could live a rewarding life in California.

By early 2012, we had our visa application under way and were waiting for confirmation of our approval from the US Citizenship and Immigration Services.

Things had been tracking along well for us as a family. We travelled internationally, we had a gorgeous daughter, and a beautiful home. Tim was doing well at work, but still Tim seemed unhappy. He was angry and taking his frustrations out on me.

His verbal and physical abuse had escalated through 2010 and 2011. It was always the same "poor me" story from him. 'They don't appreciate me at work. All I do is work. I have no *me* time,' he would complain. He appeared to have no sense of joy.

Had he forgotten he was earning in excess of $150,000 per annum and only working four days a week? Towards the end of 2011, he refused to work five days a week. He was taking Fridays off as his *me* day. Lack of money was not causing him stress, as far as I knew.

In January 2012, I took a garden rake and an edge trimmer from our family home to the Mill property to do some garden maintenance. It had become an overgrown jungle with the warm, wet weather over the Christmas break, so I spent four days with my hands dirty getting the hedges and plant beds back into shape.

At the end of the week Tim stormed into the kitchen. I had just finished feeding Bella and she was playing with a toy on the floor. He screamed at me: 'You fucking selfish bitch. What have you done with my rake? Did you take it down to the Mill without asking me? You have no right to take my garden tools without asking me first!'

Through my tears I said, 'But I was only trying to tidy the garden.' We actually had *two* rakes. He could have used the other one but I thought it sensible to keep that fact to myself for fear of inflaming his fury.

'I am so fucking sick of you,' he said. And with that, he stormed out of the kitchen, pushing three-year-old Bella out of his way and into the wall as he went.

He calmed down after an hour and apologised. I told him his response was not normal and I would not tolerate his verbal abuse and physical violence any longer, now that he was targeting our daughter. I let him know I would be calling our doctor so we could find out what was wrong with him once and for all. He offered no objection to my idea.

I never did take the rake back home. I left it leaning against the wall of the Mill as a reminder of his behaviour that day. Seven years' worth of exposure to the elements has left a trail of rusty tears down the wall.

Tim and I went to the doctor the week following his abusive outburst.

'So, Tim, what are you two doing here in my surgery today?' asked the doctor.

'We're here because I haven't been very nice to my wife,' he explained.

No shit, Sherlock.

'Um?' she said with a puzzled expression on her face. 'What do you make of this, Emma?'

'He gets angry at me – over stupid little things. He's volatile, and I get scared he's going to hit me. I don't understand where his anger comes from. I mean, we have a great life. I dunno. Is he depressed?' I said.

The doctor had Tim complete a questionnaire so she could assess whether he was depressed. According to his answers, she ascertained he was not suffering from depression.

I opened another discussion. 'He doesn't want to have sex with me,' I told her in front of him.

The doctor asked how often we were having sex. Both Tim and I agreed once or twice a year. 'So, you have a sexless marriage then.'

I found the doctor's comment very confronting. I actually enjoyed sex.

'He wouldn't touch me the whole time I was pregnant with Bella and then for months after she was born. He just hasn't been interested in me. In fact, it's been going on for years,' I explained.

'What have you got to say about this, Tim?' asked the doctor.

'Well, that was a mistake,' he said as he slouched in his chair and disengaged from the conversation.

The doctor said nothing. She sat, watched, and listened.

I was alarmed at his response. I knew he wasn't talking about Bella being a mistake. He was referring to not having sex with me as being a mistake. It was as though having sex was a conscious effort for him and he had slipped up somehow with his lack of attention towards me. His comment just didn't feel right.

'How do you feel when Tim gets angry, Emma?' asked the doctor.

'I'm terrified of him. I get worried he'll hit me. He's been pushing me into walls and door frames, threatening me with his fists, and shaking me by the shoulders. He screams and yells and swears at me on a regular basis. He even pushed Bella into a wall the other day. I'm worried it's going to get worse,' I replied.

'Is that true, Tim?'

'Well yeah, I guess so,' he said, without a hint of embarrassment or shame.

'How often are you behaving like this, Tim?' asked the doctor.

'Only ten times a year,' he said.

'So, roughly, once a month on average then?'

'Yep. That's correct,' he confirmed.

The doctor continued with her questions. 'What are your thoughts about this, Emma?'

'Well, I don't expect to agree with Tim on everything, but there's a difference between disagreement and abuse in my book. I grew up in a home where my parents didn't argue. They discussed their differences and respected each other. I just don't accept that being yelled at, sworn at, and being physically threatened is normal behaviour,' I said.

Tim interjected and overruled my opinion. 'She's not being realistic. Arguments are a normal part of marriage,' he said.

'Why are you doing this to Emma?' asked the doctor.

'It's work. I'm under pressure,' he responded.

That was bullshit.

'We're all busy, Tim. We all have pressure with work,' said the doctor.

I could sense something was eating away at him but couldn't put my finger on it.

The doctor concluded our fifteen-minute appointment with a recommendation we consider marriage counselling. She also suggested Tim would benefit from speaking to someone regarding anger management and said she would call me with a few names of professionals we might want to consider for counselling.

'So what did you make of that?' asked Tim once we arrived home.

'Well, it was insightful, I guess, but to be honest, I'm not sure anything was actually resolved,' I replied.

'The doctor said I'm not depressed. I'm fine. There's nothing wrong with me. It's got to be you then. You're the one with the problem,' said Tim.

I saw the colour drain from his face as he pursed his lips. He sneered at me and waited for my response.

I wouldn't give him the satisfaction of rising to his bait.

'You're nothing but a passive-aggressive bitch,' he screamed at me. 'It's all your fault. Don't you fucking listen? The doctor said I'm fine. I'm not depressed. It's got to be you. You're the one with the fucking problem.'

I raised my voice in response. 'Why are you doing this? I don't understand. We went to the doctor because you've been so abusive towards me. You even admitted it. And now you try and turn it around on me? Why are you destroying us? Stop trying to make me angry and turn me into someone I'm not. What's wrong with you?'

With smug satisfaction he said, 'Finally, little miss perfect is making a stand.'

He let his back fall into the pillows as he lay stretched out with his feet up on our bed. A smile of evil satisfaction unfolded across his face. I could see Tim thought he had won by getting me to raise my voice.

A week later, Tim told me he had been asked to put his name forward for a job in Sydney. According to his story, he had been headhunted when he was in Sydney for work before Christmas.

I tried not to get too alarmed by his sudden interest in moving to Australia. We were awaiting a response from US immigration regarding the business expansion visa. I naturally thought we would be moving to the United States.

On 5 February 2012, Tim was offered a full-time position as Head of Securities for an investment bank based in Sydney.

I was not informed of his job offer until a week later. I requested he reserve his decision about the position in Sydney. I had spent $20,000 and twelve months conferring with a US immigration lawyer over the visa application. We had made a decision to move to the States as a family. At no point had a move to Australia ever been discussed until Tim mentioned it in mid-January 2012.

'OK. I can wait a week or so before I give the Australians my decision,' he said.

I wasn't aware of it at the time, but he had already accepted the job. He signed his employment contract with the Australian company at the beginning of February, the same day he was offered the position. That fact came to light two and a half years later when his employment contract was provided as part of a discovery bundle for court.

Towards the end of February, we had a visitor at home. Tim walked into the lounge where we were chatting. As he went to sit down, he casually said, 'I've accepted the job in Australia.'

I was shocked but remained calm. Once the visitor left I asked, 'Why have you accepted the job without consulting me? You know we're supposed to be hearing back from the Americans later this week. What if we get the visa?'

'It won't happen. We won't get the visa. I've made my decision,' he said as he turned and headed for the stairs to his office.

The following week our application for a visa to the United States was declined.

Later in the year, one of my friends suggested that Tim may have sabotaged our US immigration visa to ensure his plan of moving to Sydney went ahead unhindered. It's possible.

Between the time Tim notified me of his acceptance of the job in Sydney and his permanent departure for Australia in mid-March 2012, we needed to find a new home for our family pet. Tim contacted the Golden Retriever Club to see whether Poppy, our beautiful dog, could be adopted. The process frustrated him. 'If I can't rehome Poppy, I'll have her put down,' he said.

I was horrified and disgusted. I didn't say anything at the time as I knew it would only cause an argument. Besides, I would never let him destroy our darling girl; I would intervene if it ever came to that. Much to my relief, within a matter of weeks, Poppy was rehomed.

On 17 March 2012, I put my husband on the plane to Sydney. He was to start his new job two days later.

Tim continued with his pressure and demands from Australia. He phoned me the day he started his new job. 'What have you done about selling our home? Did you speak to the real estate agent?' he demanded.

'Yes, I've spoken to her. I met her at home this afternoon. She wants us to spend $10,000 on marketing,' I said.

He raised his voice. 'That's ridiculous. Tell her she can go to hell. I'm not spending money on advertising. If you want to advertise the house, you'll have to find the money yourself.'

It had become apparent that I was little more than a doormat with a credit card to Tim.

Near the end of April 2012, he accessed my emails and my Facebook account. He read a private conversation I had engaged in with my friend Rob about a cop who had been given my business card from someone at a function

I had been to. The cop texted me. I told my friend Rob how nice it was to have a man compliment me for a change, but I wouldn't be going out with him or sleeping with him as I was married.

Tim woke me when he rang at 1.30 am. He screamed and yelled at me down the phone. He accused me of having an affair. But I wasn't. All I did was have a "private" online chat with Rob about a guy who sent me a text message. Tim's rant lasted twenty minutes.

He woke me again three hours later with another call and yelled at me for a further five minutes. 'If you think you can have another man, well just know that I'm moving on as well. If you're going to date anyone, I need to approve them first. I'm not having just any man hanging around my daughter,' he screamed.

But I wasn't even seeing anyone. I thought Tim and I were still married.

At 8.30 am he phoned again. He was more rational and apologised for his behaviour. He told me I was lovely and that he shouldn't have spoken to me the way he did. He let me know he had booked a flight home and suggested we attend marriage counselling.

Tim flew back to New Zealand a few days later, still very volatile.

'I've been talking to people about you,' he said. 'They told me to put myself first for a change.'

'Who exactly are these people you have been talking to?' I asked.

'My sister and her partner,' he responded.

'Really? But why would you speak to them about us? Why didn't you first come to me to talk about our problems?' I said.

'Because blood is thicker than water,' he said.

I was gobsmacked. I had given him nine years of my life. We were married, I had been faithful to him, we had built a life together, we had a daughter, and he still didn't consider me family?

Attending marriage counselling with Tim was illuminating. We arrived separately. I sat alone and on edge in the waiting room. Tim arrived almost on cue as the counsellor ushered us into her consulting room.

'So, you're expecting Emma to give up her life and sacrifice her career for yours? Do I have that correct?' asked Cora, the counsellor.

'Yeah, that's right. I was offered a great job in Sydney. They weren't going to hold it for me forever, you realise,' said Tim.

'OK, Tim. I get that. But Emma mentioned you have been mistreating her – abusing her. Is that correct?' Cora continued.

'Well yeah,' Tim replied.

'So you're abusing your wife and you expect her to throw her life away for you? How interesting.' Cora took a breath and continued. 'Look, Tim, I don't know Emma personally, but I know of her. My business is not of the scale Emma's is, but if my partner were to demand what you're expecting of Emma, well, I'd say no.'

'But it's a great job,' Tim said.

'It's not all about you, Tim. That's what we're here to establish. If you want your marriage to survive, you're both going to need to do the work with counselling to get there. Tim, you'll need to quit your job and return to New Zealand,' said Cora.

The tension was mounting. I shifted nervously in my chair. The words of the therapist hung in the air like a racist joke. I had no idea where her words would fall – upon deaf ears, dismissed and forgotten, or like a red rag to a bull with bite.

'What about my job?' said Tim. His pursed lips and squinting eyes could not conceal his hatred.

'You'll get another one,' replied Cora.

'I could do counselling via Skype from Sydney,' suggested Tim.

From the look she gave Tim, I could tell Cora was unimpressed. I was surprised with how forthright she had been. Was someone finally listening?

'Time's up,' Cora said. 'You both need to go away and give this some serious thought.'

Tim flew back to Sydney the following day. He rang me within a few days of his return. 'I've quit my job. I'm coming home to you and Bella for good. I want to save our marriage,' he said.

I was astonished and confused. All Tim's words and actions had, up to that point, been those of someone who wanted to end our marriage, not save it.

The following week, he returned to New Zealand. Two days later, he went to see Cora on his own. That evening he called me and said, 'The counselling's not working. It's a waste of time. I'm not going back to see that woman.'

My head was in a spin as nothing made sense. I recall asking him, 'But why would you quit your job and come all this way for counselling and then just ditch the whole thing in a heartbeat? How do you think we're going to resolve our issues? What are you going to do for a job? I just don't understand.'

'I'll be OK. I'll go back to contracting in Auckland,' he said.

By that stage I didn't believe a single word he was saying. I had no idea what was going on but I was determined to get some answers.

I tried putting a phone call through to his office in Sydney the following day, but my hands and fingers shook so much I couldn't execute the call.

I asked my friend Melanie (Mel) to call his office in my place. I knew Tim wouldn't be there as he was still in Auckland. But that was the whole point.

'I'd like to speak to Tim Rivers, please. He's the new guy in Securities,' said Mel.

'Oh, I'm sorry. Tim's not here right now. He's on extended leave. He won't be back until the beginning of June. Can I get a message to him for you?' replied the receptionist.

'No, don't worry. It can wait. Thanks anyway,' said Mel.

So Tim was lying. But why?

A few weeks later, after the closure of my retail store, and once the sale of our family home had been finalised, I met Tim so we could complete the division of our household furniture and chattels. I didn't say a word to him about the fact I knew he would be going back to his job in Sydney. Rather, I listened to him in silence as we both sat on the front steps of our home and waited for the removal truck to arrive and take Tim's half share of the household chattels.

He raised his voice and said, 'Just look at what I did for us. I quit my job and came back to save our marriage. I went to counselling. What a fucking waste of time that was. It's all your fault, you bitch. I don't believe you ever wanted to make the marriage work. What am I going to do? I don't have a job and I've got no income. You've ruined everything.'

He sat less than a metre from me, looking forlorn and defeated, yet I *knew* he was everything *but* forlorn and defeated. It was all a ruse. I listened and observed him in wondrous silence as he spewed a river of lies. His delivery was cold and calculated. Clearly, he was well practised at lying.

I was being shown a façade, a mask, but cracks were appearing. His decisions were not making logical sense. What was Tim hiding?

I felt defeated as I sat on the steps of the home I had spent eight painstaking years restoring. It was a beautiful home and had featured as a ten-page feature spread in an architectural magazine.

For Tim to lie to me like that, I was all of a sudden aware he felt nothing for me. My marriage was indeed over. I turned my head away from him and sighed. To challenge Tim's lies would have put me in grave physical danger. My stony face gave no sign of the contempt, disappointment, and escalating fear I felt.

three

Bait and switch

By mid-May 2012, my world had been turned upside down. I had no explanation for the chaos that spiralled around me. I was worried whether I would be able to cope under the strain of the massive changes I was facing and Tim's continued abuse.

I saw my doctor towards the end of that month and we discussed Tim's behaviour. I referred back to the consultation in January when she had assessed Tim's attitude and conduct. The doctor again explained she did not believe Tim was depressed, although in light of recent developments, she believed he had a narcissistic personality disorder. She described him as "smiling death".

In addition to the general practice work she carried out, my doctor also worked for the police. It was on her advice that I spoke to their domestic violence division. Given the severity of Tim's verbal and physical abuse, she was extremely concerned for my welfare, as was I.

A police officer warned me of the murderous capabilities of narcissists in extreme cases. She told me how narcissists are unpredictable and that I must never be alone with Tim. I asked her about having a protection order put in place. She informed me that until he attacked me with considerable force (for example, he knocked a few of my teeth out), I wouldn't qualify for a protection order. I was horrified. Who would be able to protect Bella and me if his behaviour spiralled out of control? Tim was 190 centimetres in height and weighed over 100 kilograms. I was no match for him.

I was having panic attacks. My asthma had worsened. I couldn't breathe. I was experiencing physical responses to the stress and pressure I was under.

In an effort to better understand the behaviour of someone displaying characteristics consistent with that of someone with a narcissistic personality disorder, I did some research and discovered the following:

a) Narcissists are competitive and often envious of others.
b) Narcissists are manipulative. They often lie, misquote facts and contradict themselves. When questioned about their mistruths, they will deny all knowledge of their behaviour and turn the argument on the innocent party – claiming you're lying, crazy or deluded.
c) Narcissists are dishonest and cruel. They relish the demise of others in an effort to boost their fragile egos and make themselves appear more successful or popular. Like indigestion, their abusive outbursts act like a burp and relieve their frustration. They feel better, so you should too. After the emotional outburst the narcissist may offer an insincere apology, tell you they love you and wonder why you're hurt and withdrawn.
d) Narcissists display "bait and switch" behaviour, where they will often draw you in to slap you harder.
e) Narcissists lack empathy and have little care for others.
f) Narcissists will either punish their victims with verbal and/or physical abuse or they will withdraw their affections and/or financial assistance.
g) Narcissists become more skilled with manipulation as they age and as authoritative figures that may have kept them in check die off. As a result the behaviour of narcissists tends to worsen over time. They are only restrained by the fear of damage to their reputations and/or a severe punishment.
h) Narcissists lack a sense of humour. In an attempt to be popular they will repeat jokes they have heard, but they are seldom the centre or source of warmth and frivolity. They lack joy and often have a gloomy outlook on life.
i) Narcissists have high opinions of themselves. They believe they are superior to others and they are often vain. Nothing in life is ever good enough for them – they are of the opinion that they are entitled to so much more than what they have.

j) Narcissists are generally passive and lack initiative. However, when challenged or angered, they react explosively and ferociously.

I thought about the life Tim and I shared, and I recognised Tim's behaviour as being consistent with the traits described in these points. Certain events immediately came to mind.

Three days before we were married in mid-February 2004, I sat quietly on my own at the window seat in our kitchen, while I worked on the seating arrangements for the wedding.

Tim stormed in. 'There's so much bloody work to be done. They've delivered the wrong marquee and there's no floor and no lights. It's a fucking nightmare. I can't be bothered with this shit. I'm calling the wedding off!' he yelled.

How could this be happening? I thought. I hadn't done anything to upset him. The problems he described were just logistical issues. They could be sorted out. We still had time.

What was I to do? My heart sank as feelings of sadness, failure, and fear filled me. I wondered how I was going to find the strength to call our wedding guests and tell them to cancel their flights and travel arrangements. The shock disabled me. I just sat on my own in silence once Tim left the room.

An hour later he reappeared in the kitchen. 'I'm sorry, babe. I didn't mean what I said. It's not you. I do love you. It's just the stress of the wedding.'

The following day I asked Tim to write his wedding vows. He told me I should write the vows for us both. He suggested that he would read what I had written, and he would let me know whether he agreed with them or not.

Our wedding day was fraught with challenges. The ceremony was to be on our lawn at 3 pm on Saturday, 21 February 2004. By lunchtime that day, the full force of a passing cyclone bore down on us. Our beautifully choreographed garden wedding was destroyed – along with the marquee that nearly blew away. The marquee supports broke, the car park flooded, the power went out, and there was so much mud I had to be carried from the marquee.

In early April 2004, I entered the local West Auckland Bride of the Year Competition. I was awarded two prizes that evening – a prize for the best dress, and second prize overall. The main prize was a weekend stay at a luxury boutique lodge.

Soon after we arrived home just after midnight, I told Tim of a lovely young woman – another contestant – I had met who had her honeymoon in a family member's borrowed caravan. She and her husband experienced the same cyclone we had, and their wedding day was less than ideal, as was ours. I felt sorry for her as she described the awful conditions of her stay in the caravan.

Tim and I had not long returned from our two-week honeymoon that had taken us to Dubai, France, and Ireland. As much as I was grateful for my prize, I felt undeserving of it. I told Tim I was going to contact the young woman and offer her the weekend break at the luxury lodge so she and her husband could have another chance at an enjoyable honeymoon together.

Tim's response was scary. He yelled at me. 'You're a selfish bitch! That's my prize too, you know. How dare you think you can give away *our* prize?'

I was terrified and upset. In the pitch black of night, I ran, barefoot, through the front door, down the steps, across the driveway, and along the main road. I wanted to get as far away from him as I could.

Tim eventually found me wandering along the road, in the freezing cold, at 2 am, a kilometre from home. He told me to get in the car. By that stage he was full of apologies and remorse.

I gave my prize to his parents and never mentioned it again. I was never able to see the woman I met at the competition. She could have been a lovely friend.

That night I realised I had made a terrible mistake in marrying Tim. We had been married then for just seven weeks.

I believe he was displaying a narcissistic "bait and switch" manoeuvre, whereby he "baited" me with flattery and charm, leading into our marriage. He regularly bought me beautiful bouquets of flowers. There were holidays and weekends away at sumptuous hotels in exotic locations. Tim showered me with gifts, perfume and an expensive diamond and platinum engagement ring. We bought a home together. I felt secure. I felt loved.

Once we were married, Tim "switched" his behaviour to episodes of abuse to control me.

He was jealous of the attention I had received at the Bride of the Year Competition. He couldn't be happy for me or support me in my wish to be generous and help someone with regifting my prize. He needed to undermine me and strip me of my confidence in order to dominate me.

That should have been a night full of wonderful happy memories. And yet it was not. It was merely a sign of what I was to endure for a further eight years.

I had flashbacks of planting and replanting a herb garden between Tim's efforts to destroy it with weedkiller. After six failed cultivation attempts, I gave up on my herb garden.

I vividly recall attending a wedding with Tim when I was heavily pregnant with Bella. She was a huge baby, weighing 4.3 kilograms at birth. By the time I was seven and a half months pregnant, my stomach was enormous and I was experiencing considerable discomfort.

The wedding was towards the end of January 2008. It was a stinking hot day. There was no air conditioning inside the venue – it must have been at least 35 °C indoors. I tried my best to be bright and happy but I had been on my feet all day and was exhausted. I couldn't breathe and felt nauseous. I feared I would vomit and faint. By 11 pm, I told Tim I needed to go to bed.

Tim had been drinking and immediately became abusive once we were alone in our hotel room. 'I'm sick to death of you, Emma. You don't seem interested. You could have made more of an effort with my friends. I don't even know why I bother with you.'

I needed the love and care of my husband; however, he was not willing to comfort me. My helpless state provided Tim the perfect opportunity to undermine and attack me. I felt trapped and very alone.

I rushed into marriage at my peril. As said by William Congreve in his comedy of manners, *The Old Bachelor*, in 1693: "Married in haste, we may repent at leisure."

I married Tim because I loved him. I believed Tim loved me. I was thirty-two when we met, and I thought I was ready for marriage. He appeared to offer the love and security I had been looking for. We had shared interests: we both enjoyed living a healthy lifestyle; we liked to travel; we were both ambitious and hard-working; we shared an interest in art and design. His polished manners and charm, expensive dinners, and weekly bouquets swept me off my feet.

I now realise I didn't take long enough to get to know Tim before we were engaged. I became swept along in the moment. I lapped up his attention and misinterpreted his affections. Any questions or uncertainties I had about him before we married were brushed aside. I knew he had a temper but I labelled his anger as "nerves and fear". I hoped his mood swings would pass.

I wondered about his detached and distant attitude regarding sex, but he used to explain his behaviour by saying he was tired. I had no idea I represented a façade of heterosexual respectability.

I began to wonder about his previous relationships. I was aware of one he had with a wealthy divorcée 15 years his senior. According to Tim, the relationship ended due to trust issues. I was to later learn he had refused to sign a relationship property agreement which would have denied him any claim over her significant fortune.

My advice to any young woman contemplating marriage would be to take your time with your relationship decisions and observe your partner with his friends, his family and his work colleagues. Watch and feel his reactions to stress and adversity. Is he kind? Does he put the needs of others ahead of his own? Think your decisions through very carefully. Go by your gut instinct and also listen to the advice and opinions of your friends and family – those who love you and care for your welfare. Be honest with yourself and with your friends. Never sweep concerns aside. And *never* marry a selfish, volatile man.

Why do abused women stay in marriages?

We stay for lots of reasons. I stayed because I loved my husband. I wanted to try and fix the problems we had. I also wanted our daughter to be brought up by both her parents in a nuclear family situation.

Most marriages and relationships survive through a series of intertwined incidents and daily occurrences. Selecting events to describe the whole can never provide an accurate picture, with merit.

The birth of our daughter Bella was a happy time for us. Tim was an attentive father and husband immediately following her birth.

Learning of our success at buying our first home and also the Mill was an exhilarating experience for us both. I think we both felt proud of our achievements.

We travelled well together. We had some memorable holidays, particularly our trips to the United States. We sipped hot soup from cardboard cups as we walked along Eighth Avenue in New York in freezing conditions. We watched squirrels in Central Park and sat on a massive rock and marvelled at the frozen Central Park Reservoir. I have happy memories of holding hands with Tim atop the Eiffel Tower on our honeymoon. We walked the beaches of Normandy in France and remembered the sacrifices of so many. We slept on the floor of Narita Airport in Japan, with 1,000 other people the night of the 9.1 magnitude earthquake on 11 March 2011.

We enjoyed dining out, visiting art galleries, museums, and buildings with architectural interest. At home we'd go walking together and watch TV – just the usual things couples do, I guess. In the weekends we'd work in our garden. Tim was always very regimented with his activities and his time. It bothered me a bit, but I typically went along with what he wanted to do as I didn't have the energy to fight or oppose him. I was playing the role of a dutiful wife.

I tortured myself by looking over photos of the two of us taken on my fortieth birthday. I looked so happy, with my sparkling eyes and long, glossy, dark brown hair. Within a year of that photo, my husband left me. At the time, I had no idea I was being led by the nose along a path of lies and deception.

The verbal and emotional abuse crept into our relationship over time. Tim changed, or perhaps he just let his guard down and revealed more of his true personality.

Tim became increasingly jealous of my business profile and of the attention I received. I felt he was punishing me for my ability to make my own decisions. He tried to disguise his jealousy throughout our marriage because, I believe, it was financially advantageous for him to do so.

In the beginning, the happy times were broken up by random outbursts of unexplained anger. He became increasingly short-tempered and emotionally distant.

I always hoped the Tim I fell in love with was still there. That's the plight of so many abused women – we remember the man we fell in love with and we hold on to the hope he will one day reappear.

Every time the vile verbal attacks came, they were typically followed by lashings of remorse and beautiful bunches of expensive flowers. 'I'm sorry, Emms. I didn't mean to hurt you. I'm just stressed with work,' he would say, as if somehow his apology justified what he had said and done.

I could never understand Tim's anger as there were happy moments, and I thought there was love. Yet lurking beneath his carefully crafted veneer was also pent-up anger. The look in his eyes often belied the smile on his face.

Sometimes he flipped out as though a pressure valve was being released. He'd yell and kick and throw things, while I tried my best to get out of his way. With each attack I became more withdrawn and less open to him. I was less forgiving, I guess.

My friend Becky came to visit me at the Mill one afternoon towards the end of May 2012. It was a few days before Tim was to permanently fly back to Sydney. Becky and I were having a coffee together at the kitchen table when Tim rang. I answered the call.

'Thanks for calling me back, Tim. I have something to ask of you. My aunt's coming to look after Bella while I'm in Hawke's Bay for work next week and I was wondering if it would be OK if she could use your car while she's here,' I asked politely.

He had no idea Becky was listening. He spewed venom at me down the telephone. 'I won't let your aunt use my car. You can go to hell, bitch. I'm selling my car and keeping the money for myself. You and your aunt can go fuck yourselves.'

I responded how I always did; I was shocked and said very little. I didn't react or rise to his bait.

'I don't give a shit what you do. Hire a car for her. You won't get any help from me. I'm gonna make you pay,' he continued to yell and then abruptly hung up.

With wide eyes and a shocked expression, Becky looked at me and said, 'If I wasn't sitting right here next to you, listening to that with my own ears, I never would have believed it possible.' She had met Tim on several occasions. 'Never in a million years would I have expected him to behave like that. He's filled with hate,' she said.

Becky cuddled me. 'Emms, my husband has worked in the prison system and has told me plenty of stories. I know a nutter when I hear one. You must never be alone in Tim's company again. He's unhinged and dangerous. I'll help you in any way I can.'

Tears welled in my eyes.

I sat in my chair at the kitchen table, shaking. I had difficulty speaking.

I was relieved that my friend had witnessed Tim's tirade. He was so incredibly manipulative – and so careful never to show his true hand in front of anyone. On the surface, Tim appeared courteous and polite. He was always Mr. Nice Guy. Becky was only the second person to hear him speak to me like that in ten years. And he was dishing out abuse like that to me on a regular basis.

She penned a letter about the conversation she overheard that day. Her letter was later submitted to the family court. Tim maintained the conversation never took place.

By the middle of June, my shop had closed and Bella and I were living in the Mill. It was quiet and calm. I felt I could breathe a little easier. Tim was in Australia so I was fairly confident Bella and I were safe from harm.

four

Clown

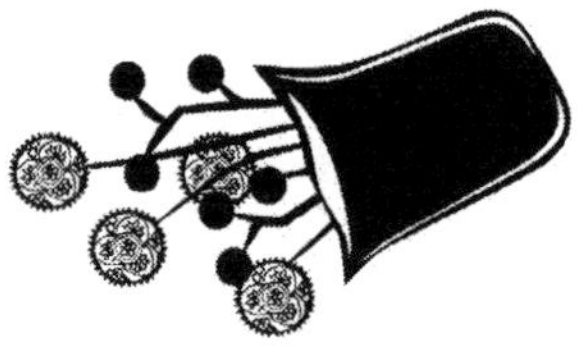

People can be deceptive. They can perfect their craft, particularly when sex, power, money, and status are all at stake.

Tim was intelligent and he was meticulous with order. He was purposefully secretive and covered his tracks well. All his electronic devices were password-protected, and he never gave me access to his laptop, his mobile phone, or his bank accounts. We didn't share a joint bank account. I never saw the need to – I had my own money and so did he. He paid the mortgage for our home, and I paid the mortgage for the Mill. He had his mail delivered to a post office box in Auckland City.

I often woke in the mornings of late 2012 with the realisation that I knew very little about the man I had just spent the past ten years of my life with. How could that have happened? How was I so blind to his behaviour for so long? Why did I not see the trail of breadcrumbs he left? Was I so busy with life, work, Bella, and running a home, that I was distracted and blinded in the process?

When little things creep into your marriage, you barely notice them. Then one day you do notice something and you think, *oh, that's odd.* But it's not a big deal and besides, you're busy trying to get the groceries unpacked and the baby is crying, so you leave it. To confront the behaviour would only cause an argument. Then you forget about it for a while.

In hindsight, that's exactly what was happening with Tim – lots of subtle and unusual behaviours had crept into his daily routines. Over time, the oddities became normalities. I lost sight of the difference.

On 6 July 2012, when Tim returned from Sydney for the weekend, I finally saw the light. On that cold, wet winter's day, we both attended the funeral of a dear friend, Gray, an elderly farmer from Helensville. Six hundred farmers and rural people were in attendance. The scene was a depiction of heartland New Zealand. There were sad and sombre, tanned, and weather-beaten faces. A sea of tweed and barely worn jackets shuffled with stooped and stocky stance. Rough hands and kind hearts met to farewell their friend.

I was seated near the rear of the church with my aunt. When a finely dressed man walked towards me I remember the shock I felt as I came to recognise him. My back arched, and I blinked over and over in an effort to adjust my focus. My head began to shake involuntarily.

That man was confident and he appeared relaxed. His face was one of familiarity. He was poised and calm as he took the seat next to me. I was stunned.

That man was my husband, and he was wearing make-up! Bright orange foundation, to be more accurate. The foundation was applied carelessly, patchy, with obvious streaks. He was dressed in what I believe could be termed as a gay man's clothing: a well-cut, tapered and expensively tailored black wool and linen-blend suit jacket with black sateen banding on the lapels, with shapely, tight-fitting matching pants.

He may as well have been wearing a rainbow-coloured onesie with a unicorn head and a sign around his neck with the words "I prefer men now".

As the funeral service continued, my heart raced and my breath became shallow and laboured. It took all my strength to remain calm and prevent an asthma attack. I wanted to run away, but I needed to stay seated and pay my respects to Gray, Laura and their family. They had all been so kind to Bella and me.

I remember preparing for the funeral that day. I hadn't seen Tim for a month, and despite his volatility and request for a divorce, I still tried to make myself look pretty for him.

I could have worn a paper bag for all the good it did. My husband looked straight through me. I meant nothing to him.

But really, why should I have expected anything more from him? Tim had treated me with indifference throughout our marriage. Today was just another day for him. As far as he was concerned, he had moved on, to Australia and his fabulous new life. I was last month's news.

People approached me at the funeral afternoon tea, asking, 'What's with Tim wearing make-up? Emma, did you see it?'

Of course I fucking saw it.

I received numerous phone calls and a barrage of questions the following week from people who had seen Tim at Gray's funeral. Our old neighbour told me her three sons always thought he was gay anyway. She casually mentioned they used to laugh at him behind his back with his over-the-top use of cologne and the extreme lengths he went to with protective clothing when he trimmed the hedge. I got the impression they wondered why I was so surprised.

It was another kick in the guts.

My world stood still, for weeks. I wondered about my worth. I struggled to process how Tim had used me. I was angry at the fact he had taken the best years of my life and worked me like a dog, all the while deceiving me as to his true identity. I felt physically sick at the thought of him having sex with men.

Later in July, I went to visit one of my wholesale customers in Hamilton. Through my tears I told my openly gay customer all about Tim's behaviour; the make-up, how he didn't want to have sex with me, how he lied about his use of tanning beds, his prolific attendance at the gym, his expansive wardrobe, the fact he was shaving his balls, his frequent visits to the dental hygienist and his obsession with whitening his teeth, his penchant for having facials and removing hair from his whole body, and the fact he was always so secretive.

My customer was very kind to me. With his gay man's nasal, sing-song lisp he gently told me he believed my husband was gay. He enlightened me as to how gay men behave and how clever they can be at disguising their lifestyle and sexuality behind the smokescreen of a marriage.

With care, he told me it was highly likely my husband had been sleeping with men for the duration of our marriage. I didn't want to believe him, but I knew everything he told me was true.

I had no choice but to accept the possibility my husband was either gay or bisexual. Somehow, I needed to come to terms with it and concede I was now a subject for local gossip.

One woman had the nerve to tell me that with being so pretty and having such a beautiful home, I was the perfect wife for a gay man. What gave her the right to say that to me? Did she consider my life and feelings were a joke? Did she think I should feel okay about being used as a cover for his lies? But people don't stop to think about how it feels to walk in someone else's shoes.

Other people said, 'Oh well, it would have been worse if he'd had an affair with a woman.'

Oh really?

I believe the significance of the deception Tim engaged in was worse than that of an affair with a woman. I believe my husband had deceived me from the beginning of our relationship. He never loved me the way he should have. The marriage was doomed from the start; it didn't stand a chance. If he was interested in other women, perhaps it would have been more of a level playing field. But it wasn't a level playing field. I didn't have a penis.

The comments from people continued in waves. I guess they thought it was a bit of a novelty. But it wasn't a novelty. It was my fucking life.

I was told of a local men's support group that met every couple of months to discuss issues surrounding living a gay lifestyle. The group was run by a gay couple who were local community identities. One of them told my friend she would be shocked to know how many married farmers – and married men in general – regularly attended their meetings.

So, was this to be considered normal behaviour now? Did people seriously expect me to build a bridge and get over it?

If I had been told Tim was gay or bisexual at the onset of our relationship, I could have made my own decision. I would have walked away from him. I should have been told.

But I wasn't. He had no right to do what he did to me – to take that choice away from me, to deceive me, and use me the way he did.

'How could you not have known?' I was asked.

The truth is, I didn't know. It never occurred to me my husband was interested in men, because he was married to me.

In respect of the signs that *were* there, I didn't recognise them or put them into any sort of context. I thought his behaviour was a little left of centre at times, but I chose not to interfere as I was trying to show him respect for being an individual. I didn't consider it any of my business to tell him what to do with his life.

I thought back to when we first started dating. We were at a burger bar in New North Road, Auckland. I sat on Tim's knee as we waited for our order. My boyfriend was being watched by two openly gay men from across the room, and I felt uneasy. I remarked to him, 'What's going on with those guys? Have you noticed them staring at you?'

'Oh yeah, that happens a bit,' said Tim.

So did that mean my boyfriend should have been accused of being gay?

He had a much lower sex drive than me. He always complained about being tired from work. He never wanted to stay in bed all day and make love to me – not even in the early years of our marriage. He wasn't into going down on me, and we never had sex in the mornings, not once.

Tim went to bed before me. He would get up off the sofa and quietly slip past me and say goodnight. He was always asleep when I got into bed, and slept with his back to me. There was never any spooning or cuddling or waking up in the middle of the night for a fevered love-making session. He hardly ever touched me.

Every weekday morning, Tim rose at 4.45 am. He was gone within seconds. There was never a good morning or a goodbye kiss, let alone sex. He was off to the gym.

I mentioned the complete absence of morning sex to one of my male friends well after the separation. He responded, 'Seriously, Emma? Wow. But morning wood is the best. All I can say is, if he wasn't having sex with you in the mornings, he was definitely having sex with someone else.'

Over the years, Tim had successfully eaten away at my self-esteem to the point where I believed I was unattractive. I thought *that* was the reason why my husband wasn't interested in me sexually. I also assumed there must be a decline in sexual drives of married men. In my naivety, I didn't realise the situation was so far removed from normal behaviour.

I believe Tim tried to be straight at the beginning of our relationship. We had sex two or three times on our twelve-day honeymoon. He didn't want to have sex with me in our hotel room in Dubai, and yet he seemed attentive and held my hand as we visited tourist landmarks.

We travelled on to France and spent some time in Paris, the so-called City of Love. I remember the bored expression on Tim's face when we were photographed together over lunch on my 33rd birthday – we had been married for just over a week. My eyes were bright, my face full of hope. His eyes looked dead, vacant, and angry. Bitter, even.

In Normandy, we stayed at a bed and breakfast in a quaint country village. I loved the simplicity of the interior furnishings and architecture, the smell of time, and the rickety furniture. Tim refused to have sex with me (again) that night. I felt rejected. I ended up sleeping on the lumpy sofa in the lounge.

We continued on our honeymoon with a brief three-day trip to Dublin. He was ambivalent towards me as we lay in bed together. I guess I got used to the rejection. It crept up on me and swallowed me whole before I had a chance to understand what was going on.

Did he ever really love me? Perhaps he manufactured a version of love to enable his participation in a heterosexual marriage? Did he resent me for being the necessary front and distraction from his true feelings and urges? Is that where his anger came from? Did it become harder for him to deal with the stress of his deception as time went by? Was gay sex a pressure valve for him? I tortured myself over the unknown.

I thought about his preoccupation with his looks. He always looked so tanned. I sometimes asked him whether he was using sunbeds. Of course he denied it, yet some days he was bright red all over; some days he appeared to be brown all over. I thought it was weird.

One morning in early March 2012, as I stepped out of the shower, I observed Tim standing naked and bent over the basin as he brushed his teeth in our bathroom.

'Um, Tim, you have tan lines under your bottom. You *have* been using sunbeds. Why have you lied to me all these years?' I said. I tried to be neutral in my tone and leave out any sarcasm or judgement from my voice.

'Just fuck off,' he said, as he spat the last remnant of toothpaste from his mouth into the sink and calmly placed his toothbrush in its holder. With his eyes still cast down, he turned and strode confidently out of the bathroom. He didn't even look at me as I stood naked and wet before him. My gaze followed him out the door.

In late 2012, I desperately tried to make sense of all the pieces of the puzzle; was he actually attending the gym at all? For a guy who went there every weekday morning, he wasn't exactly "ripped" or "buff". His muscles were there but they were a bit spongy, with a decent covering of fat. Perhaps he was meeting men for other leisure pursuits in the mornings?

I remembered back to May 2008. Bella was two months old. Like any new mother, I was frustrated with and concerned about my "baby weight".

'How about I join your gym? I really need to shift these extra kilos,' I said, grabbing a fistful of fat from my ass. 'What do you think? It could be something nice for us to do together.'

'No, that's not happening. You're not joining my gym,' he replied.

My heart sank as I looked up with surprise. I knew I wasn't looking my best, but really, was I that ugly?

I didn't want to argue with him so I never mentioned it again. I went walking and reduced my calorie intake instead and lost six kilograms.

By 5 pm from Sunday to Thursday, Tim would leave his suit hanging on a hook by the front door. His gym gear, toiletries, and his lunch, similarly lay in wait for his early morning departure to the gym. You could set your clock by him.

Every now and again, I said to him, 'Wouldn't it be nice if you didn't go to the gym in the mornings so we could have breakfast together?'

Tim flatly refused. 'Look, the gym is what I do in the mornings. Don't interfere,' he would say.

In April 2016, I had a coffee with the guy who owned the gym Tim went to for the years through our marriage. I casually mentioned Tim's name.

'Oh yeah, I remember him. He was a bit of a pretty boy,' the guy said.

During our chat he volunteered, 'I'll go check out his membership for you.'

He called me the following day. 'I checked out Tim's membership. He was here at 5 am twice a week over the eight years he was a member.'

Wow. I was stunned. Twice a week at the gym, huh. Not five times, as I was led to believe.

I had no proof as to where Tim was, or what he was doing three mornings a week. I can only assume he was meeting men for sex. I doubted he would have met women for sex at that time of the morning.

And then, of course, there were the times I was away travelling. Tim would have had plenty of opportunity to either venture out for sex or have men back to our house. Bella was either at home with Tim, or she was with my friend Laura while I was away.

'Do you think he was paying for sex?' remarked my American friend, Kiera. 'I mean, that would make it simple and uncomplicated for him. He loved that, right – clinical and unemotional?'

'Yeah, could be,' I replied. 'Who would know? Maybe they were paying *him*?'

'Oh no way,' said Kiera. 'But my God, that could be it.'

'Maybe,' I said. 'It's possible. It'd kill two birds with one stone – keep his fuck buddies quiet and line his pockets, in one fell swoop.' I struggled to keep the snide tone of contempt and disgust from my voice.

The information about Tim's morning routine, in respect of his absence from the gym, threw me for months. It's one thing to witness the disintegration of your marriage, but to learn it was highly likely my husband had been fucking men behind my back for possibly the whole duration of it was a deception on a completely different level. The knowledge was soul-destroying.

My confidence was in tatters. And to make things worse, I could see my husband had set me up to destroy me financially as well.

I had flashbacks of what had happened over Christmas 2011. Tim developed a condition called prostatitis. At the time, he told me it had arisen through some strenuous gardening he was doing. I was too naive and too busy to do any research over and above accepting his explanation that he had strained his prostate while gardening. I have since read up on the condition, and I now understand prostatitis to be an inflammation or infection of the prostate gland, which can be brought on by rectal intercourse.

In early July 2012, when I saw Tim stride into Gray's funeral wearing make-up in front of six hundred farmers and country folk, it was as if a light suddenly switched on. I saw all the pieces of the jigsaw puzzle. They jostled and moved their way into an image I could finally make sense of. An image that screamed at me: *You've been married to a gay or bisexual man!*

If it quacks like a duck, if it waddles like a duck, if it looks like a duck, and people tell you to your face they think it's a duck, then it's hardly going to be a chicken, is it? Even when the duck is secretly paddling in a pond with other ducks and is having some type of middle-aged duck identity crisis, all the while emphatically telling you it can't be a duck because it's a chicken ... it really *is* a duck. Because we all know chickens don't swim.

I tried to find answers to the madness swirling inside my mind. My Google searches typically read as follows: "signs my husband is gay", "married and gay", "how do you know you are gay", and so on.

All the websites I searched had lists of key indicators or signs which could suggest your husband might be gay. My husband displayed the following signs from the lists I came across:

a) Decline in sexual activity early in the marriage
b) Sexual performance more mechanical than passionate
c) Prioritising spending time at the gym
d) Working hard at changing his appearance
e) Preoccupation with image and grooming, e.g. using beauty therapists for facials, waxing and eyebrow shaping, tanning beds, teeth whitening

f) Erasing computer search history
g) General secretiveness
h) Apparent midlife crisis
i) Moodiness and depression
j) Failure to notice how beautiful his wife is

In July 2012, Bella drew a picture and explained it as follows: 'That's me, that's my Daddy, and that's Daddy's willy in his mouth.'

I needed advice as I was in shock and had no idea how to handle the situation. I made an appointment with my doctor. 'You need to go to the police and report him,' she said.

My reaction was more considered. Rather than reporting Tim to the police, I took Bella to see a child psychologist. After a series of appointments, the psychologist told me she had inconclusive results regarding the drawing. She was unable to conclude whether Bella had, or had not, been sexually assaulted, or whether she had witnessed her father engaging in sexual activity with men, or whether she had seen anything at all.

I was angry, but also desperately trying to stop myself from overreacting or being vindictive towards Tim. I was determined to think clearly and objectively about what was best for Bella.

Without proof of any abuse, or any change in behaviour from Bella, I came to the conclusion she had not been sexually abused. What I do believe is she may have witnessed her father engaging in sexual activity with other men at our home while I was away for work, or she may have seen him watching gay porn. For those reasons, I chose not to report the incident to the police. My barrister later commended me on my decision and how I had handled the situation.

When the drawing was discussed with lawyers, Tim made no attempt to explain himself or Bella's drawing. He made no enquiry as to Bella's welfare, and he did not ask to speak to, or meet with the child psychologist, or ask to see the notes of the therapy sessions.

In September 2012, I finally summoned the courage to ask Tim over the telephone about the fact he was wearing make-up. 'Tim, I need to ask you something. It's personal and I would appreciate it if you'd remain calm. A number of people have told me they have seen you wearing make-up. I've seen you wearing it too, several times. I've been asked whether you're gay. Hey, if you're gay, that's OK. I don't have anything against gay people. But you're my husband. You should have been honest with me.'

'I'm not gay,' he responded with a condescending tone.

'All right then, can you please explain the make-up wearing?' I asked.

'It's not make-up. It's tinted moisturiser,' he said.

'Really?' I replied.

'Yes, it's Dale's,' he said. (His sister's.)

What a load of bullshit. 'OK, then,' I said, 'I need you to be aware of what you have put me through. I had to have an AIDS test.'

He said absolutely nothing from then on. Not a single word. Then he hung up.

I told one of my girlfriends about his response. She told me any heterosexual guy, if asked whether he was gay, would say something like, "What the fuck are you talking about? Are you fucking nuts?"

She then said if Tim was straight and wasn't playing around on me, he would have said, "Why the fuck have you had an AIDS test? Have *you* been playing around on *me*?"

I was in shock for months. The afternoons lingered the most. I went in and out of concentration with my work. I was present in person but my mind was never really there. I tried to make sense of all the uncertainty. Over and over I repeatedly asked myself: *Why? What does it all mean? How could he have done this to me?*

I closed the curtains and lowered the blinds. I snapped shut all the blades of the white window shutters. The interior of my home was as dark and as isolated as my soul. I needed to cry my ocean of tears in private. The tears came in waves and they wouldn't stop.

I felt utterly deceived and completely defeated.

I lay face down, like a starfish, on the floor. Emotions oozed from my body as I wrote the word *why* through salty pools of tears. I ran my fingers through the shagpile rug. The coarse, textural threads left indentations on my face. My chest heaved. Snot trickled down the back of my throat, and tears of pain streamed down my face. I was hyperventilating. I couldn't breathe. My whole body convulsed.

I pulled myself up the side of an armchair and crouched on my knees. I looked at the reflection I saw in the mirror on the wall and did not recognise the person staring back at me. Her eyes were red, puffy, raw, and destroyed, her bottom lip quivering uncontrollably. Streaks of luminous melon-coloured lipstick smeared her face. Most shocking of all was the river of black lines running in crazed patterns down her cheeks – they were mascara-laden streams of tears.

I stared at myself as it slowly dawned on me that I was the sad clown to be laughed at and shamed.

My mind wandered back to Tim and his make-up wearing. I thought of how smug he was. Wasn't it so "rich" of him to turn up in that way and disrespect me, and also to disrespect our friend Gray at his funeral? Wasn't that such a "queer" thing to do?

Clown

Make-up for all the world to see
"So rich"

Applied as only a man would
"Boorish"
With such blatant disregard for my concern
"So queer"

To have suffered for so long
At his malevolent hands
My layers of hurt
"Are"
Far deeper than those of his all-consuming vanity

Shattering lives
My fate unclear
Where has he gone?
"Why?"
He doesn't care

I see a face
Wretched with fear
Show me a clown
"I am"
Already here

I slowly came to understand why Tim had been so horrible to me. I believed he felt trapped and sexually unfulfilled while he was shackled in marriage. With his narcissistic tendencies, he was never going to blame himself for his unhappiness. Naturally, he took his frustrations out on me.

I was able to make sense of what he said towards the end of May 2012. 'Oh, you really are so lovely, Emma. You've been a wonderful wife, but I need to be in Australia. It's better for all of us. And for what it's worth, I'm sorry for what I'm putting you through.'

I remember those words as if he had spoken them yesterday. His eyes conveyed emotions of release and relief. They were not eyes filled with sadness or regret.

Even more disturbing was his attempt at justifying his decision to abandon Bella. 'I need to be in Australia – so I can reach my potential. What's good for me is good for Bella,' he said.

How could any father say it was in the best interest of his child to be separated from them? Perhaps Bella *was* better off without him living too close to her. At least she would receive unconditional love from me, and I would never abandon her.

Through her tears, Bella asked, 'Mummy, what did I do wrong? Why did Daddy leave me?'

At those times, I cuddled her and said, 'Daddy and Mummy love you dearly, darling. You haven't done anything wrong, sweetheart. Daddy had to go away for work. That's all.'

Bella was four years old. I was torn apart. So was she.

I was stuck in a vacuum during that year. I couldn't make sense of anything. Each day I battled to hold on to my sanity and my physical strength. I became skilled at dealing with my pain in private, away from the public, away from Bella. I let the grief out with my poetry, going for runs in regional parks, and sitting for hours feeling the wind claw at my face in open spaces. I was somehow comforted by the salty sea air and the streams of tears that bit my raw and reddened cheeks. I had to let out the pain that welled in bottomless pits within my heart. I spent weekends away on my own, wandering through the kauri forests of Northland. The permanence of the thousand-year-old trees told me my issues were temporary, that this time in my life would pass. I found peace and freedom with nature and was able to breathe and just "be". I needed that time and space to grieve my loss.

I felt dirty and violated by Tim's betrayal. It was humiliating to learn of his deception. The stigma of a failed marriage to a man you suspect is gay or bisexual is quite a cross to bear. I tormented myself trying to find answers to a situation I didn't understand.

With great sadness, I was eventually able to accept that my best was not, and never would be, good enough.

PART TWO

CHAOS AND LONGING

five

Mel, what are those dark marks on your chest?

My bestie Mel and I are a comedy act on four legs. When we're together, we're in our happy place. It really doesn't matter where we are or what we're doing, we make our own fun. Mel tends to be the dominant troublemaker. She always strides out ahead of me. Her boobs tend to head us both off by a few seconds. Well, that's my story and I'm sticking with it. She would say otherwise.

Mel lost her beloved brother to suicide in January 2012, and the wheels fell off my marriage and life shortly after.

A year later, in February 2013, we put stress and sadness aside for a few days and travelled to the United States for some girl time in Los Angeles and Las Vegas. To cover the cost of the trip I booked space at a trade fair in Las Vegas with the intention of selling my father's wholesale range.

We stayed with my American friend Kiera in LA and had hours of fun window-shopping in Beverley Hills, eating out in Santa Monica, and watching the LA Lakers play at the STAPLES Center. We went backstage at the *Jimmy Kimmel Live!* show and were in the audience to hear Ellie Goulding perform live to a group of approximately 100 people.

Mel and I were in our element in Las Vegas. We took our credit cards and our bodies to the limit. We bought gorgeous cocktail dresses for as little as $80 and relished the delight of playing dress-up before departing for dinner each night.

The two of us are always up for a laugh and a new adventure. We both appreciate a fine-looking young man, so it was inevitable we found ourselves front row and salivating at scantily clad young men at Sapphire Las Vegas Gentlemen's Club.

Half an hour into the show, and with a few cosmopolitans already under my belt, I was approached for a lap dance.

I was a little sceptical at first, but Mel encouraged me to let my guard down. I am easily led, it seems.

Brad, the stripper, was in his mid-twenties. He was in great shape – toned, attractive and sexy. I'd never had a lap dance from a man before. I had no idea what to do. I didn't know where to look.

Brad took my hand and led me away to a more private, darkened area of the bar. He swayed his hips, he shook his booty, and he began to slide his manhood up and down my thigh. He slipped his thumbs beneath the band of his Calvins and teased me by pushing his underwear down below his hips.

I felt nervous and uncomfortable. I was heading for an asthma attack. 'Ah, Brad,' I said, 'you know what? You're hot and all, but I'm not sure I'm cut out for this. Do you mind if we go back to my table?'

He escorted me back and sat with me while I reached inside my evening clutch for a $50 tip. I was so embarrassed about my freak-out, I just wanted to crawl under the table and not come out.

Meanwhile, my very much married friend Mel had disappeared into the darkest corner of the club with a well-built and handsome young black man by the name of Noah.

Back at our table, Brad plied me with alcohol and flattery. 'Gee, Emma, I never get to meet lovely women like you. I wish we hadn't met here. I wish we had met somewhere else, you know, like at the library.'

There were three things going through my inebriated brain at that point. 1) No one uses libraries any more, 2) It wouldn't really matter whether we had met at the library, the supermarket, or a petrol station, because I had no intention of dating Brad, and 3) I was amazed at the level of attention and flattery my $50 tip had bought me. Perhaps, they were just some well-rehearsed lines?

'Oh, that's sweet of you Brad,' I said. Aargh.

Mel eventually reappeared a good twenty minutes later. Her revealing top displayed her flushed and ample breasts. Beads of sweat scurried and disappeared within her cleavage, and a deliciously satisfied smile was plastered across her face. She was struggling to breathe.

'Mel, are you OK?' I asked.

'Ah, yeah,' she replied. Her eyes darted nervously as she dropped like a stone into her chair. In the dappled lights of The Sapphire Club her breasts continued to heave and glisten.

'Hun, are you sure you're OK? And, um, what are those dark marks on your chest?' I asked.

'Oh, I dunno,' she said as she glanced down at her surging bust. 'It must be his fake tan,' she said as she carried on wheezing between her gasps for air.

Mel wiped her brow with the cocktail napkin she held in her right hand. With her left hand, she fervently reached for her drink. Her right hand then began to dab at her breasts. She tried to erase the trace evidence with her napkin. But what exactly were those dark marks?

'Are you sure that's fake tan, Mel? Um, did you not notice that guy was black?' I could barely get the words out through my laughter.

'I'm not sure black guys wear fake tan, Mel. Jesus, girlfriend, what the hell *are* those marks on your chest?' I asked.

By that stage I was bent over in my chair, in pain with laughter.

She never did own up to what the black marks were. And she has never told me what she got up to in the deepest, darkest corner of The Sapphire Club with the gorgeous young black man named Noah. I can only guess.

Noah gave Mel his business card. I recall watching her stroke and flick that card with her painted fingernails several times that night and over the following few days. Was Noah on your mind, Mel?

We carried on our antics well past midnight. At 4 am, we found ourselves seated at one of the cocktail bars at the Bellagio. My mate was smoking a stogie cigar. I sat right beside her and sipped on yet another cosmopolitan while I chatted to Carol, who was on holiday from the United Kingdom.

I woke at 8.30 am, alone in my luxurious super king bed back at the Venetian Hotel. Mel was across the room, asleep in her own super king bed. Did we take a taxi or did we walk back to our room? It took me three days to remember how we had manoeuvred our path from the Bellagio across the road and down a bit to the Venetian. We were two girls behaving badly.

Later that day, we had to construct our stand at the trade fair. Mel found herself a chair and took great hilarity in directing my every move. I was up and down ladders and trestle tables with a staple gun in hand, erecting signage and laying out displays. I was so badly hung-over, my headache lasted two days. I even fell asleep at the restaurant over dinner that night.

The trade fair wasn't exactly successful. Feeling unwell for the first day would have had something to do with it. I remember verbalising my thoughts to

Mel: 'Doll, I don't even want to talk to these people. My head is pounding, and I think I'm going to be sick.'

Mid-afternoon on day two of the trade fair, Mel announced, 'I need a massage.' A few hours later, we both lay naked and face down on our respective beds in our hotel room. Starched white sheets preserved our modesty.

As my masseuse finished kneading my back, she tapped me on the shoulder and said, 'Roll over, please.'

In a dream-like state of relaxation, I rolled over and struggled to open my eyes. I glanced over to where my friend lay.

I froze like a raccoon in headlights. With wide eyes I stared in disbelief as I caught sight of Mel. She lay naked on her back with her upper body fully exposed. Her masseuse stood over her from behind with outstretched arms and two hands either side of her left boob. The masseuse threw her body weight into massaging my friend.

'Are you paying extra for that shit?' I asked Mel as I began to chuckle.

A few days later we flew back to LA to see Kiera. I had always admired Kiera's flawless skin, and I said to her, 'Honey, whatever you're doing, whatever you're taking or injecting, well, I want some of what you've got.'

We made our appointments and taxied to her beauty therapist. I requested the therapist inject a little filler into my cheeks and some Botox into my forehead. I paid for the treatments and we left.

On our way to LAX airport the following day, Mel, Kiera and I enjoyed a casual meal at one of the many Cheesecake Factory family restaurants. Towards the end of the evening, Mel looked across the table at me and said, 'Oh my God. Rivers, what's going on with your eyebrow?'

'Huh? What do you mean, Mel?' I replied.

'Babe, your left eyebrow has moved halfway up your forehead,' she exclaimed, cackling with laughter.

Sure enough, she was right. I could have walked from the set of a reality TV series: *Botox Gone Wrong*. My seemingly harmless dabble with LA appearance medicine had gone horribly awry.

As soon as I got home to New Zealand, I plucked the offending eyebrow off and pencilled in a replacement. There was no way I was leaving the house looking like that. It really did look ridiculous.

A couple of months later, my darling Bella started school. She was such a delightful child, and I remember with fondness walking her to and from school each day. As

I held her hand, she told me about her day. Looking up at me with a cheeky grin, she said, 'Mummy, I wore your knickers to school today.'

I couldn't believe my ears. I thought she was making it up.

As soon as we got home, Bella lifted her skirt. She stuck her tiny bum out and said, 'See, Mummy, I really did wear your knickers to school.'

Sure enough, she was wearing a hot-pink cotton G-string I had bought as a joke for four dollars at a souvenir shop in Las Vegas. In silver writing on the front were the words: "If you are reading this, you must have bought me dinner."

six

And so, the show begins

Two months after Tim unilaterally decided to divorce me, I tried to secure a financial settlement with him.

In July 2012, I offered him $430,000 in cash. That was a clean split down the middle of our property assets. I didn't go after the $82,000 in cash he had already taken with him to Australia – money from his work superannuation scheme. Technically, $41,000 of that was mine.

I left my businesses out of my settlement offer, but, then again, they had been wound down; there was minimal stock, the retail store had closed, and I had told all my customers and clients I was moving to Australia. The businesses weren't trading and they were worthless in their current state.

I didn't ask for a contribution towards the business loan of $85,000 I was repaying to the bank, even though the money had been borrowed through the businesses to fund the renovation of the Mill. In essence, I was being reasonable and fair.

In July 2012, there was $117,000 between the amount he wanted and what I was prepared to offer. Tim threw my offer for settlement in my face. He refused to accept it or to negotiate with me.

In August 2012, Tim threatened me. As he passed Bella back to me at the Henderson Pak'n'Save supermarket car park, he said, 'I know you've restarted your businesses and you're using your father's company as a front. If you don't do exactly as I tell you and give me everything, I'll destroy you.'

I was served with legal proceedings on 21 February 2013. Tim was taking me to court. To maximise my pain and suffering, he chose to have me served on our wedding anniversary.

Tim claimed that the collective value of all three of my businesses was $745,000. He suggested I was free to keep them, and in exchange for that, I was to immediately sell the Mill and all proceeds from that sale would go to him. He said he would only accept offers for sale of over $1,150,000. He also proposed he should receive the $430,000 that was sitting in a lawyer's trust account, being the proceeds from the sale of our family home. Tim indicated he would also get to keep the $82,000 superannuation he had already taken with him to Australia. He made no mention of the $85,000 business debt.

Tim had devised a plan that would leave me with a four-year-old child to care for on my own, with no home, nowhere to live, with no job, no means of income, no assets, and with debt of $85,000. I had some personal credit card debt at the time as well. In exchange for that, he was proposing to take $1,112,000 in cash with him to Australia. He was being paid a salary of AUD$218,000 per annum for his job in Sydney. He had the use of a company car, was receiving superannuation benefits, was being incentivised with an annual bonus payment as part of his salary package, and would receive five weeks paid holiday per year. With no childcare responsibilities, Tim was footloose and fancy-free.

I had worked extremely hard and made significant sacrifices to get us to where we were financially. Most of the equity we had accumulated in our properties had been paid for with the proceeds from my businesses. I had thrown all my energy into my marriage, my family, and building the companies for our shared benefit.

But Tim made a critical error of judgement. He had overlooked my gritty determination – the very quality that had fuelled my success in the first place. I was not about to hand all I had worked for over to him and start again from scratch.

I launched the businesses in 1998, well before I met Tim. I had a vision, some skills, and endless amounts of motivation and energy. To this day, I still remember the desk I worked at in the flat I shared with Mel. That was where it all began. I incrementally grew the businesses from that desk, to a shared commercial office, then to my own commercial office, then to a retail store. I had no angel investor – all the business growth was funded through careful management of the business cash flow. For years, I barely took holidays, and I routinely worked eighteen-hour days.

I almost lost everything in the 2008 GFC. By the time Tim launched his legal attack against me at the beginning of 2013, I had earned my place in business twice over already. I had no intention of losing everything to Tim and starting from scratch, again. Little did I realise that the legal onslaught would bring me to my knees, regardless.

The validity of Tim's claim was irrelevant at that stage. He never thought I would have the financial means or the emotional strength to be able to defend myself against his legal attack. Tim thought I would simply submit to his demands, that he would win and take everything. Well, he was wrong.

So, what were my choices exactly? To not fight back and defend myself against Tim's ludicrous claim would have meant certain and immediate defeat. I would have lost everything. However, to go into battle against him provided no guarantee of success. I had no idea how much it was going to cost in legal and professional fees to defend myself, and there was no assurance of financial security at the end of it for Bella and me.

There was no middle ground with Tim. He didn't want to mediate or compromise. It was all or nothing. I *had* to defend myself. I had to at least try.

I chose to fight. For Bella, for myself, for our future.

The injustice of the legal system hit me, as a tsunami. I was to learn if one party (the plaintiff) initiates proceedings and the responding party (the respondent or defendant) decides not to defend their position, then the aggressor (the plaintiff) automatically wins. In a nutshell, if you do not have the financial means to defend your position, you are stuffed. Where is the fairness?

To have Tim manipulate, lie, deceive, and threaten me the way he did, literally made my blood boil.

I made a decision: I would do whatever it took to prevent Tim from achieving his goal of taking all our combined assets.

I made a pact with myself never to give up.

Time and time again over the course of the following four years, I recited aloud: 'You cannot defeat a person who will not give up.'

I centred myself mentally and harnessed my anger. I caressed and concentrated every ounce of the frustration and despair I felt and threw it back at Tim with all the strength I could muster.

Tim weakened me, he threatened me, and then he thrust his boot on my throat. I guess he figured if I was put under enough financial pressure, to the point where the mortgage and taxes weren't paid, the Department of Inland Revenue (the government Taxation Department/IRD) or the bank would step in and force the sale of the Mill property. He thought I would eventually give up.

Tim was to discover I was a lot tougher than I appeared.

Between June and December 2012, I had received so many hateful and threatening telephone calls, emails, and texts from Tim, I was reluctant to pick up the phone. Every point of contact with him tore off the Band-Aid that covered my open wound. He planted his daggers where he knew they would hurt the most – over the care of our daughter and the trash he left of our marriage. His power was, in part, being fuelled by the terror, emotional pain, and financial hardship he was able to inflict on me. I had to put a stop to it.

I instructed my lawyer to send Tim a letter notifying him that he was not to contact me via telephone, text, or email. All his correspondence would need to be delivered through my lawyers. He was furious. His texts, phone calls, and emails continued. A total of six letters instructing Tim to cease all communication with me were sent to his lawyer before he stopped.

He then decided to email my lawyers over trivial matters with the sole purpose of burdening me with unnecessary legal costs. For example, he emailed my lawyer to find out what time Bella finished school one particular Friday. He could easily have phoned the school or checked on their website. Each time Tim contacted my lawyer, that single gesture cost me money in legal fees, as my lawyer was required to contact me then report back to Tim in writing. It cost him nothing.

In an attempt to try and justify his claim of 50% ownership of the companies I set up well before we were married, Tim wrote of his day-to-day involvement in running them. He asserted he was responsible for stock control, pricing and merchandising within the retail store. It was the stuff of fantasy.

I read documents detailing what he believed he was entitled to. Tim noted I had accrued loyalty points on my work credit card. He wanted his share. I did some research and discovered I had enough loyalty points to buy a 12-month magazine subscription.

Tim secured the domain names for the business websites early on in our marriage. When it came to renew the licences for the domain names in January 2013, he refused to transfer the management authority for them over to me. All three of the company websites nearly crashed. It took pressure from my accountant and other male business associates before Tim relinquished his authority.

Tim never declared a profit for the businesses over the nine year period 2003–12 when he acted as the company accountant. I am not entirely sure how he managed to do that, considering the companies were turning over more than $1 million per annum for a few years prior to the GFC.

The turnover ebbed and flowed, and I did my best to manage cash flow and expenditure accordingly. There were challenging times, particularly when the full force of the global crisis hit. Turnover plummeted. Within a few months, architectural project work disappeared altogether. The combined turnover halved within a year. From 2010 to 2012, I was only ever able to drag the turnover back to 60–70% of the pre-GFC figures.

When I read his claim that my businesses were worth $745,000, I wondered how he thought he was going to prove their worth. Businesses that don't make a profit are generally not worth a lot.

He reported the businesses had next to no stock and no assets. In fact, they were left with a debt of $85,000 to the bank. I was fairly certain Tim would struggle to access financial evidence to back up his fabricated claim. When my lawyer demanded Tim hand over the historical financial records of the companies, he declared he didn't have them. Without comprehensive financial documentation as evidence in support, why didn't my lawyers make a demand for Tim's case to be thrown out of court?

Despite his lack of evidence, and with no opposition from my lawyers, Tim successfully launched his legal attack. I was directed by the law firm to seek the expert opinions of court-approved valuers and employ forensic accountants to disprove his claims. It became apparent that if I was unable to access funds to pay professionals and file a defence, I would lose. I would lose, irrespective of whether there was any truth to Tim's claim or not.

The direction the law firm sent me in abruptly slapped me in the face when, in February 2015, I was presented with an invoice for $11,500, being part of the total $35,000 I would eventually pay to a court-approved business valuer. The valuer requested I pay his invoice so he could progress with the preparation of the business valuations that would later be released to the court.

I rang my barrister. 'Katherine, I don't have $11,500. What will happen if I don't find the money to pay the valuer and the report doesn't get filed?'

'Without the valuer's report, you will lose, Emma. I'm sorry,' she said.

I had to call my parents. I had no choice. It was either a matter of finding $11,500 within three days to pay the valuer, or let Tim walk away with over $1.1 million and have Bella and me face destitution.

Fortunately, my parents were willing to assist.

I very quickly came to understand that the outcome of a civil legal matter is not an indication of who is right and who is wrong. The outcome will often be decided by who has the financial means to afford the best and most sustained defence, and/or attack. The outcome is also dependent on who is prepared to lie.

Tim made mistakes. He underestimated the level of support I had and my ability to access money through my family. He misjudged my huge reserves of mental and physical strength, my intelligence, and tenacity.

To give myself a chance of surviving Tim's assault, I had to channel my energy, work hard and maintain my position. I needed to earn enough money through my father's newly incorporated companies to pay the mortgage and our basic living expenses, and stay mentally and physically well enough to see the matter through to the end. Tim had no concrete evidence to use against me to back up his claims. I had nothing to do with the accounts. Everyone knew that. There was no way Tim could make the financials say the companies were worth anywhere near $745,000 based on the figures he presented to the IRD.

If Tim was to stand up in court and say the companies were in fact making money and that he had effectively "cooked the books" with the submission of inaccurate business records to the IRD, well that would be the end of his fabulous finance career in Australia. I couldn't see him taking a risk like that.

Every time his lawyers delivered a letter to my legal team, I was certain he thought he was wearing me down to the point I would break.

Sure, I was feeling the pressure. It was intense. I liken it to being woken every morning with a bear spread across my chest. It was suffocating. I tossed and turned in bed at night, writhing in fear. I could almost feel snakes crawling beneath my skin everywhere I went. I was forever on the lookout for another killer blow. I couldn't escape Tim's threats and torments, whether they were direct or not. His clammy, spiteful, oppressive aura followed me everywhere I went. I couldn't shake him. Day and night, he lurked in my mind.

There were relentless emails and meetings with lawyers, accountants and valuers that didn't seem to end. I spent whole weekends documenting facts, figures and events so my professionals were fully abreast of the detail and context of each situation.

With the exception of a few days off with Mel at the beginning of 2013, when we travelled to Las Vegas to the trade fair, I had not been on holiday since Christmas 2011. The situation worsened with time; legal and accounting costs continued to escalate, and my energy reserves waned. I had to forget about holidays.

Tim commenced child custody proceedings in the family court around the same time he initiated proceedings regarding our relationship property.

With the child custody proceeding, he requested he spend one weekend a month with Bella. Over and above those weekends, he wanted one additional full week a year with her, plus every alternate Christmas. He also requested the court enforce his request to have Bella spend one weekend a month with his sister or his parents.

In response, I offered him four weeks a year with Bella, being one full week over each of the four lots of school holidays, plus every alternate Christmas with her. I also offered him two weekends a month so he could spend one weekend a month with Bella and take her to his family for the other weekend. Tim turned down my offer and continued with his legal action and request for *less* contact time with his daughter. Interestingly, he wrote in various legal documents that his daughter was his number one priority. I failed to see the correlation.

The child custody action provided Tim with another vehicle through which he could attack me. He was able to cause me emotional distress and further bleed me dry of money in the process. I am convinced his strategy was to wear me down with the child custody action so I would be less able to afford to defend myself with the relationship property action. It had to be that. I mean, what man takes his ex-wife to court to secure *less* contact with their child than what is being offered? It's nonsense.

How did the child custody matter even end up in court given the ridiculous demands Tim was making? Was this again just a clever revenue-generating exercise being exacerbated by lawyers and barristers? Given my emotional fragility and legal naivety, I was easy prey.

With little relief from looking after Bella, my time was either spent caring for her, working at my day job or working on my legal defence. I couldn't afford childcare and Tim rarely saw Bella, so I was unable to go out and have a regular social life. Any dates I went on with men mostly happened over coffee throughout the day, or when Bella was staying the night with my friends.

In comparison to my situation, Tim was leading a very carefree lifestyle in Sydney. It took him less than two months, from the time I confronted him over his suspected bisexuality in September 2012, to find a girlfriend. Interestingly, she was a lawyer who owned a residential property in one of the most sought-after suburbs in Sydney. Within a year of meeting, his new partner had successfully become pregnant through IVF. They got engaged.

Did his new partner ever wonder why a guy would choose to set up a new life in a city and country where he knew no one? Did she ever wonder what he was running away from? Or what of his past he was trying to conceal with his new life and location? Was she unconcerned that he left his young child behind in New Zealand?

Not surprisingly, Tim actively prevented me from meeting his new partner.

seven

DTF? WTF!

Time stood still for me when Tim appeared wearing make-up at the end of June 2012. For the six months that followed, I felt tormented with uncertainty. Was my husband gay? Was he having sex with men throughout our entire marriage? How did he get away with it? Did he ever love me? Why didn't I see it? Did my subconscious know all along and was I too weak to confront him? Was I imagining the whole thing?

I felt worthless, and I felt used. On a confidence scale of zero to ten, I was sitting at a meagre negative five.

My friend Rob was wonderful to me over that time. He and I have always had a magical friendship, one based on kindness and a shared mischievous zest for life and fun.

Rob called me. 'Hey, Rivers, we're going out – on Friday. And you're not wearing any of those hideous tents that make you look like Nana Mouskouri. I won't have it. I won't be seen in public with you if you look like that.'

'Don't be so mean to me,' I said. 'You know I'm not finding any of this easy. Stop riding my ass.'

Rob laughed at me down the phone. 'Nope. Not doing that. Those are the rules, Emms. You've got a fantastic figure. Stop hiding it. You've got two days to get a babysitter. Now go.'

He took me shopping and educated me as to what clothing men find attractive on women. I had lost all sense of myself and how I was perceived by men.

Rob talked me into buying an above-the-knee, skin-tight grey dress with black embellishments on the shoulders, and a pair of four-inch heels in a garish combination of crimson and purple suede.

'But I can't walk in these stupid shoes. Hun, they're hurting my feet,' I complained.

'They're supposed to hurt,' he said. 'You're actually not meant to walk in them, ya egg. They're only good for sitting at a bar.'

'Well that's ridiculous,' I said.

'Oh dear Lord, what's it going to take to get through to you? You're not living on the farm now, young lady.'

When Rob and I were out together there were times when he was momentarily distracted at the bar or he wandered off to the bathroom. At those times random men approached me. They offered me drinks or they'd just stand next to me and tell me I was gorgeous. I had no idea how to handle the attention. I was lost and overwhelmed. Most of the time I just wanted to crawl away and hide.

Navigating my way back to dating as a forty-something solo mother had me searching for answers. In September 2012, I visited a clairvoyant. She mentioned a horrific legal battle that I was going to have to contend with. 'Don't worry, Emma. Karma is your friend. You'll be fine, but take a deep breath because what you have ahead of you will cause you considerable heartache.'

She picked up on the presence of a young man and described the arrival of a baby.

I wondered what on earth was going to happen. Was I going to have another baby? Oh God. Who with? I hadn't had sex for ages. Would it be an immaculate conception? Jesus Christ? Literally. Really?

In October 2012, I received a call from my friend Kate. 'Hey, Emms, do you remember that young guy who was at the bar with us on Friday night?' asked Kate. 'You know, the guy who was talking to you.'

'Ah, I think so. Was his name Nick?' I replied. 'Does he have olive skin, and gorgeous pale-green eyes? The young scaffolder you work with – is that who you're talking about?'

'Yes, that's him,' said Kate. 'Well, he just walked into my office and asked me for your mobile number.'

The kid was twenty.

'Oh no way! Seriously? Stop it, Kate. You're joking, aren't you? Please tell me you're joking,' I said as I struggled to get the words out through my laughter. 'What on earth did you say to him?'

'I told him not to be so bloody stupid. That he obviously doesn't realise how old you are and, besides, you're well out of his league. I told him to forget about you, get the hell out of my office, and go back to work,' replied Kate.

'You're so harsh, Kate. I hope he's OK,' I said as I continued to chuckle.

I couldn't believe such a handsome young man would even notice me, let alone have the guts to ask Kate for my number.

A month later I went to the races with my girlfriends. Going to the races is always great fun and a good excuse to play dress-up for the day. I didn't place any bets. What was the point of betting? I could barely tell one end of a horse from the other.

As Kate and I sat in the afternoon sunshine, sipping on champers with four of our girlfriends, handsome young Nick wandered over to our table. He pulled up a chair and placed it right next to me. He was very chatty and incredibly attentive. I was intrigued by his behaviour – did the stunning young man not have a mother?

I couldn't stay long as I had to pick up Bella – she was with my friend Skye for a few hours. Nick walked me to my car. As I went to open the driver's door, he took me in his arms and kissed me on the lips. It was a long, slow, passionate kiss. It was so hot. He was so hot. And then he kissed me again.

What was happening? Was I suffering from heat stroke? Did the handsome young man just kiss me?

Nick told me he knew how old I was and that he didn't care. He thought I was beautiful and he wanted to date me. I drove off questioning whether I had just imagined the whole thing.

Oh Lord, he was stunning: tall, part-Māori, with divine, smooth olive skin, dreamy pale-green eyes and a wide beaming smile. His broad chest and divine muscles personified youth in all its glory.

My friend Skye had a joke at my expense later that afternoon. She suggested it was possible the young man the clairvoyant had foreseen was also going to be the father of my new baby. As she threw her head back and laughed, she said, 'I can't wait to overhear *that* phone conversation when you call your parents and tell them you're having a baby with a twenty-year-old.'

It never happened. I was not the one who had the baby.

Nick stayed over at my place one night but I didn't have sex with him. He was very sweet and innocent and probably just what I needed at the time – a decent young man who wasn't out to use me.

Mel reminded me of a text I sent to her one morning before 6 am at the time I was seeing Nick. It read: *OMG. Naked 20 y o in my bed. Gorg. Dreaming? WTF should I do?*

Dad phoned me just before Christmas 2012. 'Your mother and I have been chatting. We're concerned that you're not eating enough. You've lost too much weight. We know things haven't been easy for you, but you have a daughter to look after. You can't afford to get sick. Now come on, you need to eat.'

'Thanks, Dad,' I said. 'Look, I get that you're concerned, but really it's not that simple. I'm very busy and quite often I don't have time to stop and eat, particularly when I'm travelling.'

My father replied, 'Get a chilly bin. Put it in your car.'

I had little tolerance for my father's lecture that day, and I thought I knew how I would be able to shut him up. 'Hey, Dad, yeah, I get it about my eating. I'll try harder. But look, while I have you on the phone, there's something I should tell you. Um, I think I'm dating a twenty-year-old.'

There was a brief pause on the other end of the phone. Then my dad said, 'Well, Emma, you really *are* going to have to eat some more, aren't you. Because if you're seeing a twenty-year-old, you're going to need your strength.'

I was shocked. 'I can't believe you just said that to me, Dad!' My reply came as a wheeze through my laughter.

'Well, it's the truth, isn't it? Just eat some more and get on with it. I'll chat to you later,' he said.

Clearly the concept of me dating a twenty-year-old was not going to be a lasting thing. I was forty-one at the time, old enough to be Nick's mother.

I never actually had sex with that stunning young man. Our brief liaison was over in a matter of a few months. I'm not sure which one of us was more scared. My gym friend, Tayla, found great hilarity in the situation. She told me I had just ordered a delivery pizza with all the extra trimmings and left it sitting on the bench to go cold.

Looking back, the whole experience was surreal. I was grateful to have had those moments with Nick. Without him ever realising, he gently helped me take my first steps back to rediscovering my sexuality.

Sometime in March 2013, I visited my friend Skye and her husband Dan. We all sat around their dining table. With tears streaming down my face, swollen eyes, and a fistful of tissues, I said, 'How am I supposed to move on? How do I start dating? I never meet anyone. I might never have sex again.'

Skye told me later that after I left, Dan laughed and said, 'All this shit about Emma never having sex again? Somehow I doubt it.'

It seems ridiculous, but that's honestly how I felt. I had no idea men found me so desirable. My husband barely touched me sexually throughout our marriage. I grew to feel transparent.

I didn't know where to start with dating. With the exception of the attention I had received from young Nick, it had been ten years since I had been on a date.

After weeks of agonising over my decision, I put together an online dating profile. Within a few hours of launching it, I had over a hundred men trying to message me. I was flabbergasted and a little freaked out.

On the particular dating site I was on, it was possible for people to pass photos directly to each other through the website. Within a day I had received three "dick pics" of fully erect penises.

What had I started? Thankfully these men knew nothing about me apart from a fake profile name and a couple of pretty pics of my face. I blocked the penises from contacting me.

Without a doubt, one of the most wonderful things to have happened when I started dating was the distraction it gave me from the chaos and hurt of the legal action that was unfolding around me. Dating gave me a chance to breathe, to feel human, connected, alive, valued, and wanted.

Agreeing to go on a date gave me a reason to look forward to the weekend, when, for a few hours, I could exist in a world that did not involve work, childcare, and a vindictive ex. I escaped my grim reality and pondered over which of my divine cocktail dresses I would wear and which shoe and jewellery combination I could match to my selected dress. I lathered myself with delectable Burberry Body scented oils and spent time on my hair and make-up. I always left home with a spring in my step and a twinkle in my eyes.

Being in the company of interesting and attractive men became quite addictive. I soaked up the attention like a parched sponge. My dates generally buttered me up with a slew of compliments, and most of them gave me a kiss goodbye. None of them suspected how much they were helping me recapture my joie de vivre.

I hid my insecurities well. I rarely spoke of my marriage. I never spoke of my family. I tried to appear confident and composed, yet my nerves got the better of me at times. I had several asthma attacks over my standard order of a glass of Sauvignon Blanc with chicken Caesar salad. Clearly dating was more stressful than

I gave it credit for. As time went on, the severity of the asthma attacks worsened. I put that down to the increased pressure from the legal case. The stress was slowly but surely wearing me down.

With the exception of four men, all those I dated were younger than me. They were young enough to still have a broad chest, a pert butt and a flat stomach, yet they were mature enough to know how to treat a woman and to be able to contribute to some interesting conversation.

I was barely drinking so I never lost control, and always drove myself home.

Mel was fascinated by my tales of dinner dates and dashing young men. She wanted to know names and details. In a fever, she began to record their names. As the list grew to approach 30 names, I announced, 'Mel, I need a shower.' I was starting to perspire at the thought of some of the hotter dates and all those missed opportunities.

I yelled out to her from the shower, 'I've got a couple more for you, doll.'

We were at the supermarket one afternoon when, midway through loading Diet Coke bottles into the trolley, I suddenly looked up at her and said, 'Nipple Steve, Mel. How could I forget Nipple Steve?'

Mel's next question was, 'What's your number, Emms?' In other words, she wanted to know: Of the men I had been on dates with, how many of them had I slept with?

'I'm not sure, hun. A couple, I guess,' I replied.

She expressed her disappointment in me and remarked, 'Don't go saving yourself, girlfriend. You're nearly middle-aged, for heaven's sake. You should be making hay while the sun shines. Now look, while your vagina is still wet and wanting, your nipples are still pointing straight ahead and not down to your toes, and while you still have enough brain capacity to remember the men you've slept with, you're actually governed by an unwritten moral obligation to set an example of hope for all the solo mothers out there. What in the hell are you waiting for?'

'I'm all about quality, not quantity, thanks all the same,' I responded.

'Give me strength. Would you just stop it for once?' she chuckled.

There were a lot of guys who put it out there that all they were interested in was sex, with no relationship or commitment attached to what they were potentially offering. I had to educate myself about the concept of DTF.

Some guys overtly wrote they were on the dating site for DTF; others said they wanted fun with NSA (no strings attached). Others described themselves as MBL (married but looking), WTR (willing to relocate), and with a GSOH (good sense of humour). Some men described themselves as aiming for an LTR (long-term relationship) while others said they were still LITPB (living in their parents' basement). There were people who described themselves as SUB (submissive) and DOM (dominant). These people were into sadomasochism, bondage, and discipline.

The one I couldn't work out, though, was DTF. WTF? DTF? What the fuck did DTF mean? I had to ask my eighteen-year-old boarder, Harper, for advice.

Harper stared at her geriatric roomie in disbelief. 'What, Emma? Seriously? Don't you know what DTF means? Get with the programme. It means "Down to Fuck".

Wow, so there was even a glorified term for a one-night stand these days. I was clearly a bit out of my depth.

DTF

STUFF IT
I'm done with you lot
You're all basic, drab, and uncouth
You drink too much
And you rate yourselves
GOOD LORD
Have I just seen
Middle-aged spread?

You expect it all
In return for NOTHING!
This solo mother is angry
For she is honest

I can't say the same for you lot
With your loosely veiled lies
And your DOWN TO FUCK

Not falling for your crap
I'm way way waaaay too smart for that
Gonna just write me some lines
Get outta my way
All you're doing
Is wasting my time

I found the use of terms such as DTF offensive. It seemed to me sex was easy come, easy go. Sexual opportunities were so freely available over the Internet that people had lost the art or need for any type of courtship. I was told it went both ways; there were men *and* women putting it out there openly that they were purely seeking casual sex.

It's as though people moved almost immediately to sex and then worked backwards to a relationship and trust. Should anything go wrong with the relationship, the bonds quickly broke and people swiftly moved on to the next option.

A lot of the men I came in contact with got off on sexting and were blatant and predatory with it. Their messaging became very suggestive very quickly. They'd throw out baited lines with the hope I might be interested.

Lecherous Longing

Who are you really?
Beyond another wanton
Lust-fuelled lover

You covet me
Craving carnal knowledge
Of my most private and intimate self

I am bombarded by your
Lyrics with lewd lecherous longing
Your fervor-fired fantasies
And salacious sensuality

Words
Flow as fountains
From your loins

Who are you really?
Strip back the poetic posturing
Are you kind?
I would really like to know

Dating as a mature woman was such a different experience if I compared it to dating as a young university student. At over forty years of age, I was considered a MILF, a "Mother I'd Like to Fuck". I sat on the invisible line of age acceptability: attractive enough to be a target for the thirty-year-old guys who liked the idea of an older woman, yet too old for a man wanting a family. But I was physically and mentally too young for an older man.

I felt a lot of the middle-aged men on the dating sites were on the midlife crisis continuum. They'd invariably post photos of themselves engaging in all number of sporting pursuits, for example, competing in multisport events, surfing, hiking, or standing next to their mountain bikes wearing tight pants and helmets. I'd scroll through photos of their cars, motorbikes, tattoos, fish they'd caught, or wild pigs they'd slaughtered. It was common to see naked torsos and pics of them cuddling up to cats (because they're so fond of "pussy"), or schmoozing with attractive women in bars. I found it all a bit too predictable.

I began to realise men of my age who had succeeded financially were generally very guarded about their personal lives. These men were battle weary. They generally had a string of ex-wives, girlfriends, mistresses, children, and staff clamouring for their attention and money. I understood they were time poor and they needed to put their children and careers first. Any potential partner would only ever be viewed as a sexual convenience until a later stage when a bond developed. To put masses of energy and time into developing a relationship before sex was simply unrealistic for them. They were always pressing for sex within the first two to three dates. They never wasted much time in deciding whether they liked me enough to stick around.

I also observed that quite a number of the more mature and successful men on the dating sites were not really looking for a woman of equal intelligence and ambition. They didn't appear to want the complications of an equal, as they had challenges in other areas of their lives. Rightly or wrongly, I believed most of these men were on dating sites hoping to hook up for casual sex.

As I sat in the sun having lunch with one of my male friends, he told me all about the dating site "Seeking Arrangement". According to him, the dating site worked on the basis of agreed arrangements between "sugar daddies" and "sugar babies" where sexual favours were exchanged for money, gifts, and experiences. Women as young as eighteen were willingly entering into arrangements with one or more sugar daddies.

I heard how funds were being put towards university fees, deposits for first homes, and investment properties. I was told of a young lawyer who was "seeking arrangements" to pay off her student debt.

For a mere few hundred dollars, a man would have the sexual pleasure of a beautiful young woman. He'd enjoy the glow of a firm, youthful body, with a warm and open smile that carried no sign of resentment or disappointment. Her bright eyes, luscious hair, and sexual energy were uncomplicated and compliant. For many men, a sugar baby was a practical and logical solution.

These arrangements were always by mutual consent. Contact was restricted to securing a time and date to meet. Outside of the agreed time they spent together, each party to the arrangement went back to their normal everyday lives. Sugar daddies could be married and also dating via the use of more typical dating websites.

The more I learnt from my friends, my acquaintances, and my own personal dating experiences, the more sceptical I became. At any given moment, how was I to know the guy I had just been on a date with over the weekend didn't have a wife *and* a sugar baby. My trust and faith in men was eroding.

Men told me of their frustrations and how they were so over middle-aged Kiwi women with their borderline alcoholism, hostility and bitterness.

These women typically laid down the law over a coffee: "You have to realise, my kids are my life. They come first. And then of course with my job on top of the kids, well, you know, I'm just so busy I barely have time to date at all. Look, if you want to date me, we'll have to fit it in around *my* schedule. Do you like dogs? I have a dog. I love my dog. My dog's family, too, you know. If you don't like dogs there's just no point in us seeing each other."

Dating seemed to be problematic for both men and women. I clearly wasn't alone.

I could have dated a typical Kiwi male who worked a nine-to-five job with average ambitions. But realistically, I knew better than to try and ease a square peg into a round hole. I was far too ambitious and had far too much energy to have a relationship with an average guy.

Most men like to be the dominant force in a relationship. After all I had experienced, there was simply no way I was going to have my self-determination taken away from me.

I came to see I was showing signs of becoming hostile and bitter myself.

I understood I needed to be with a man who inspired me, a man who challenged and extended me intellectually. I had discovered I preferred athletic types, men who had an ongoing interest in sport and nutrition. I lived a very healthy lifestyle, which was important to me. I preferred a man with muscles and a decent sex drive.

Rob said to me, 'Emms, you're hoping to meet a male equivalent of yourself, and that's just not being realistic. You keep overlooking the fact that most men just don't really give a damn about anything over and above sex, money, their car, rugby, motor sport, fishing, alcohol, their mates, and their kids. Seriously. And in that order. Stop setting yourself up for failure. You'll be single forever if you keep this up.'

I laughed. 'Oh, just shut up will you. Did I even ask for your opinion?' I said.

I told Rob about a meme I had seen on Facebook. It read as follows: *The key to happiness is low expectations. Lower. Nope, even lower. There you go.*

Being the ignorant fool, I told him, 'I'm aware that I'm different. But there must be someone out there like me, or a man who suits me. If I exist in the female form, there must be my alter ego out there somewhere.'

I persevered with online dating for two and a half years. My enthusiasm for meeting random strangers began to wane, and my focus shifted as time went on. There were, however, some truly funny and bizarre things that happened with the online interactions and dates I had over that time. Some of my experiences were funnier than fiction.

1) I was offered money for sex several times. The thing I struggled to make sense of was how my perceived market value was rising with my age. I put that down to all the working out I was doing. My best offer was $600 for an hour of my time. I told one of my male friends about my potential career opportunities. Without hesitation, he offered to be my pimp. I declined all offers.
2) I met five strangers for dinner one evening. We had been 'matched' through a dating agency. As a means of relieving nerves, we exchanged funny dating stories over dinner. I had been sitting chatting to James for a good twenty minutes before he launched into his story. 'About a year ago, I emailed a very pretty woman. I asked her out on a date but she turned me down, saying she didn't think we would have that much in common. She said she saw I was into motorsport and that wasn't her thing. I messaged her a couple more times, telling her I wasn't that much of a petrolhead. I really tried with her as she was gorgeous but nothing seemed to work – she kept brushing me off.' James then swung his head around and looked straight at me and said, 'And that was you, Emma.' Oh my

freaking God. I literally laughed so hard I wet my pants right there as I sat at the restaurant table. Clearly the Auckland dating scene was a goldfish pond, not an ocean. Was I going to have to move to a bigger pond?

3) I was emailed by a 62-year-old guy from Taranaki, with long grey hair and a beard. 'You're hot,' he said. 'How would you like to have some fun with me and my daughter Jade?' I blocked him. I couldn't make this up if I tried.
4) A faceless dude with no profile pic told me he likes to entertain bored housewives. He said he was handsome, well hung, married, and had a secret pad. He was after NSA sex. Wow. Just pay for a hooker and be done with it, you arrogant jerk.
5) I got asked to join in with several married couples. I was fair game for lesbians too. Sorry. Not interested.
6) I was asked out on dates by men from the age of eighteen to seventy-four and everything in between. When I politely explained to one 68-year-old that he was almost as old as my father, he responded by telling me his name. He suggested I should google him. 'I'm quite well known,' he said. Did I google him? Hell, no. Next.
7) I was told by one guy that with my looks and education I would be a perfect match for him. He seemed to think he was a successful businessman. My bet was he was into pyramid selling and sold vitamins and powdered meal replacements. At the end of the day I was not interested in being a kept woman. He was short and looked a little like Mikey Rooney. He wasn't my type at all.
8) I have been emailed by men with skulls tattooed on their necks and men with dreadlocks who wore orange fluorescent high-visibility jackets. They all seemed to think I would be interested in them. They should all stop smoking weed and meth, if you ask me.
9) Why did so many men hold dead fish and slaughtered pigs in their profile pictures? Was it some throwback to hunter-gatherer caveman days? I just didn't get it.
10) I was told by a pilot that most men won't be interested in my personality. He said that, because of my looks, all a guy would be thinking when he saw me was, I want to fuck her. My heart truly sank when I heard that.
11) I had coffee with a corporate guy in Auckland one day. His name was Steve. He leant over the table and quietly asked me whether I had big

or small nipples. I thought a mature businessman might have a bit of class, but I was wrong. My friends wanted to know what I would do if "Nipple Steve" started stalking me. 'Oh that's easy,' I said. 'I'll tell him about my 24 rescue cats and how I save money by milking them rather than waste money on cows' milk.' They laughed and told me to stop being so immature.

12) One guy went on a rant over dinner about his ex-wife's spending habits. 'She just wouldn't stop buying café-made coffees,' he explained. What a mean-spirited creep. He was from Hamilton. I should have known.
13) I was set up on a blind date by a well-meaning acquaintance. As I sat and sipped on my skinny latte, my date told me with complete nonchalance, how he had left his wife because her cancer changed her. He went on to explain how he divorced her before she died. I remember sitting across the table from him, staring at him in disbelief. How could someone be so cruel?
14) When I'm 43 and you're 36, and you say you're fit, yet when you're two minutes into having sex with me you say you want to stop because you're short of breath and have got a stitch … well, all I have to say is this: 'Get the hell out of my bed and don't bother coming back until you're in better shape.' In fact, why don't you just leave. You're annoying me.
15) Mental note to self: Google search the full name of your potential date before you agree to go out with him. That might aid in the prevention of accidentally dating criminals.
16) Taking me on a date to a food hall and spending $10 on my meal will not impress me. Not even a little bit. As you sat with your elbows on the table, chewing with your mouth open and dangling your fork in front of your face, you said, 'Wanna come stay at my place tonight?' You almost wore your cashew chicken and rice that night.
17) Lying about your height is not only pointless, it's pathetic.
18) Bringing your rat-like bitzer Hairy Maclary clone of a dog named Suzie to my home was bizarre. Having Suzie sit at the end of the bed while we were having sex was truly crazy. Discovering the guy had a nipple ring and a partially removed tattoo of his ex-girlfriend on his left pec really made me want to bolt from the room. The trouble was, I was kind of naked and committed by that stage. I was torn between wanting to slap the guy across the face and kicking Suzie off the end

of the bed with my foot. Luckily for Suzie, my coordination wasn't that great, given the pressure of the situation. I resigned myself to the hope that the trying ordeal would end swiftly. Suzie lived to see another day. I refused to return that guy's phone calls.

19) Stripping me almost naked, then refusing to give my underwear back was kind of hot. Except for the fact they were expensive knickers and now my set doesn't match.
20) Inviting me back to your place to have me discover your girlfriend's bra in your bedroom was sloppy. I left, obviously. Six months later you texted me and expected me to be glad to hear from you. 'I don't have time for your nonsense,' I said. 'Oh, but you're such a lovely woman, Emma.' You just wouldn't accept no for an answer. 'I'd really like to see you again,' you said. Oh just fuck off.
21) Having multiple text conversations with several women at the same time and accidentally calling me Stacey will only ever end with one word. Delete.
22) Going into great detail about how you and your best mate enjoyed a threesome with a chick he met online was rude, considering I barely knew you. And when I asked if you were feeling me out for the same, you didn't deny it. Well, maybe that's okay for some women, but it's not okay for me.
23) Referring to my beloved daughter as a SOCK (Some Other Cunt's Kid) is never going to be okay. Not ever. Not under any circumstances. And these guys wonder why they are in their late thirties and still unmarried and childless. It's not rocket science. Treating people with respect and showing compassion would be a good first step.
24) Telling me you like to wear women's underwear while you're having sex is not a turn-on for me. Trying to sell it to me by saying other women like it just makes it worse. It's not my gig. Move along.
25) Discovering you were using a fake name on your Tinder profile was disappointing. It only took me a few days to work it out. There was simply nowhere for our "relationship" to go. Delete. Again.
26) I was alarmed when you told me over the phone that you'd had a heart attack eighteen months earlier. When I asked what you were doing when you had the heart attack, you informed me you were having sex at the time. I really had to cut you loose for your own sake. If I had dated you, I would have killed you, for sure.

27) I was "catfished" a number of times by balding, bearded men with dad bods, who were using ten-year-old photos on their dating profiles. That's simply false advertising.

Mel was intrigued by the fact I had been on dates with a Frenchman, an Italian, an Argentinian, a German, two Americans, a Chilean, a Canadian, and guys from all walks of life. I tried to explain to her that I am all about embracing multiculturalism and broadening my horizons these days. She just looked at me, rolled her eyes in disbelief and laughed.

Dating was a delightful and entertaining distraction. There were plenty of wonderful, positive experiences that came with my re-entry to the dating scene. I have always loved learning about people so it became a little like a glorified school project in some ways.

Most of the guys I went on dates with wanted to see me again. That was good for my ego, in light of what I was going through with my ex-husband.

When I began dating, I confused the sexual drives of some of these men with genuine interest, and I fell victim to a few who were purely flattering me to get me into bed. It didn't take long for me to wise up to it, and I became more discerning.

For all the crazies, the assholes, the players, and the ones who "catfished" me good and proper, I also met a number of wonderful men who have become special friends.

I Remember Their Eyes

I see all their beautiful and handsome faces
I remember their eyes and
How they spoke to me and made me smile
They gave me hope and sometimes
More reason to carry on

Looking no more forward than
The following day
Their reassurance and kindness
Saved me over and over again

I cannot see "his" face
I see "their" faces
They have shown me love
Often in subtle and meaningful ways
Distracting me with laughter
And changing my light bulbs
For I am too short to reach

They stacked wood in my shed
'It gets cold in winter,' they said
A special few have fed me
When I was too distressed
To properly care for myself
They have held me tight for just long enough
And reminded me of my beauty
They said still shone through mascara streams of tears

Day by day I began
To feel more human again
I give thanks for the souls of the wonderful men
Who stood by me
And gave me confidence
So I could begin my long slow journey back towards
Believing in myself once again

Subconsciously I yearned to fill the void in my life that Tim's absence had left. I naturally thought I needed a replacement for him, as I had been used to having the presence of a male in my life.

With time, I realised I was able to care for Bella on my own. I saw the added stress of having a man constantly influencing my decisions was, in some situations, more of a hindrance than a convenience. I needed to conserve my energy for the legal fight.

It was going to take someone truly special to capture my attention and have me commit to a relationship.

For the time being, I remained open to opportunities. I have never claimed to be a nun.

eight

Get fit, get even

I have always exercised. It's just what I do. When I have had the odd break from the gym, I have led such a busy life and have always eaten "clean" so my weight has never gone any higher than 60 kilograms. Except during my pregnancy, of course.

Exercise is the powerful tool I turn to when I am dealing with stress. Physical activity is my go-to antidepressant drug of choice.

When Tim left me, I naturally felt sad and overwhelmed. I never recognised these emotions as symptoms of depression, but more a result of the shock and trauma of Tim's abandonment. My problems were situational as opposed to being a chemical imbalance in my body.

The human body is nothing more than a complex system of cells. Cells require energy and nutrients in defined amounts for peak performance. To maximise your own potential, it's advisable to fuel your body correctly: eat properly, get plenty of rest, stay away from drugs and alcohol, and participate in regular physical activity.

Physical activity assists in the production of two naturally occurring mood-elevating chemicals – serotonin and dopamine. The production of these chemicals is also enhanced when we expose ourselves to natural sunlight, and eat certain types of food. It's science.

Eating eggs, whey protein, bananas, fish, and chicken will assist in the maintenance of serotonin levels that naturally occur in the body. B vitamins support the production and function of serotonin, so it's a good idea to supplement your diet with vitamin B complex. Interestingly, St John's wort works as a natural SSRI (selective serotonin reuptake inhibitor) by preventing the breakdown of serotonin in the brain. I took one St John's wort tablet and one vitamin B complex tablet each day.

With the exception of my university years, where I indulged in alcohol with my friends at parties, I have never been a heavy drinker. Within a year of Tim's permanent departure to Sydney, I had all but given up drinking alcohol. It didn't make a lot of sense for me to drink, when even one small glass of wine was enough to upset my system. Alcohol had begun to make me feel ill.

In September 2012, when my doctor asked how I was coping with the stress of my marriage breakdown, there was no way I was going to have her medicate me with antidepressants.

Despite the stress, I was actually doing okay. I was tired, bewildered, and I had lost a lot of weight, but I was okay. I was having anxiety and asthma attacks, but they were not at a level that I considered life-threatening.

I understood antidepressants would probably relieve some of my distress; however, I couldn't allow drugs to cloud my thinking. It was essential for my mind to stay sharp for the legal battle I was facing against Tim. Somehow I had to find an effective way to cope with the escalating stress without relying on medication.

I decided to "spring-clean" my diet. There was no more pizza or takeaways. Instead, I ate lean red meat, chicken, vegetables, fruit, a little cheese, low-fat milk, and healthy cereals. I reduced the amount of bread and carbohydrates I ate. There was no butter, no cakes, no ice cream, no sweets, and no fries or potato chips. I got my skinny white ass back into the gym. I got fit. I got really fit.

Three to four times a week, I attended 60-minute Body Attack high-impact cardio classes, as per the Les Mills group fitness programme. After a couple of months, I threw in a few interval training programmes with weights and boxing elements, plus walking, and running on the treadmill.

By early 2015, I was on the hunt for another challenge.

A few people had suggested over the previous eighteen months that I should enter a bodybuilding competition. I thought about it for a few months, and one night in early April I filled out the requisite forms, paid my fee, and sent off my entry form.

I remember looking for a novice category for my age group. I checked the form a few times yet there didn't appear to be a novice category for over 35-year-olds. It took me a few minutes of consideration before I realised there never would be a novice category for over 35-year-olds – no one in their right mind would enter a bodybuilding competition for the first time when they are over 35 years of age, let alone when they are 44. What idiot would do such a thing? Me, I would do that.

I spoke to some people at the gym, and I was referred to a Pro Bikini bodybuilding competitor who was based at the Les Mills gym in central Auckland. Her name was Courtney and she was about to become my nutrition and fitness coach.

I had some preliminary fitness and body composition testing done. My starting total body fat was 19%. My muscle mass was 75%, weight 57 kilograms, my visceral fat was just under 3%. The computer at my local gym seemed to think I had the equivalent body composition of a 29-year-old. Courtney told me I was starting from a great position (in respect of muscle mass and fat percentage). She just needed me to do the weight training, follow her dietary advice, and watch my muscles grow.

My weight training programme and nutritional plan was rigid and detailed. It took me a few days to wrap my head around the diet. I had to rethink my eating, again. I was required to weigh all my food and introduce eggs, bananas, plain chicken breast, nuts, broccoli, and loads of other random things to my diet that I wasn't used to. Courtney had me taking fish oil capsules, which actually made me want to heave from the awful fishy aftertaste. I was required to eat protein powder on cereal and in smoothies, which I blended with water and ice. I had never tasted protein powder before. I grew to enjoy it.

There was so much food. I had to eat every couple of hours. It was weird, as sometimes I was so incredibly full all day but I'd wake the following morning feeling leaner. I discovered I could eat an enormous lean steak and a plate of steamed broccoli only to feel hungry a few hours later.

My body reacted quickly to the change in diet and the intense weight training sessions. Within a few weeks, my muscles were noticeably bigger. I even had "guns".

Work and life had to continue around my weight training. There were days where I drove 500 kilometres, saw four customers, sold $4,000 worth of stock, and still had to drive in the dark to find a motel, unload my car, then venture out again to find a gym. I channelled my thoughts and told myself the weight training gave me something to look forward to at the end of the day.

With my earplugs in, and Spotify on, I left my worries at the gym door. I walked and ran and pumped crazy weights until my muscles ached with fatigue. I'd crawl back to the motel, have something to eat, then zone out with mindless TV, or write poetry until my eyelids refused to stay open any longer.

As the weeks of training continued, I watched posing tutorials and bikini bodybuilding competitions on YouTube. All the competitors had incredible physiques, luscious long hair, heavy make-up, and beaming smiles. I wondered whether I had what it took to present myself in a similar way. I thought, *Yep, I can do that.*

I admired the colours and styles of the beautiful Swarovski crystal-encrusted competition bikinis. Mel and I wasted valuable hours of our lives in deep discussion as to whether I should wear a red or navy-blue bikini onstage. Mel was convinced I should wear a blue-based red. I couldn't decide.

We talked about what jewellery I was going to wear, and what style of sparkly competition shoes I preferred. It was all ridiculous, trivial, girly chit-chat, yet it really helped to keep my head in a positive space while I dug deep for the onslaught of the legal battle.

I hadn't entered the bikini competition to win. I figured as long as I was able to walk onto the stage without making a complete fool of myself, I would be happy.

As the weeks progressed, my muscles gained in size; however, I was still tiny in comparison to most people at the gym. The fat drained from my frame, and I took delight in seeing some impressive muscle definition taking shape. Sadly, my boobs completely disappeared. It became apparent I would need to somehow create a set of artificial boobs for myself without the use of surgery.

I loved learning about the competition posing, even though I found it difficult to master. Courtney instructed me on how I should rotate my hips, point my toes, stick out my butt, and position my shoulders. I was required to tense my muscles, smile, look ahead, and *not* down to where my feet were going. I gave it my best shot. I was not going to have anyone say, "Oh dear, what a disaster. Good for Emma, though. At least she tried."

I used the publicity I generated from my bodybuilding training to raise money for my friend Mia – my friends donated dollar amounts for every percentage of body fat I lost. Mia had battled kidney issues her entire life and was required to undergo dialysis three times a week to stay alive. She had missed out on the day-to-day things we all take for granted – university, jobs, boyfriends, parties, children, independent living and travel. Through the generosity of my friends, we were able to raise a significant amount of cash for Mia. Tickets to a Fleetwood Mac concert were donated, complete with a backstage meet and greet with Mick Fleetwood.

Mia stormed into my life as a boisterous and adorable six-year-old when she and her dad lived next door to me. I was 26 at the time. She took a shine to my cats and would routinely kidnap them and claim them as her own. Mia stole my cats and stole my heart in the process. Ever since then, I have played a steadfast role in Mia's life, supporting her as best I could through her lifelong struggles. She was one of my bridesmaids, along with my friend Mel, when I married Tim. I loved her with all my heart.

On 2 August 2015, I flew to Hong Kong to attend a two-day trade fair. The disruption to my routine was difficult. The time difference meant I was awake at odd hours. I generally woke at 2 am and went to the hotel gym, where I would spend hours walking on the treadmill and pumping weights. My body rhythms were completely out of sync with the local time zone.

Having to walk past the 30-metre-long pastry and cooked breakfast smorgasbord in the hotel restaurant for the three mornings I was there was challenging. Courtney had reduced my calorie allowance to 6,000 kilojoules per day for the final six weeks leading up to the regional championship. I was truly hungry for around 20 hours of each day.

Despite the temptations, I stuck to Courtney's diet and training schedule. Every few weeks I checked in with her. She pinched my fat with callipers and had me jump on the scales in the changing rooms. By 18 August, exactly a week before I stepped out onto the stage at the regional champs, I was 55.3 kilograms with 48.3 kilograms of lean muscle mass (87.3% muscle mass). I had 12.8% body fat, with a miniscule 0.5 mm layer of fat on my stomach. My abdominal muscles were clearly visible.

I barely ate for a whole week before the regional champs. I was so hungry. My stomach grumbled and moaned constantly. It felt as though my insides were eating themselves. Even so, I refused to eat anything over and above the carefully measured amounts of chicken, rice, vegetables, salt, and water on the last few days leading up to the competition.

Courtney had me swallow fat burners, diuretics, and skin tighteners. Food was going straight through me, and my skin shrivelled up like a prune. To counteract the wrinkled look of the shrinking skin, I drowned myself in Bio Oil to keep my skin looking fresh and supple. For the most part, it seemed to work.

I weighed myself on the morning of the Auckland Regional Champs. I weighed 54 kilograms. I was at 11% body fat. My head looked enormous in comparison to my tiny frame. I felt fragile and tired, yet I was exhilarated at the thought of the day that was about to unfold.

nine

Lame excuses

I expected more from Tim in respect of our daughter. How he was able to extract himself from Bella's life with seemingly no remorse, I will never understand.

Leading up to the child custody hearing at the end of April 2015, both Bella and I were required to be interviewed by Child, Youth and Family (CYF), being a unit of the government Ministry of Social Development.

Our interviews were a standard condition for any child custody matter. So, too, was the requirement for Bella to have an independent barrister assigned by the court to represent her. Bella's barrister was paid for by the New Zealand taxpayer.

Given I was doing all I could to protect Bella from abuse and neglect, it was unsettling having my parenting skills and lifestyle choices scrutinised by a CYF case worker.

I was equally affronted to learn the "lawyer for child" had visited and interviewed Bella at her school several times without my knowledge. I would have preferred to have been able to tell Bella to expect a visit from "the lady in the very smart suit" and to gently let her know she was not to be afraid.

Tim was asked by the CYF case manager why our marriage had failed. *Emma travelled for work. Emma was away from home four nights a month on average. Because Emma was away from home, I didn't feel nurtured in the marriage*, he responded in writing.

Seriously now, Tim? Did he really think anyone would accept his fabricated bullshit as a justifiable reason to end a marriage? As a narcissist, he probably did.

For the week leading up to the Child Custody Hearing, my barrister attempted to have Tim commit to dates when he would spend time with Bella for the remainder of 2015, bearing in mind it was already near the end of April and he hadn't seen Bella since the previous Christmas.

Late in the afternoon on the day before we went to court, his barrister sent a document saying Tim had actually used up all his annual leave for 2015 with the birth of his other daughter in Australia. As a consequence, Tim was unable to see Bella at all for the remainder of the year, outside of two weekend visits that were still unconfirmed at that stage.

He still took me to court, even though he knew he had no intention of adhering to the minimal levels of contact he was seeking.

The final terms of the parenting order provided for Tim to have one weekend a month and one week a year with Bella. The one week per year was to be taken out of her school holidays. Over and above that, he was to have her for one week every second Christmas, and her Christmases with him could be spent in either New Zealand or Australia.

Tim was also required to provide and pay for a mobile phone for Bella in order to either have FaceTime with her, or call her on Sunday and Wednesday nights at 7 pm.

He pressed hard to have a provision included in the court orders which would require me to take Bella to his sister's or his parents' home one weekend a month. I was advised by my legal team that the court can only make orders in respect of the relationship with the parents and their child, not other family members.

With a view to being reasonable, I agreed for Bella to have contact with Tim's extended family by mutual agreement (which meant the provision was not enforceable by the court). His sister Dale was to contact me independently of Tim to arrange visitation with Bella.

Tim spent three weekends with Bella during 2015. He failed to see her for his allocated week during the year or his week at Christmas.

Between April 2015 and November 2019, I received no phone calls, texts, or emails from Dale. Either Tim had failed to inform his family of their opportunity to spend time with Bella, or Dale chose not to contact me.

And the telephone calls and FaceTime Tim was to have with Bella? Well, there were problems with the phone Tim provided. After many weeks of putting up with his belligerent refusals to assist me in fixing those problems, I simply paid for a new one and instructed Tim to call her on the new number.

I believe he engineered the whole situation to cause me grief and to allow him the opportunity of direct contact with my lawyers in order to escalate my legal costs. Tim insisted on keeping his lawyers out of day-to-day contact issues so in comparison, it cost him very little.

Tim generally called Bella once every week to ten days. According to the call logs, the calls lasted between three and six minutes. He asked her what she had been doing at school, he talked about his work and travel and he described the excursions and activities he engaged in with his other daughter.

Bella was usually very quiet after she spoke to her father. Sometimes she cried. There were times when she simply refused to answer the phone when her father called. It was an impossible situation in the respect that I couldn't "fix" the problem for her – I couldn't make her father care. And I couldn't sit there and tell her how I truly felt about him either. I held her tight and encouraged her to think of all the wonderful things happening in her life. I told her it's always best to think of the good things, and then the hurtful things wouldn't seem so big any more.

I wondered about the long-term impact of her trauma on Bella's self-esteem. I worried how her own personal relationships would be influenced by the absent and rationed affections of her father and the needless tension between her parents.

I was careful to reassure Bella that she would always be my number one priority. That I would be there to listen and guide her with her choices and decisions. I said I trusted her, and I believed in her. She was beautiful, kind, and so worthy and deserving of love.

Tim made a mockery of the court system. He used it and the child custody action to cause me financial and emotional hardship. It was never about him securing quality time with his daughter.

ten

The Builder

I met the Builder online.

He invited me to join him for dinner at a local restaurant. It was a typical small, rural-town Indian restaurant with mandatory oversized flat-screen TV high on the wall, belting out Bollywood entertainment. I sat in the brightly coloured but worn dining chair and experienced sensory overload with the smells, the lights, the dancing, and the chanting of the singers on the screen. The room began to spin. All I wanted to do was focus on my hot date, not the wild warbling and gyrating hand and hip movements of the dancers.

I evaluated the Builder over the steaming chicken korma that rested in a round copper dish on the table in front of me. He was polite. He was handsome; he had short, dark-brown hair in a fairly trendy style (for a builder), piercing blue eyes, a sun-kissed tan, a chiselled face, great teeth, and some fairly attractive muscles that were no doubt a by-product of his daily work. He had a noticeable scar above his eyebrow – a rugby or workplace injury perhaps? Whatever it was, it just made him more appealing. I sat across the table from him thinking how rugged he looked.

My glass of Sauvignon Blanc was doing its job, and I began to relax. The conversation was easy. He buttered me up with some smooth, well-rehearsed lines. 'You're a honey,' he said. We were off to a good start.

Twenty minutes into our date, I began to tire of tales of his American ex-wife and her obsession with keeping exotic pets indoors. She was a vet, apparently, and she kept a menagerie of reptiles, rodents and amphibians. My eyes began to glaze over.

All of a sudden Jordan, the Builder, changed tack. Perhaps he could see he was losing ground with me. 'You're really rather lovely,' he said.

'Oh. Thank you,' I replied. Perhaps he was impressed with my listening skills.

'Um, yes, you really are lovely, Emma,' he continued, 'and it's a problem for me.'

'Pardon me?' I said. 'I don't understand, Jordan; you've lost me.'

'Yep, it's a problem for me, Emma,' he said as he shook his head. 'I thought I was coming out here for sex tonight, and you're too good for that.'

Wow. Welcome to dating in the year 2013.

Maybe Jordan thought he was paying me a compliment? I don't know. I was shocked and a bit pissed off at his display of disrespect. How dare he speak to me like that. And what's with the "too good for sex" comment? I love sex.

I tossed aside Jordan's offhand comment and let him kiss me goodbye as he walked me to my car. But that was all. I wasn't about to prove his theory of me wrong.

We stayed in touch but I knew exactly what drove Jordan. It was perfectly clear he'd taken me on a date with the intention of having me as his hook-up but for some reason he'd changed his mind.

He was hot, though, and I was tempted by his looks and his brooding sexuality. At 190 centimetres, he was pretty much 90 kilograms of perfect, pure muscle. Jordan was a great kisser. His bright eyes, sharp wit, and gorgeous beaming smile had me captivated.

Every few days for around six weeks after our date, he texted me. He was desperate to see me again, but I wasn't sure I was ready for the whole hook-up scene. It had never been my thing, even through my twenties. I just wasn't that girl. And although I was now older, I didn't know whether I could handle the self-esteem graveyard that went hand in hand with a hook-up arrangement.

I refused all Jordan's advances.

Four weeks rolled by. I happened to be in Ponsonby meeting another guy for a drink. The dude was boring me to tears. While my date was in the bathroom, I texted Jordan: *Hey. What r u doing?*

At home watching rugby, he replied.

OK. I'm in Ponsonby. I'm leaving in 15. Want me to call in, say hi on my way home? I inquired.

You won't come, he said.

I'll come. I just need your address, I replied.

Holy shit, really? Great, came his reply within seconds.

I pulled into Jordan's driveway and knocked on his door. He proudly showed me around his home and described his renovation plans. It was very much a builder's work-in-progress bachelor pad. There were no feminine touches – just a lonely leather sofa, a coffee table, a massive flat-screen TV, a dining table, and two chairs in the lounge. The other rooms were uninhabitable with half-finished walls and builder's tools lying scattered everywhere.

We sat and watched television. He offered me a beer.

After ten minutes he said, 'Babe, come with me.'

He took my hand. As we walked past the dining table towards the door, he put his hands around my waist. He lifted me up and sat me on the table. He drew his hands up my thighs and beneath my dress. He kissed my neck and drank his fill of lust before carrying me to his bedroom.

We had sex, many times. We talked and laughed and enjoyed each other. I felt happy and at peace.

I left in the morning and texted him later in the day: *Thank you for making me feel wanted again.*

My pleasure. Anytime, he replied.

Jordan drove to my home the following day. I greeted him at the door wearing three-inch crystal encrusted heels and a tiny silver-sequinned, off-the-shoulder cocktail dress. I wasn't wearing any underwear.

We didn't make it to the bedroom. He took me on my kitchen table, and I orgasmed five times within the hour. I never got my shoes off.

Jordan messaged me. *When can I see you again? Babe, you're so fucking hot, I need to have you again. I can't get your perfect butt and your velvet pussy out of my mind.*

I loved the way Jordan spoke to me. It was intoxicating, being wanted like that. No man had ever spoken to me like that before. I loved the urgency and the want in his words.

I humoured him for nearly two weeks after that. 'Look, I realise there is no relationship attached to this. We've had fun but I'm really not that girl. You need to move on.'

He didn't take the rejection well and I didn't expect to hear from him again.

Two months later, he texted me: *I just can't get you out of my head.*

I reiterated my position. He said he was aware of what I wanted. He continued by saying he is a man who needs a lot of great sex in a relationship. I should be prepared for that. He then asked me out for dinner.

I thought he had considered my position and was willing to give us a go. I agreed to meet him.

Less than an hour into our meal, he said, 'Let's go back to yours for my dessert.'

I don't know – maybe it was a subtle gesture with a hint of disrespect, or a fleeting look of insincerity in his eyes that triggered my question. I looked at him. 'Jordan, you still view me as a hook-up, don't you?'

'Well, yeah,' he responded. His tone spoke as though I should have known.

'You're unbelievable,' I said. 'What's your problem?'

'I want a family. And you're too old for that,' was his reply. He was blunt and to the point. Misinterpretation was not on the menu that night.

I simply stood up. I turned my back on him and walked straight out of the restaurant. I left him with the bill for our meal and I didn't look back. He infuriated me. I never thought I would see him again.

But sure enough, another two months went by and he was trawling again. I always knew when he was between girlfriends, as he messaged me.

Shortly after Christmas 2013, Jordan was drinking with his mates when he fell and severely sprained his ankle. His leg was in a plaster cast, and he was required to elevate and not move it for weeks. He was stuck at home – horny, lonely, bored, and sweltering in the summer heat. I offered to visit and keep him company for a few hours.

I was prepared for his banter. As he lay back on his sofa with his leg up, he said, 'Come on, babe. Help me out here. You're killing me with that cute ass of yours within my reach.'

'I don't fuck cripples,' I said with a smile.

I made Jordan laugh and brightened his afternoon. We didn't have sex. We drank coffee, ate chocolate muffins, and watched cricket together. We were just two mates hanging out. We had a really nice afternoon.

He apologised for his rude behaviour two months back. 'I'm sorry about what happened at the restaurant, Emms,' he said. 'I handled it all wrong. Look, the thing is, you put my head in a total spin. You're so fucking gorgeous, and I can't get enough of you, but I want kids. I admire you but I just can't have you. Why the hell can't you be 32?'

What was I to say to that? For goodness' sake, Jordan. At 37 years of age, had he not worked out that life doesn't come perfectly packaged exactly how you want it, exactly when you want it? Do us all a favour and grow up.

The trouble was, I liked the guy – if not for his delivery, at least his honesty. Jordan was to the point. There was no bullshit with him. He always told me exactly what he thought. Our banter was always fiery. I enjoyed his humour and his sharp wit. He was a sexy dude and a great fuck.

I accepted his apology. 'Thanks for that, but I think you're kinda missing the point.' I sighed and gently rolled my eyes. 'Jordan, I am the way I am *because* of my age. Fabulous doesn't happen in five minutes, you know – it takes a bit of time,' and with that I began to chuckle. 'Look, younger women are needy because they want marriage and children. They want security. I'm not needy because I already have the marriage and baby T-shirt. I'm also financially independent.'

'Yeah, maybe,' he said with that blank look only a man is capable of.

'Jordan, when I'm with you, I want you. I don't *need* you, and that makes a difference. You're into me because I'm everything you're really not looking for.'

No words from Jordan this time. His eyes darted to the TV. Someone just hit a six over cover into the stand.

'Hey, you'll work it out. You'll be fine,' I said. I took another bite of chocolate muffin.

As the months rolled on he continued to tell me he wanted me. I was grateful to him for our sexual journey and for the confidence it brought me, but I couldn't see us together. That boat had sailed and I told him so. I knew that falling into a friends-with-benefits situation with him would not be good for me.

He missed me. He told me I was amazing. Perfect even. And I was the fuck of a lifetime, apparently.

Oh, really? How much of what he said was because he was desperately horny and I bothered to listen to him?

It was a shame he was on the hunt for a womb, as I think we would have been great together. But I would not risk my heart. My chances of being dumped for a younger womb were about ten to one and those odds were not in my favour. It would not be a matter of if, but when. I had been through enough. It was time to make the hard decisions to protect myself.

Oh, how he did amuse me, though.

Jordan and I remained in contact. He messaged me until the small hours with discussions ranging from personal issues, to house renovations, and American politics. His opinions were always informed and considered. Regardless of whether I agreed with his viewpoint or not, I was always guaranteed a challenging chat with him. He was no oxygen thief; he didn't waste a word.

Deep down, he was a decent guy. He just chased his cock around, and discarded women under the pretence of finding "the one". It's a good excuse but it didn't wash with me. If he was looking to find the one to settle down and have babies with, then why had he taken a 42-year-old out on a date?

I had overlooked the fact I was aging until I met him. With being so fit and healthy, life and age had never slowed me down. It came with considerable shock to be enjoyed, judged and discarded – and in that order. I came to understand the concept of being a MILF.

Sometimes people surprise you.

Jordan called me the day my dad died suddenly in November 2015. He was worried I would be on my own and wanted to make sure I was okay. He arrived at my home late in the afternoon with a beautiful bouquet of flowers. Jordan and my friend Kate stayed and kept me company all evening. I don't remember a lot about that day, but I do remember the people who were there for me. And Jordan was one of those.

Life doesn't always deliver what you ask for; however, it often gives you what you need.

eleven

Digging in

I'm mostly peace, love, and light
And a little go fuck yourself

Anonymous

In September 2013, I paid $1,725 for ninety minutes of time with one of the toughest female divorce lawyers in the country. I wanted the best strategic legal advice, so I went to the best.

I was well prepared with a 15-page brief of information for the lawyer, which I emailed to her before our meeting. I also took several printed copies with me.

I wore a power suit, as I was not going to be outdone by another woman, even if she was wearing Chanel from head to toe and charging me $1,000 plus GST per hour. I power-walked in my power suit up Shortland Street in Auckland's CBD and rubbed shoulders with some of the most astute and lethal legal minds in the country.

From my seat in the lawyer's office, I viewed the Waitemata Harbour through floor-to-ceiling windows. I could see out across the top of the container wharf, to

Waiheke and Rangitoto Islands, I viewed the harbour bridge and beyond. It was a clear, sunny day with a radiant blue sky. I almost forgot about the fact my every syllable was costing me money as I was being distracted by the magnificent view.

I remembered the lawyer from my early years in retail in Auckland City. She strode into my store one day and negotiated with me over the cost of a $3,600 possum fur throw. She was an haute-couture-clad street hustler, and I needed her on my team.

Her office was more like a luxurious hotel suite than a place of business. I patiently sat and marvelled at her Terry Stringer bronze sculpture and her Toss Woollaston painting while she reviewed my document.

'Have you heard of spousal maintenance?' Her questions were short and sharp in their delivery.

'Nope. I can't say I have heard of that. What is it?'

'Spousal maintenance is a living allowance paid by the higher-earning spouse to the lower-earning spouse from point of separation until eighteen months after divorce. Spousal maintenance is paid to ensure the lower-earning spouse is able to lead a similar lifestyle post-separation until such time as the divorce and relationship assets are divided,' she informed me.

Tim had devised a plan that saw the destruction of my businesses and my career. His actions and manipulations had forced me to relinquish ownership of my companies and seek employment with my father, or face destitution. I was earning a paltry $249 per week from paid employment from my father's company.

In comparison, Tim was earning AUD$218,000 per annum, and receiving bonuses and perks as part of his salary package.

The lawyer advised me I had a sound case for spousal maintenance.

I connected the dots myself later that afternoon and realised that if I was to bring the spousal maintenance action to court, I would be able to argue the case for that and the relationship property action with one set of information. Arguments for both matters would be based on actual documented facts and figures that Tim could not dispute, because he himself had prepared the accounts.

When Tim took that first shot at me, he should've made damn sure I never got back up.

twelve

The Gangster

It is said, "Best to quit while you're ahead."

For some unexplained reason, over the summer of 2013–14, I began to watch back-to-back series episodes of the US television drama *Sons of Anarchy*. I was being drawn to the violence, the brutal characters, the leathers, the swagger, the rough sex, the Harleys, and the lead character Jax Teller. Maybe I was just horny, and the fantasy of a bad-boy biker was a better option than the Internet dating disappointments that had been wafting in and out of my life in recent months?

One Sunday morning in February 2014, Jax Teller stepped out from my television screen and paid a visit to my world.

The man I was about to cross paths with, the Gangster, could easily have passed for a movie star. He was just as good-looking as Jax. Yet the Gangster was something Jax would never be; the Gangster was real.

I was travelling through the South Island for work when he initiated contact with me. I felt his strength and energy in the first line of his message. His sentences were short. His words were sharp. The tone of his conversation was direct. He was not interested in my feelings, and his inquiries as to my life and experiences were token. He wanted photos and the more, the better.

I was guarded with the pictures I sent him. He wanted to know how someone of my age looked ten years younger than my actual age. He said most of the women of his age (34 years) look ten years older in person. I guess he wanted reassurance and was over being "catfished".

The urgency and direct nature of his communication captivated my attention. I felt drawn to him. He was four photos, a series of texts, and 1,500 kilometres away from me at that moment.

What could he possibly do to me? My subconscious cautioned me to be wary, but I was curious and I wanted to meet him regardless.

He told me he was an athlete; he worked as a personal trainer and was an international gold medal winner in martial arts. He knew I was a sportsperson so we had a shared interest.

I have to meet you, he texted.

I gazed at his photos and wondered about the man behind the sparkling yet haunting ice-blue eyes. The Gangster's face was open. His mouth was wide with delicious, full lips. He had perfectly straight white teeth; it was a mouth that screamed sensuality. I saw multiple personalities in his eyes and could sense an inner conflict from his photos and his interaction. I was intrigued – where was the air of steel coming from?

His near naked body was glorious to look at – he was 195 centimetres tall, with smooth, lightly tanned skin, and long limbs that were toned and full. He was delicious, and I wanted him.

When the Gangster asked to meet me, I felt my heart race. And yet, within seconds, my brief flirtation with excitement was superseded by thoughts of despair and hopelessness. *Oh, here we go again*, I thought. The impossibility of my situation would surface. He would learn of my constraints, and our relationship would be over before it had begun. Outside of work and caring for my daughter, there really was so little time for dating. Still, I was curious to meet him.

The Gangster was big. When he walked through my doorway I knew I was only seeing fifty per cent of his potential and yet his energy still filled the room. To say there was an air of menace about him would be too harsh. I was unsettled by his presence – perhaps I was just nervous.

We decided to go grab a bite for lunch. He handed me his spare helmet and I mounted his Harley. As my hands slid beneath his jacket and my arms wrapped around his firm abdomen, I could barely contain my excitement. All the while I said very little and acted somewhat aloof. It was just a short five-minute ride to the restaurant in Helensville.

We sat outside in the sunshine, ate a light meal and drank one alcoholic beverage each. He paid. The conversation was polite. He told me his mother had died of cancer. He had been in one serious relationship with an older woman (similar in age to me, at forty-two years). I knew there was so much more to his story, but I knew better than to dig. Besides, where exactly was our relationship going in the space of five hours?

Back at my place we sat side by side on my sofa. We talked. We smiled at each other. I wasn't about to make the first move, and he wasn't either.

'You're reasonably quiet, huh?' I said.

'Yeah, I'm a bit shy, I guess,' he responded.

I knew that was bullshit. I humoured him and shrugged my shoulders.

Another minute passed before he looked me in the eye and quietly said, 'Come here, babe.'

I leaned forward just a little. His hands gently cupped my face and he kissed me tenderly on my lips.

My body relaxed. My subconscious exhaled. He was profoundly sensual. My head fell back and he began to kiss and lightly lick my neck.

'I want you so bad,' he murmured. 'I'd hoped our chemistry would be great, and it is.'

With effortless strength he lowered me back onto the sofa. His right hand slipped underneath my shirt. He pulled my bra aside and revealed my left nipple. He bit it gently. As my back arched and my head fell back, I knew I was powerless against my desire for him.

'Can we move to your bedroom?' he asked.

How long did we have? I thought. *Another two hours?* I couldn't say no.

Like a feather, he carried me to my bedroom and laid me gently on the bed. With practised precision, he peeled layers of clothing from my body. He complimented me on my jeans.

I apologised for my tiny breasts. He brushed my comments aside and said I could always get implants. In the heat of the moment, he wasn't concerned about the size of my breasts. My insecurities were all of my own making.

I felt his lips tickle my ear. With warm and wanting breath he whispered, 'Oh God, you're so sexy.'

Side by side, we lay naked and entwined. I let the vision of his stunning physique seep into my bones. The moment, the emotion, the desire I felt, all carved a canyon deep within my soul.

His fingers explored, caressed, and teased. His hand bit my ass as he slapped it with force. His lips, nose, and tongue trailed my nipples. He carried on in circles over my stomach and then buried his face in the crevices of my vagina. He inhaled me and quenched his thirst with my wetness.

He feathered his fingers so gently across my cheek. Then back up over my forehead, down my long dark hair, down my back, across my buttocks and my thighs. His fingers yearned and explored.

Full attention was paid to my tiny breasts, with a squeeze, a pinch, and a firm tug with just the right amount of pressure. His massive palms washed my stomach before they descended and gently spread my legs. His fingers teased and fondled gently before he thrust them deep inside me. With a surge of heat and lust to near split me in two, I thought I might die from my desire. I let out a delicious moan and quickly climaxed. The man had a gift, and we had only just begun.

He told me he wanted all of me. I was being hesitant – a little selfish perhaps? I told him I wasn't sure. My response frustrated him, and rightly so.

It's the internal conflict of being a woman – wanting to uphold your virtue yet battling as a slave to sex. I just couldn't say no. Besides, with a man of the Gangster's enormous power, I could feel his urgency. He was a hair breadth from taking me anyway, whether I was willing to submit or not.

I gazed with longing at his manhood. His penis was perfect; the perfect length, girth, shape, and tone. His pubic hair was soft and light in colour, with just the right quantity – not too much and not too sparse. My moist lips gently kissed his penis. I allowed the tip of my tongue to tease the V at the tip and circle the rim of his hood. With my left hand I gently cradled his balls. I salivated and flicked my tongue from side to side as I slid along his shaft. I applied pressure to his prostate. With that he let out a deep groan of satisfaction. I felt the tension of his hand on the back of my head. The elixir of his masculine smell filled my lungs. I lost myself to his glorious cock.

My eyes trailed his fingers as he rolled a condom down his thick, erect shaft. He lifted me with the immense power of his forearms and lowered me effortlessly onto himself. As he entered me, I let go all over again. He filled me sublimely. We fell together onto the bed. With his right hand he took my long dark hair in his fist and twisted it behind my head. With a forceful tug my head jerked back. I was his. He had total control over me.

'How do you like it, babe? Hard or slow?' he asked with a shallow, wanting voice.

'Hard and fast.' I could barely breathe for my lust of the man.

I relaxed into the rhythm he set. He drove deep inside me and found places I never knew existed. His rhythm and momentum was to perfection. His penis caressed and teased; we moved in unison, and with every thrust he brought me closer to euphoria. We became a single being.

We went somewhere together that afternoon. It was a place I had never been before. I drowned there, lapping up the tension as he pulled my hair and pounded my body in the most magical way. It was a perfect mix of lust, strength, longing, and desire.

I climaxed again, beautifully and powerfully. I told him I was his and he could do whatever he wanted to me.

It was a scorcher of a day. The sun burned without mercy beyond my windows. We quickly exhausted all the air in the bedroom.

He rose from the bed and gasped. 'It's so hot. I can't breathe,' he said as he reached to open the French doors.

I lay admiring him in all his glory. He swept back the curtains and unlocked the doors. Fresh, cooling air rushed in.

As he stood naked in the door frame, his magnificent body luminesced in the streaming afternoon sunlight. Steam hovered around him as a rising blanket of mist. Sweat glistened and was there, because he wanted me.

He drew his hand across his forehead and wiped his opposing palm across his glorious chest. Droplets of sweat sprayed the room. And then he turned. His butt cheeks were pert, full and rounded. His entire body was blemish free – no tattoos, scars, moles or freckles.

The Gangster wanted me on top. He wanted me any way he could have me. I savoured his magical cock. He was, quite simply, intoxicating.

I was still feeling a little self-conscious of, and insecure about, my small breasts. He just didn't seem to care and kept telling me how fantastic and sexy I was. I mentioned that he wasn't seeing my "A" game as I was still so exhausted after my mammoth sales trip.

'Well, if this isn't your A game, I can't wait to see it. You're great,' he purred.

Oh, the things I ached to experience with that man; bondage and discipline would be electrifying. He would dominate me, and I would gladly be his slave. I could see us being risqué – anywhere, anytime, anyhow.

We lay together.

'When can I see you again? Later this week? How about I come over and you cook me dinner?' he said.

I humoured him. 'OK. I'll see what I can do.' All the while I knew how impossible that was going to be as I would have Bella with me.

I nonchalantly asked the Gangster for his full name, his surname in particular. Despite the fact he had just given me the sexual experience of a lifetime, I still only knew his first name. Kyle.

As I lay naked on the bed next to Kyle, my mind drifted to a place somewhere between reality and make-believe. I was in a post-coital haze and found it difficult to concentrate. I had to get him to repeat his surname. I wanted to be sure of it for some reason. I detected a subtle nervousness in his response.

We showered together.

He put his arm around me and drew me near as we walked through my lounge to the front door. 'You like me, don't you, Emma?' he said.

Never being one to show all my cards at once, I replied with, 'Maybe,' and a coy smile.

'Well I really like you,' he said. 'We're going to be great together.'

He helped me carry some heavy sample cases from my car then sped away. The rumble of his Harley echoed into the distance.

When I collected Bella from Tim half an hour later, I must have oozed sex as I swaggered across the Henderson supermarket car park. What Kyle gave me in five hours surpassed anything Tim had been able to offer over the ten years we were together. I felt alive. At peace. As though I was finally free.

Kyle messaged me later that afternoon. He wanted to know what night he could see me. I said I would have to get back to him as I was in for a very busy week with work and personal issues.

The following day, he messaged again. I read his text as I sat in my car outside my lawyer's office. I'm not sure why, but I decided to google his full name before responding to his text. I frowned and shook my head. I thought, *What? That can't be right. My man's ex-girlfriend was in jail. My man also has a criminal past and some seriously bad connections. Surely not. That can't be him.*

I almost messaged him to ask if he knew the woman in jail, as there must be another guy with his name. In a split second of reconsideration, I decided not to press send as it occurred to me … what if Detective Google was correct? Who was that man? How dangerous was he? What had he done? How did I fit into that picture? What didn't I know? How vulnerable was I? What about my daughter?

The impact of my discovery was immediate. I was stunned. I felt as though someone had just reached through my chest and twisted my heart. No! Not Kyle! Please, not Kyle, my eyes pleaded.

In my heart I knew what I had read was correct. It was as though Google had connected some dots for me; the deception of saying he was shy when he was clearly far from it, a hint of apprehension when I asked him for his full name, asking me about my security cameras at home, the expensive Harley on his gym instructor's income, and the scant information about his personal life.

I was experiencing a degree of shock that afternoon. I knew what the revelation meant – I would never be able to be with Kyle again.

I reached out to some friends and family for advice. They all said the same thing; I was to stay as far away from him as possible.

I was upset, and yet I asked myself, why was Kyle and the experience of being with him so important to me?

Perhaps being with Kyle had confronted me with what I had missed out on with Tim – how men did find me so desirable, which just heightened the hurt of Tim's deception. I felt a real sense of loss at not being able to see Kyle again. I needed his strength and our sexual connection to heal or release me in some way. But I simply could not have him; for Bella's sake above all.

The next three to four weeks were torturous for me. My emotions wavered on a pendulum; I wanted Kyle, I needed him, and yet I actively pushed him away with feeble excuses as to why we could not meet up. For one of the few times in my life, I honestly tried to listen to, and act on, the advice of those who genuinely cared for me. It almost ripped me in two.

I had fleeting moments where I imagined myself riding with Kyle on the back of his Harley. Whenever I allowed my mind to wander along that carefree path of romanticism, I was quick to slap myself back to reality.

I understood Kyle's contacts in Sydney had the ability to threaten Tim and have him back off and leave me alone. With one phone call, my problems with Tim could all be over. As tempting as it was, I knew better than to travel down that path. Crime, drugs, and violence had not, and never would be, a part of my life.

I don't know what shocked me the most. Was it the fact I came so close to being drawn into Kyle's world, or was it my realisation of how much I wanted to be with him? Was I drawn to him, or was I being drawn to the risk? I connected with his bad-boy persona, the Gangster, on a purely sexual level. And yet in the cold, harsh light of day, beyond the steamy bedroom acrobatics, there was just no way I could be involved with someone from his world.

Being with the Gangster was one of the most wildly erotic and satisfying sexual encounters of my life. He taught me things I didn't know about myself. And although our relationship was brief, I missed him. Perhaps I missed the "what if" and our chemistry. He was unique and interesting.

I unexpectedly ran into him at an underground bar in Auckland just over a year later. I knew better than to approach him. He didn't see me in the dim lighting, but I was able to observe him from behind from a distance of less than three metres.

I Could Have Whispered Your Name

Fire to your ice
I sat with disbelief
In the bowels of Tanuki's Cave
I never thought
We would meet again

Three metres separated our worlds
I could have
Leant over to your ear
I could have
Whispered your name

Your silhouette;
Mightier than any man I have known
You appeared;
I was thrown back to our time

You didn't see me
In the dark
As you sat
At the bar
I faced you
With your back to me

To your left
An attractive petite brunette
With cascading locks as mine
I am "your type"
I was told

In my mind
I saw you stand
And face me with your
Naked magnificence
A private show
For my eyes only

Sensuous lips
Massive hands
Your chest
Your tongue
Devouring every inch
Of my soul

Delirious in lust
I gave myself to you
So perfect
And still
So wrong

Reality bit
When you led my clone
To the door
As if a dream
You never knew
I was there

Four years later, as I was serving a customer in my retail store, Kyle dropped by to say hello.

I sometimes wondered whether the chemistry between us had been merely a figment of my imagination. But it wasn't – time had changed nothing. Once again, I felt drawn to his darkness.

My voice wavered, and I miscalculated his change as he purchased a candle for his aunt for Mother's Day.

When he messaged me the following day with an invitation to join him for coffee, I stood at a crossroads.

Handsome rider near' led me astray.

thirteen

Liar, liar, pants on fire

Three days before the spousal maintenance hearing in early May 2015, my barrister withdrew as my acting counsel. She cited workload pressures. With complete nonchalance for the bombshell she had just dropped on me, she told me to call my instructing solicitors at the law firm and see what they could do for me. The replacement barrister was a staff solicitor from the firm who happened to be seven and a half months pregnant. Given her physical condition and lack of preparation, she was in no fit state to represent me. She had one working day to prepare for court.

The business valuer who was engaged upon recommendation of the law firm to have the business valuations prepared as evidence for the spousal maintenance hearing did not in fact have the reports completed in time for the hearing.

The law firm should have sought an adjournment for the hearing, given my original barrister had withdrawn her services and the business valuations weren't ready. To my knowledge, the law firm never filed an adjournment request. My representation was severely marginalised as a result.

Narcissists have an advantage within a courtroom setting. They tend to attract like-minded lawyers who fuel their narcissistic supply. Narcissists often win disputes due to their refusal to accept responsibility, their self-righteous confidence, and their convincing lies. It takes a long time and a lot of money to prove otherwise, with little or no consequence at the end for the dishonest narcissist.

Watching Tim's performance in court was something to behold. He was desperate to avoid paying maintenance. Lies and manipulations were standard procedure for him, and I was curious to see how the judge was going to handle him. I prayed the judge was sufficiently experienced to be able to detect a liar when presented with one.

I hoped the financial information I had access to would be adequate to reveal enough of his ruthless and deceptive character, and the desperate situation he left me in when he abandoned Bella and me.

The subject of Tim lying about quitting his job at the end of the first week of May 2012 to come home and save our marriage was raised. I had been racking my brain regarding how I was going to prove he was lying about quitting his job. The recollection of Mel's phone call through to his work in Sydney, where it was revealed Tim was on leave and had not quit his job after all, was not going to be enough to prove he was lying.

I don't recall when the idea came to me. Maybe I was in the shower? Perhaps I was blindly wheeling my supermarket trolley down the coffee aisle? One minute I didn't know how I would prove his lie; the next minute, the solution was crystal clear. The proof I needed would be documented within Tim's payslips. If he had quit his job, as he said, his final payslip would indicate that.

My lawyers obtained his payslips. They clearly showed Tim had taken three weeks "leave in lieu" of pay from 7 May to the end of May, 2012. His regular monthly salary payments resumed from the beginning of June 2012.

The submission of documented court evidence made no difference to his hardened denials – he refused to fall on his sword.

'But Your Honour, I *did* quit my job in Australia, and here are the emails to prove it,' he pleaded with agitation and anger.

'I have read those emails, Mr Rivers, and all I can see is some chit-chat between you and your boss where you say you're off to New Zealand for a few weeks, and your boss says he will chat to you when you get back,' replied the judge.

The dialogue between Tim and the judge was quite something to behold. Only a fool would argue with a high court judge.

He still wouldn't let it go. I smiled in silence at another email he had sent to his boss in Australia in early May 2012, stating that he had been advised by his lawyers to attend marriage counselling as a prerequisite to separation and divorce. He told his boss that he had to go back to New Zealand for a while and that he *may* have to resign from his job. His boss replied with the suggestion they should talk more about it when they were both back in Sydney.

I couldn't understand why Tim voluntarily passed over that piece of correspondence, as the email suggested it was his lawyers who had instructed him to attend marriage counselling. Don't normal couples make a joint decision to attend counselling with the aim of saving their marriage? And don't normal couples call in their lawyers months and sometimes years down the track when all attempts at resolution have failed? Tim had provided evidence that he had indeed set me up for his lone, permanent departure from our marriage to Sydney. I believe his attendance at marriage counselling was merely a cover put in place on the advice of his lawyers.

My barrister should have pounced on Tim's evidence as proof of his lies and intention to leave me financially and emotionally marginalised. But she didn't say a word. Instead, she passively sat and said nothing.

Tim was putting on a good show; he appeared sad in court. 'But I attended marriage counselling, Your Honour. I tried to save the marriage,' he said.

He was displaying the narcissistic trait of "projection" by refusing to take responsibility for what had happened. According to him, none of it was his fault.

As he sat in the witness box, he became increasingly frustrated – his manipulations were being viewed with scepticism.

Then the tears started. Tim cried in court. Twice in fact. He told the judge how he was struggling financially as a result of the $50,000 he had spent on the court action. The same court action he had started.

He argued he shouldn't have to pay spousal maintenance because he was having difficulty meeting the financial demands and responsibilities for his new family in Australia.

'Your Honour, it's very expensive to do IVF in Australia, what with the costs of medical care and health insurance for my family, on top of the legal costs,' he complained.

'Are you providing health insurance for your wife and child in New Zealand, Mr Rivers?' asked the judge.

'Well, no, Your Honour. I have a new family now,' responded Tim.

In some warped parallel universe, he thought having a new family in Australia dissolved him of the responsibilities he had for his original family in New Zealand.

I almost gasped with shock and amusement when the judge responded to Tim's whining. 'Well, Mr Rivers, not that it is any business of mine to comment, but is it really sensible for you and your new partner to be having another child when you say you're struggling to support your existing family? And besides, we're not here today to discuss the needs of your new partner and family in Australia, we're here to discuss your responsibilities to your wife and child in New Zealand.'

Little did I (or the judge, or my barrister) realise at the time, but Tim had actually divorced me behind my back on 17 March 2015. I was no longer Tim's wife when I appeared in court that day. Nobody knew but Tim, and possibly his barrister. They never mentioned it.

'She's been dragging out the court action on purpose, Your Honour. To cost me money. And that's why I haven't been able to visit my daughter – because I can't afford to,' he said.

Seriously now, dude? Really? As if anyone was going to believe that.

'It was your decision to take the job in Australia, though, Mr Rivers,' continued the judge. 'You would be able to find work in New Zealand again, I assume?'

'I guess so, but what about my family in Australia?' Tim said.

'Mr Rivers, you didn't have a family in Australia when you made the decision to move there, now did you?' said the judge. She was rapidly losing patience with him. 'As I have already said, this is not about them. This is about your wife and your daughter in New Zealand.'

He claimed he barely took any furniture with him to Australia. According to Tim, I was in possession of 80% of the $182,000 worth of household chattels we jointly owned. It was stuff of fantasy. To start with, $182,000 was an insurance valuation for full replacement at current retail values. It was not an accurate valuation for chattels that were ten years old and in various states of wear. He had also mysteriously forgotten about the $5,165 he had paid to furniture removers to have furniture and personal items moved from our home to Sydney in May 2012.

When Tim packed up his possessions from our family home I didn't pay too much attention to what was being wrapped and moved. It was weeks later that I realised he had taken all our gardening equipment to his parents' home. Tim tried to justify his actions by saying I didn't like gardening, and yet I had an established garden to maintain at the Mill and I was the one doing the work. My lawyers asked Tim to retrieve the gardening tools and equipment and return them to me. He never did.

Why didn't my barrister submit as evidence Tim's lawyer's letter from June 2012 where Tim stated all household chattels had been evenly divided? And with the copy of Tim's $5,165 invoice for freight that my lawyers also had, how was Tim able to argue in court that I had 80% of $182,000 worth of household chattels?'

'I believe you have denied all Mrs Rivers' requests for access to funds from the sale of your jointly owned family home. Would you care to explain your actions, please?' the judge asked.

'Well, Your Honour, as far as I can see, Emma will just spend the money on legal fees. I thought it would be easier to get her to settle if I didn't give her access to the money,' he replied.

'Mr Rivers, I suggest you approve the release of funds to your wife. It is her money, after all. If I hear you have continued on this path of obstruction, there will be serious consequences for you,' said the judge.

Tim sat in the witness stand looking like a sullen five-year-old.

I had been trying to prove to the court that he had launched a nonsense relationship property claim with the hope I couldn't afford to defend myself. I believed it was his intention to plunder all our joint assets. He had all but admitted that to the judge.

My barrister remained silent and seated. *Come on! He just handed us "his intent" on a plate. You need to drive that home to the judge*, I silently screamed at her. *Do something! Say something!*

Tim and I were joint trustees of the trust that owned the Mill. When the trust took out the mortgage for the Mill, the agreement allowed for one trustee to solely change the terms of the mortgage. I was initially unaware of this provision. When the mortgage came off fixed term in May 2013, Tim was able to refix the rate for the Mill at the bank without my knowledge or approval, and by doing so he committed me to huge, ongoing principal repayments.

Due to the fact Tim and I were joint trustees, Tim's refusal to contribute to the mortgage meant I was solely responsible for meeting our financial obligations with the bank. If I stopped paying the mortgage, the bank would have forced the sale of the Mill. Bella and I would have had to move.

'I understand you refixed the mortgage at the Mill property without consulting Mrs Rivers. What is your explanation for this, please?' the judge asked.

'Well someone had to do it,' said Tim.

'Again, I caution you, Mr Rivers. If you continue to engage in this type of conduct there will be repercussions. Do I make myself clear?' she said.

'Yes, Your Honour,' said Tim, as the scowl on his face worsened.

It took three years from date of separation before Tim agreed to change the mortgage repayments to interest only, and even then he would only commit to an interest-only repayment period of six months.

When the mortgage came off fixed rate again, in May 2016, Tim refused to allow it to be set at interest only. It was originally taken out with the bank with the intention of having it paid off within fifteen years. Because Tim would neither agree to extend the repayments over a longer period nor agree to interest-only payments for the duration of the relationship property matter, I was required to pay hefty monthly interest and principal repayments of $5,400 per month.

Midway through the morning of the second day of the hearing, Tim and his barrister could sense their arguments were losing credibility. Tim was annoying the judge.

Upon recommendation of my lawyer and as a requirement of the court, I had paid a business valuer $35,000 to assess the value of my three original companies and also the three newly incorporated companies owned by my father. Despite numerous reminders regarding the urgency and importance of having the valuations ready for court, the valuer did not make them available, so we had to apply to the judge to have alternative financial documentation submitted to the court. Tim desperately tried to block the evidence from being discussed. As we were about to break for lunch, the judge ruled that my financial evidence could be presented and it would be dealt with in the afternoon.

Tim was fearful of this as he knew the financial position he left me in was dismal.

Over the lunch break, he made me a paltry offer for settlement of the spousal maintenance matter. We turned Tim's offer down. Considering the judge was scheduled to preside over the relationship property matter later in the year, we agreed it was important for the judge to hear my evidence that afternoon.

There were inconsistencies and gaps throughout Tim's evidence. He claimed he was paying the mortgage for their property in Sydney while his partner was pregnant and not working. And yet there were no mortgage payments coming out of his bank account. When my barrister questioned him on this, he then changed his story and explained his partner had extended her mortgage and borrowed more money from the bank. He also said he had borrowed money from his partner to cover his legal costs. None of his evidence made any sense. If his partner was financially stable enough to provide him with funds for his legal costs, then why was there an issue with servicing the mortgage?

In late 2015, when Tim received $100,000 from the money held in trust from the sale of our home, I could see that amount deposited into his Australian bank account. The $100,000 was immediately withdrawn in five lots of $20,000. When Tim was asked where that money went, he said he repaid his partner for the monies he borrowed to fund his legal costs. And yet we never saw $100,000 coming into his account from his partner. Besides, hadn't Tim just told us he'd spent $50,000 on the court action, not $100,000? I think the five lots of $20,000 were transfers to his investment accounts.

I do not believe Tim's partner ever had a mortgage on her property. And I do not believe he ever borrowed money from her. He was simply attempting to weave an elaborate web of lies to try and have the judge think he was suffering financial hardship and therefore should not be expected to pay spousal maintenance.

I did not cry when I sat and gave evidence in the witness box. I was cross-examined for six hours, over two full days in court. I was grilled about the accounting reporting of six companies, two trusts, my own personal finances and the accounting reporting and interconnections between all nine entities. I answered every question to the best of my ability. I assured the judge that I was being asked to comment on reports I did not prepare. I also made it quite clear that I was not an accountant. I told the judge if I was struggling to answer the questions, it was because I either did not understand the question, or because I wasn't sufficiently schooled in accounting terms and processes to be able to answer. It was not because I wished to deceive the court.

I delivered my answers in a calm, concise fashion. I spoke slowly as I needed to think very carefully about the evidence I gave. My voice wavered through fear. I thought I would vomit.

Tim capitalised on the fact I was in court without the business valuations. He spewed lies and outrageous claims of how successful the companies were prior to his departure. According to Tim, I was living in apparent luxury in his absence.

'Now Mrs Rivers, I see you have an expensive hobby,' said Tim's counsel.

She was a dishevelled train wreck masquerading as a barrister. Her hair was untidy, her clothes were too tight, with buttons straining across her voluminous breasts. Her handbag, shoes, and briefcase were all worn and well past their best. I noticed the look on Tim's face when she arrived in the waiting room at court that morning. By his look of surprise and distaste when he shook her hand, I was sure it was their first meeting. He must have hired her from an out-of-date photo and a brief career biography from the Internet. All it took was a five-second Google search for me to work out Tim had been "catfished" by his own barrister. Oh, how I chuckled in silence. Tim never did like a sloppy woman.

'Excuse me? An expensive hobby? I'm not sure what you're referring to,' I replied.

'Look. Here, on your bank statement. There's a regular weekly payment of $17.95 from your personal bank account for a gym membership,' the bitch said as she pointed her fat finger to the page and shoved it in my face.

She was close enough that I could have effortlessly leant forward and slapped her, hard. As I glared at her puffy, reddened, alcohol-infused face, I imagined the sting in my palm and the searing welts my fingers would have left on her cheek. In my mind, I heard her shriek in pain.

I took a deep breath. I centred myself, and said, 'You seem to have overlooked the fact that, with almost no warning, my husband decided to move to another country without me. He abandoned us. I had next to no financial support from him and no assistance with childcare. I was not getting help with any jobs or tasks around the home. That's a lot for anyone to contend with.'

I looked the slovenly bitch in the eye and, with an ample helping of sarcasm, said, 'I would think $17.95 per week is a very small price to pay for my health and my ability to complete these tasks, now wouldn't you agree, Leanne?'

It was disrespectful of me to have called an officer of the court by her first name. I did it on purpose. As far as I was concerned, she was a rodent and belonged in the sewer along with her client.

'Mrs Rivers, did you ever ask your husband for financial assistance, particularly with respect to childcare for your daughter?' asked the judge.

I dropped my sarcasm. 'Your Honour, my husband has launched two legal actions against me and is doing everything he can to destroy me. I thought to ask him for financial assistance would be rather a waste of time,' I replied.

As proceedings continued towards the end of the second day, Tim continued to pout from the witness box. At 6.15 pm and with no warning, Tim abruptly swung his head to face the judge and declared, 'Your Honour, you do realise she had an affair.'

Tim told an unsolicited, unprovoked, unwarranted, barefaced lie. This time he wasn't even massaging the truth. Tim knew it. I knew it. My barrister knew it.

The judge looked at me. She was trying to read my facial expression and capture the emotion in my response. I looked straight back at her in shock.

In response to Tim's lie, my barrister said nothing. She never defended me or challenged Tim's lie. I didn't know what to do. Was it acceptable for me to interject and challenge Tim of my own volition, or was I to wait for my barrister to respond and restrain myself in the meantime?

I waited. No one said another word.

The judge wrapped up proceedings; she stood up, turned, and as a bat, disappeared into the night. I saw the back of her head and black gown disappear through the rear door at 6.20 pm.

But what about Tim fucking men behind my back? What about the fact he liked to wear make-up? I had proof he was registered on the dating website Ashley Madison while we were together? Was that irrelevant? What about how he abandoned Bella and me and commenced a new relationship in Australia and had a baby with his new partner while we were still married?

Did Tim believe telling a lie about me having an affair would justify his abandonment of us?

Well, it didn't.

fourteen

Softly, softly, catch that tiger

The experience of appearing in court over two days for the spousal maintenance action at the beginning of May 2015 was nothing short of harrowing. I was shocked to witness Tim stoop so low as to lie and wrongfully accuse me of having an affair when his own behaviour had been so questionable. To have my lawyers advise me the court would not be interested in hearing about Tim's suspected bisexuality and how he verbally and emotionally abused me was damaging to me.

Tim's abuse had an impact on me. It weakened me and allowed him to manoeuvre me into a vulnerable position, for the whole unfortunate sequence of events to happen and unfold as they did. That mattered.

In July 2015, when the judge released her interim decision concerning my spousal maintenance application, she wrote that she believed I had planned to move to Australia to be with Tim; however, I changed my mind. I am sure she came to that conclusion due to Tim's lie with regard to my alleged affair. Without objection from my barrister, Tim successfully cast doubt over my integrity. The judge explained that she needed more financial documentation and information about the performance of the businesses before she could reach a finding. In other words, she wanted access to the business valuations.

She requested Tim provide information relating to his own personal circumstances – his living arrangements with his new partner, proof of any debt on their home, proof of his new partner's income. Interestingly, I later submitted all requested documentation to the court, but he did not.

I vowed I would not rest over being wrongly accused of having an affair. I was determined to get Tim to recant his statement. It took some time, but he eventually conceded that I had received a text message from a man while he was in Australia in April 2012. He stopped short of admitting perjury. Clarification regarding Tim's lie was never submitted to the court as evidence in an affidavit.

In the meantime, the judge who heard the spousal maintenance case suffered a heart attack, so she was unable to continue with our case. Continuity was lost.

It was interesting to see Tim write in later legal documentation that he claimed my spousal maintenance action was thrown out of court. Well, that's not what happened. It was incredibly frustrating to have to continually deal with his constant barrage of lies.

In mid-2015, I had my lawyer request approval for the release of $50,000 to me, being part of the cash proceeds from the sale of our home.

His lawyer put pressure on me to drop the spousal maintenance case in exchange for their approval and subsequent access to my own cash. They tried to argue that if I had access to my own cash then I wouldn't require spousal maintenance.

I refused to submit to their threats and demands. I was not going to allow Tim and his lawyer to blackmail me.

I instructed my lawyer to continue to press for the release of my own money as an issue independent of the spousal maintenance action. Tim was wallowing in his ability to play God and put me through financial hardship. I felt sickened by his remorseless displays of cruelty and greed.

Around that time, Tim invited me to enter into a mediation to settle the relationship property matter. The timing of this was interesting and telling.

I was only a few weeks away from receiving the official valuations for the businesses. He was attempting to lure me into a negotiation before I had the evidence from the valuations to sink him with the proof that he had been lying about them all along.

My lawyers turned down Tim's offer, explaining how a mediation would be futile, given Tim's unrelenting bullying and unrealistic demands.

I wasn't about to be cornered into a beat-down negotiation. Forget it. He started the legal process, and I would finish it. I would see him in court before a judge. I deserved to be heard, and I deserved fairness, not that I was ever going to see it.

When I put up resistance to Tim's claims and fought back, his volatility and narcissism began to get the better of him.

As my lawyers picked at the scabs of his inconsistencies and lies, he began to lose control. His affidavits – I had the feeling he was writing his own – did not make sense, and there were often emotive rants with little substance being presented to the court.

Slowly but surely, his lies and deceptions began to tighten, as a noose around his neck. Softly, softly, I vowed I would catch that tiger.

fifteen

The Player

Two Cures for Love

1. Don't see him. Don't phone or write a letter.
2. The easy way: Get to know him better.

"Two Cures for Love",
from *Serious Concerns*, Wendy Cope

Cameron (Cam), the Player, and I had unfinished business. There had always been the tease of "what if" between us.

I have wrestled with a tangled labyrinth of emotions over knowing what is right and what is good for me, with respect to him. So much of what happens between men and women doesn't make any sense at all. Given my track record, was it any wonder I found myself travelling the same self-destructive path with him as I had in the past?

We met on a building site in Auckland, many years ago, at an age when Cam was tall, willowy and confident, bursting with cocky exuberance. I was naïve, cautious, and ripe with youth. We were instantly attracted to each other. It was more of a curiosity at first. He employed me to do some architectural drawings for his construction company. He was, and still is, a builder.

We enjoyed a number of intimate liaisons but we never slept together. He moved away from Auckland and we lost touch.

I never forgot Cam, and even through the years of my marriage I got goosebumps whenever I heard his name mentioned. We had a few mutual friends and acquaintances. I assumed he was married with children.

It wasn't until early July 2014 when I heard from Cam again. We were friends on Facebook, and he had seen a photograph of me taken at the races. I was wearing a stunning red dress, a fascinator, matching red lipstick, and a beaming smile. He always had an eye for a pretty girl.

Cam invited me to join him for lunch at an Auckland beachside café. It was the first time we had laid eyes on each other for thirteen years. As you would expect from two old friends, the conversation flowed easily. We had a lot to catch up on.

'It's so great to see you again, Emms. You're still just as gorgeous as I remember you,' he said.

'Aw, thank you. That's kind of you to say so. I have to work at it these days, you realise,' I responded with a smile.

'Well, hun, keep it up; whatever you're doing, it's working. Let's order,' he said. 'I don't know about you, but I'm starving. God, it's great to see you. How many years has it been?'

'A few,' I said.

'I'm sorry to hear about your separation. Can't be easy on your own with a kid. I thought I'd have kids by now,' he continued.

'So you never married? No little mini-Cams running around in far-flung reaches of the world then? Really? I find that hard to believe,' I teased him.

We both knew what he was like. It was no secret he enjoyed the ladies.

'Nope. No kids. No wife. I guess I just haven't met the one.'

What a crock of shit. How many times had I heard similar excuses and denials from late thirty-something-year-old men who can't let go of their womanising ways? I just looked away and pretended to peruse the lunch menu.

Cam held my hand as he walked me to my car. He took me in his arms and kissed me. My lips had memory. Dormant emotions rushed back as if we had never been apart.

We made love for the very first time two weeks later. He was all the man I had imagined him to be.

The Scent of Morning

My mind drifts to a time
When I would wake to him
Lying next to me
Such a handsome man
Asleep and at peace

I trace patterns of my thoughts
Over his nakedness
My fingers find pathways
Across his broad and manly chest
My hand rises and falls as he breathes

He imbues that decadent
Scent of morning;
Clammy and smug
With the stench of sex

It takes every ounce of my control
Not to wake him
I wait
Watching
Savouring
Each moment

He stirs
His arm curls around my neck
Behold
The magic begins
Again

Over the following few weeks, Cam was in constant contact with me. He invited Bella and me to his fortieth birthday party. He also asked me to join him in Queenstown to go skiing for five days. I was excited. I hadn't had a break in a very long time, and with the pressure of the court proceedings I was really looking forward to some time away.

Two days before his birthday, Cam returned to Auckland.

We caught up for dinner; however, something had changed in his attitude towards me. There was a hint of restraint to his voice and body language as he spoke of his ambitions and plans for the future.

I was surprised to hear him mention he had just paid for his season pass to ski in Colorado and that he was leaving for the States in January. He hadn't booked a return airfare. He didn't know whether he would be coming back to New Zealand. There was no mention of "us" in his future plans.

I cried on my way home.

I was so confused.

How could I have misinterpreted the situation and his feelings for me so badly?

The following day, I told Cam I wouldn't be travelling to Queenstown with him. I didn't see the point when he had made it so obvious that our relationship was going nowhere. I couldn't put myself through the free fall of emotion I knew would go hand in hand with spending more time with him, only to miss him when he left.

Cam convinced me to still come to his fortieth birthday party.

I reluctantly agreed but decided not to take Bella. Considering the temporary nature of our relationship, there was no way I was going to throw Bella into a situation that would only confuse her.

We partied hard that night. I had a great time, and all Cam's friends and family were warm and welcoming. I wasn't drinking so I drove us back to my place. We arrived home at 3 am and made love for hours. His need for me was intoxicating. I felt like a teenager experiencing love, lust, and sexual hunger for the first time, all over again.

We rose again for breakfast at 8 am.

Our routine continued. I was almost out of my mind with sexual satisfaction.

Oranges Not Oranges

I really love oranges
The way the flesh
Erupts all over my face
Cascading syrupy juice
Down my chin
So

Indulgent
Delicious
Satisfied
I wipe away the spoils
With the back of my hand
And catch sweet nectar
With my tongue
So
Erotic
I had almost forgotten
How much
I really love oranges

We chatted later that morning. Cam sat back on my sofa and beckoned me to sit on his knee. He explained his reasons for going to the States, saying he would probably come back to me. It was hard to sit and listen to him speak. Did he seriously think I would wait for him?

My heart and mind were on a collision course with the mixed messages he had on offer. Nothing he had to say made sense to me, and yet I was still drawn to him.

I drove Cam to his mother's home. We sat in my car in her driveway, and he cupped his hands gently around my flushed cheeks. He looked through my eyes into my soul and he wouldn't let go of me.

With tears in his eyes, he said goodbye. He turned and slowly walked away. I had no idea whether I was ever going to see him again.

For two weeks my emotional pain ebbed and flowed. I felt physically sick. I barely ate.

My question invariably remained the same – with our connection, how could he just walk away?

I understood Cam had a basic instinct to reproduce and as much as he kept getting sucked into my "sexual vortex" (his words, not mine), my age eliminated me as a potential long-term option for him.

It really didn't make any difference as to the why. The fact was, he left with no indication of when he was coming back.

Maybe it was all my problem? I seemed to be drawn to narcissistic types. *Grow up, Emma, and walk away. Do yourself a favour for a change*, I told myself.

Cam and I saw each other again six weeks later. We spent the following three weekends together. It was always the same between us – mind-blowing sex with about 80% emotional engagement from him.

By that stage we had fallen into the most amazing sexual rhythm; I was letting myself go as I trusted him sexually, and he was hungry for me.

We lay naked in bed in a motel room. We were both spent. My mind drifted with the realisation that Cam would soon leave for the States.

I raised my thoughts with him. 'I don't believe what you're looking for is in the States,' I said. 'If you think I'm going to sit back and watch you fuck women from one coast to the other and you think I'll have you back, well, you're mistaken. I'll move on. It saddens me that for all the years we've known each other, it has come to this.'

I dressed. I packed my bag and walked towards the door.

'Can I help you down to your car, Emms?' he asked.

'No, thank you. I'm perfectly fine on my own,' I replied.

In the weeks and months that followed, I thought of Cam, my expectations of him and how I thought I was getting to know him. I wrestled with my gut-wrenching realisation that I knew so little of what drove him, outside of his raw lust for me and possibly a raft of other women. I thought about the measured levels of emotion he rationed out and how I was left feeling unfulfilled.

I pondered the concept of "*why?*" Why had I allowed myself to become so emotionally involved with Cam when he had already demonstrated to me, all those years ago, that he lacked the conviction to make a stand for me? I suppose there was the familiarity factor; I already knew him, so I trusted him to a degree. Then, of course, there was the undeniable chemistry we shared. He made me feel young again. Being with him took me back to a time before Tim, before so many crushing disappointments.

I had imprinted my own emotions and expectations onto Cam, and I'd assumed he felt the same way. Well, I was wrong.

False Idol

I thought
I knew you
I thought
I loved you

With hindsight
I now know
That I was wrong

The man
I thought I loved
Is not the man before me
More an idea
Of who
You really are

All fault lies with me
I need to meet with reality
You never were
The man
I imagined
You
To be

I could have played the victim and agonised as to why he had chosen *not* to be with me. But that would have been a futile waste of energy. I wanted to be happy. I wanted to be with a man who really loved me, a man who could not walk away from me, a man who would do everything to protect me and share his life with me.

I understood I needed to keep my focus on the future and not be drawn into the past. I was done with the past. Things didn't work out with Cam when we were young, so why had I expected anything to be different this time around? That was my lesson.

My poetry flowed as a river of my emotions. I was able to express how I felt through words, the euphoric highs and also the emptiness I felt with Cam's departure.

I wrote of the uncertainty I felt for my future and the gaping hole he left in my heart. There were times when I felt his presence as though he was a lingering ghost.

Ghost of My Broken Heart

I sat today
Gazing
Into the eyes of a stranger
As WE dined on delicacies
And fine wine

The earnest stranger
Implored with gusto
To my whims
HE was too eager
To appeal to MY vanity

The handsome stranger spoke
And yet
I saw YOUR piercing eyes
Your energy bore down on ME
Oh how my body ached for the fire of OUR chemistry;
Our all-consuming passion

As YOU slouched in the stranger's chair
You mocked and tortured me in part
For allowing your company at HIS table

I am trying so hard
To dismiss YOUR absent charms
You have relinquished any right to be here

I must stay strong and vanquish YOU
Be gone
Ghost of MY broken heart

Months went by. They stretched into a year. I received a few texts from Cam. I blew him off. I couldn't bring myself to speak to him or return his messages. I was still hurting.

Another year went by.

From his Facebook posts I could see he was partying in Colorado. He had a native American girlfriend. She looked very like me with her flowing long, straight dark hair, her warm brown eyes, and her radiant smile.

There was a Facebook Messenger phone call from Cam one afternoon in July 2016. I was surprised to see his name appear on my mobile screen. *Why would he be calling me?* I wondered. My curiosity got the better of me. I swiped my phone to take the call. 'Hello,' I said.

I was greeted with a softly spoken woman's voice with an American accent. She introduced herself as Cam's girlfriend and got straight to the point. 'Why is there a naked photograph of you on my boyfriend's phone?' she asked.

'Um …' I was stalling for time. 'Don't you think you had better ask *him*?' I replied. 'I don't know why you're calling me. I haven't seen Cam in almost two years. It's not really appropriate for you to be calling me,' I continued.

She was an intelligent woman, a pilot in fact. *What on earth was going on in her mind?* I wondered. If she was jealous, she had nothing to be jealous of. I no longer wanted him.

I suggested she would be better to concentrate her energies on a man with a stronger character. I wished her well and said goodbye.

What naked photo? Jesus.

I scrolled through our old text messages. There were some saucy exchanges to and fro but there were no naked photos – of *me* at least.

I checked Facebook Messenger and scrolled through our historical online chats. There was only one sexy pic of me. In the photograph you could make out the lean, muscular curves of my back, my legs, and my ass.

I smiled.

Within six months, I could see Cam had changed his online Facebook relationship status. He and his American girlfriend were no longer Facebook friends. He was back in New Zealand, and he was single again.

sixteen

The piss cup

A sea of beauty queens had entered the bikini category of the August 2015 Auckland Bodybuilding Regional Championships. Some stunning beauties – 130 in all – had gathered to strut their stuff and see just how far their hours of weight training and dietary sacrifices would take them.

The Masters Bikini category is a small class in comparison to the other Bikini classes. I guess by the time most women get to thirty-five and over, and have had one or more children, the thought of walking on stage in a bikini and being judged for your physical appearance is not exactly appealing. I totally got that. Considering I was forty-four and competing for the first time, how and why I found myself doing bodybuilding was a bit of a mystery.

I weighed myself on the morning of the competition. I was 54 kilograms. I felt dehydrated, starving, and exhausted. I looked sensational.

It was pitch black outside and freezing cold when I left home at 6 am. I was booked in for a spray tan at the venue at 7 am.

I was naked beneath my thin black satin robe as I stood barefoot and in line with fifteen to twenty similarly naked and starving individuals on the cold concrete floor.

My name was called and I was ushered into the flimsy three-sided spray tan booth that looked a little like a tall, makeshift tent for one. A stern young woman stood by the booth and rested the spray gun on her hip. She told me to disrobe inside the tent. I stood with outstretched neck, arms, and legs as she swept the spray gun over my body. Within a few minutes I was covered in a cold, sticky, wet brown goo that had the most unusual smell.

As I held my breath for fear of inhaling the disgusting brew, I noticed a young guy loitering in the distance. Every now and again he glanced over to me as he played on his phone. I tried my best to avoid eye contact with him as I stood naked inside the booth.

I was almost bursting with embarrassment. In all seriousness, most of the women who enter these competitions have fake breasts. I definitely do not have fake breasts. In fact, it was debatable whether I had any breasts at all that morning.

I once had an ex-boyfriend describe my breasts as two Disprins on an ironing board. My two little Disprins were not looking particularly voluptuous as they clung to my skeletal chest. I was sitting at 11% body fat. What could I possibly expect?

Still, I sucked up my pride and tried to ignore the young man who was perving at me with sideway glances.

'Turn around and bend over,' instructed the authoritative, efficient woman with the spray gun. 'I have to spray your back and I don't want you getting any lines under your butt.'

Oh, for God's sake, I thought.

With my back turned, I was sure the nice young man had a wonderful view of my naked posterior and vagina as I bent over.

Make-up was next. I thought I was mentally prepared for the stage make-up but I wasn't – not even close. I had massive false eyelashes applied, and by the end of it I looked like a cross between an orange Ooompa Loompa and a drag queen, albeit a short, very skinny drag queen with Disprins.

I was nervous and excited as we waited for the competition to begin. I found it hard to believe I actually looked okay standing next to all the other beautiful young women. It was a little like being backstage at a Miss World contest. Not that I have ever been backstage at a Miss World contest, but hey …

At one point a prominent Kiwi sportsman and his friend wandered over towards me as I filled in time. The two men wanted to chat to me. Yes, to me. Of all the Miss World contestants they could have chatted to that morning, they chose me. They introduced themselves and one of them said, 'Gee, Emma, your husband must be so proud of you.' He assumed I was married.

My eyes immediately fell. I responded with a simple thank you as I struggled to fight back tears. I wanted to fall through a crack in the floor. If only I'd had a husband who cared. I felt very alone.

Much of the day was spent waiting around. I amused myself talking to the Bikini competitors. A delightful Irish woman told me all about the "piss cup" she had made. Twenty-six-year-old Aishling looked ravishing with her cascading auburn curls and her copper-coloured, crystal-encrusted bikini. Aishling was a full-time personal trainer.

I smiled from ear to ear as I saw the humour in the situation. Sitting next to me was a drop-dead gorgeous bombshell of a woman going over the finer details of how she had perfected the construction of the piss cup – a polystyrene cup with the bottom cut out. She described how she pressed the top to her girlie bits and pissed into it. That helped direct your piss straight down towards the bowl of the toilet. If you got a dribble on your fake tan, it was immediately ruined. The cup helped avoid such a tragedy. I thought the whole concept was a total hoot. Aishling made one for me while we waited backstage.

As midday approached, I heard the adjudicator call out Masters Bikini. Midday was our scheduled time to walk onstage. I happened to be on the toilet right at that very moment, having my tenth nervous wee with my piss cup. I panicked. I thought, *Holy crap, don't tell me I have just spent four months training my guts out, not eating cheese, muffins, pizza, wine, and anything with a hint of carb and fat decadence, to then miss my call to go out onstage?*

I ran out of the toilet with my cup in hand. I couldn't see a rubbish bin anywhere so, with no time to spare, I literally threw it into the middle of the women's changing area. I didn't stop to look. I had just sprayed my piss from one side of the room to the other, quite possibly over a few of the Miss World contestants. I ran to the stage and surprised myself with how quickly I could move in my four-inch stage heels.

I was beyond relieved to realise the marshal was merely heralding our first call to assemble. We weren't due on stage for another ten minutes.

Masters Bikini was the first bikini class to compete. Of the 130 competitors, guess who was first to be called to walk across the stage that day? Well, yes – me.

I was so nervous. There were hundreds of people in the audience – not that I could really see a lot; the stage lights almost blinded me.

I made it up the steps and onto the stage without tripping. As I cautiously strode across, I was careful not to look at my feet. I didn't want to disappoint Courtney and mess up my routine.

I fell into drill mode. The hours of practice paid off, all bar my inability to stop my left leg shaking. My friend Kate told me later that evening that she had noticed my quivering leg from her seat in the audience. The judges would have noticed too. Oh dear.

I caught sight of Bella's beaming smile. She waved at me. I instinctively waved back. I probably wasn't supposed to do that either. Double oh dear. I loved my wee girl and I was so pleased she was there. I waved some more.

I placed second that day. I had just secured my qualification to compete at Nationals.

Wow. Seriously wow! I was going to compete at the New Zealand national championships later in the year. Never in my wildest dreams did I think that would happen.

I called my parents to tell them my exciting news. As an elite sportsman himself in his younger years, Dad was delighted.

'Well done, Emms. I'm so happy for you,' he said. 'Make sure you have a good sleep tonight. You deserve it. Now I'll just pass the phone over to your mother so you can tell her your great news.'

'Hi, Mum. You know how I was competing at the Regional Champs today. Well I was placed and I've qualified to compete at Nationals in October!'

'Oh. OK. Well you don't want to go and get all obsessive about it now, do you,' she said in response.

seventeen

National Champs

Mel flew up from the South Island to be with me for Nationals. My friends Skye and Mia were also in the audience that day.

Nationals was an experience all of its own. There was palpable tension in the air as New Zealand's elite bodybuilders channelled their energy and pumped their muscles in preparation for the competition.

For many athletes, their performance onstage that day was the culmination of years of dedication to training, diet, and lifestyle choices. I was very much a beginner in comparison. I had only been doing weights for six and a half months. I was actually shocked I had qualified to compete alongside such dedicated sportspeople.

There were too many competitors to allow segregated changing rooms for men and women at the convention centre. Instead, we all jostled together to change our clothes and prepare in various meeting rooms. I had near-naked men and women all around me and the spaces were cramped. The most lingering memory of the changing facilities was the revolting smell – a mixture of testosterone, fake tan, and sweat. I liken it to being held in a room with fifty "roaring" stags.

Individuals prepared themselves as best they could. Two Indian men lay on the floor with their heads close to my feet. They were resting their legs halfway up the wall in an attempt to drain fluid from their limbs. As I changed out of my activewear and knickers into my bikini, I could see the whites of their eyes darting towards my naked vagina. I felt uncomfortable, but what choice did I have? There was nowhere else to go.

Compared to the Regional Champs some eleven weeks earlier, I was able to improve on my posing and shoulder positions for Nationals. I broadened my smile and did my best, but with all I had to remember, I forgot to wave to the judges as I finished my routine. I would have been penalised for that.

Every single day from 5 April to 17 October 2015, I pushed myself to my physical and mental limit. I focused my thoughts and controlled every aspect of my diet, my lifestyle, and my daily routine. I thrived on the experience and felt physically and mentally stronger.

I was one of the top seven competitors in New Zealand for Masters Bikini when I strode confidently across the stage that weekend at Nationals. Mel filmed my prejudging routine, and I have watched my performance from time to time since then.

Although I never received a medal, I was immensely proud of my achievement. I had accomplished something truly extraordinary, considering my age and lack of experience. I felt like a winner.

eighteen

Distractions

Mel has been my rock of support for as long as we have known each other. Without hesitation, she has been at my side to help me through many of my personal challenges. She stayed with me over the tumultuous period when Tim left Bella and me – helping me pack up my home, my retail store and moved Bella and me into the Mill. Mel travelled to the United States at the beginning of 2013 to assist me at the Las Vegas trade fair, appointing herself as Director of Logistics, Public Relations and Nightly Activities for the duration of our tour.

My friend generously gave her time to fly to Auckland and support me through six court hearings during 2015. She sat outside the courtroom with my dad and waited for hours to ensure I was okay. Mel has sacrificed her time to care for Bella so I could travel domestically and internationally for work. I appreciate with my whole heart what she has done for me and I cherish her friendship.

It was through the consistent encouragement of my friends and my father that I was able to face my fears and draw upon the strength I needed to fight Tim in court. They reassured me and gave me confidence to rebuild my life. It was their love that led me along a path to freedom through our laughter and my tears.

I remember the afternoon of the child custody hearing. Mel was left in the waiting room that adjoined the lawyers' conference rooms. She sat immediately next to the paper-thin walls of Tim's lawyers' room.

Mel could clearly hear their conversations. She vigorously texted updates to me as I waited on my own inside the court.

Half an hour went by before my barrister pushed her way through the courtroom doors with outstretched arms. 'Can Melanie hear Tim's lawyer? Is she texting you information?' she demanded to know. As a schoolteacher her razor-sharp eyes glared at me with disdain.

I cannot tell a lie to save myself. 'She can't hear much,' I responded weakly.

As soon as my barrister turned and left, I texted Mel. *They're on to us! You had better back the bus up, girlfriend.* I quickly deleted our texts.

We laughed about that for weeks; we felt like two naughty little kids who had been caught texting in class. But it felt great to see the humour in the situation, and it helped me get through that traumatic time.

On 28 February 2015, Rob called and offered to take me out for lunch for my birthday the following day.

We met at a café on the Auckland waterfront and had a wonderful time chatting and laughing together. After lunch, he suggested we go for a walk along the beach.

Rob was dying to show off his new acquisition. As he drove through St Heliers in his black Mercedes sports car, we admired the palatial homes and gardens along our route. He pulled over, parked, and said, 'It's a bit of a walk to the beach, Emms, but you'll be OK. I brought some towels. Grab your bag. Let's go.'

I was wearing an elegant, sleeveless chiffon blouse, a below-the-knee, flowing floral taffeta skirt with a tulle petticoat, and high heels. I hadn't considered a walk along the sand when I decided on my wardrobe for my birthday outing. I followed along behind Rob as best I could.

The walking track wasn't well maintained. The ground became more uneven as we went along. The gravel gave way to a dirt track with tree roots and other pitfalls. It was tricky keeping up with Rob given the three-inch Swarovski-crystal-encrusted Michael Kors heels I was wearing. Suddenly the track disappeared, and all that remained was an aluminium ladder that descended vertically down the rocky cliff.

As Rob's head and torso appeared to levitate down the ladder, I called out to him. 'You've got to be kidding me. I know what you're up to. There's a nudist beach down there.'

'Just lift up your skirt, woman. Use those gorgeous legs of yours and get your ass down here!' he yelled.

'You're crazy. I'm going to fall,' I called back to him.

'Come on. Hurry up, Rivers. I haven't got all day,' he berated me from the bottom of the cliff.

I must have looked absurd as I descended the ladder in all my birthday finery.

There were a few people on the beach that day. It was a bit of a smorgasbord of ages and body types. All I could do was lie back naked on the towel and try to pretend it wasn't really happening. I shook my head and had a good chuckle.

'You're attracting attention, Emms,' Rob said.

'Oh, just shut up will you,' I said, 'and don't even think about bringing that weapon of yours over here.' I saw the humour.

'You can't blame a man for trying now, eh?' he said.

'What's it been, hun? Seventeen years we've been friends? You're killing me – this has gotta be your best attempt to date,' I said as my voice wheezed with laughter.

While I lay nude next to my friend, my eyes scanned the shoreline. I soon fixed my attention on a man who could be best described as a short, fat, lawyer type with glasses. His dwarf-like legs worked overtime as he scuttled past us like a fevered crab on the sandy shore. His head swivelled from side to side, stealing glances as he went. I took a photo of his wobbly white ass and texted it to Mel.

Almost immediately, she responded. *Where r u Emms? Isn't it your bday? Why is* that *guy in* his *bday suit? Who is he? Not your type! WTF?*

There were so many questions from Mel. I could tell she was concerned.

I'm out with Rob. And yes, it's my birthday, I replied.

Oh. OK. Be gd. LOL. Happy bday hun, she texted.

Mel again flew to Auckland in mid-2015 to support me for another of my many courtroom appearances. As we dragged half her house across the arrivals area and out to my car, I said, 'I've got some news for you, girlfriend. Rob called as I was waiting for you. He wants to meet us at his favourite club at 11 pm.' I raised an eyebrow and gave Mel a sideways glance.

'Oh my God. No way. Shit. I'm not wearing my sexy knickers,' she said.

Rob was about to introduce us to the Auckland swinger scene.

The entrance to the club was inconspicuous. There were no signs, just a solitary downlight above a darkened, nondescript door. As we gingerly stepped inside, we were required to leave our mobile phones and our prudish reservations at the door.

The owner made a poor attempt at feigning a first-time meeting with Rob as he went over the rules of the club.

We were ushered through a series of doors into a dimly lit room. A cocktail bar swept along the room to our left and a large, round metal cage hung from the ceiling to our right. Inside the cage were two naked women. One of them was on her knees, the other had hooked one of her legs over the first woman's shoulder. The woman kneeling was giving head to her cage mate.

The bar was heaving with bodies; some were clothed, some were not. No one looked overly excited. Everyone moved slowly and appeared relaxed.

Seated to my right on a long booth seat was a middle-aged woman with large, sagging breasts. Her skin was pale and uneven. The glasses and sensible shoes she wore sang a verse of her life. I had visions of her working in accounts at Auckland Council.

There were white-haired, balding men with skinny legs stripped of muscle, proudly parading swollen bellies. I found their confidence astounding. Still, who was I to judge?

Younger alpha males walked confidently through the bar, leading beautiful women by the hand.

Rob, Mel, and I sat at the bar and sipped on cosmopolitans, all the while observing our surroundings. We didn't say too much to each other. Just the odd knowing glance, a raised eyebrow, and wry smiles were exchanged.

We wandered into a room where six people were lying naked and entwined on a large bed having sex. I whispered to Rob, 'Is it really OK for us to watch?'

'They want you to watch, Emms,' Rob assured me.

As I stood watching the orgy with fascination, Mel picked up an electric drill with a massive, flesh-coloured vibrator attached. She turned it on and nearly jumped out of her own skin with fright.

'Get that thing away from me,' I shrieked as Mel ventured towards me, with the wobbling, whirring gigantic mechanical cock in hand.

We left that room shortly after and moved to a more private area where we watched an attractive young man and woman have sex with each other. The couple had stamina. They were a pleasure to watch.

Her wrists were handcuffed and positioned above her head. She lay in a movable sling with her legs elevated in stirrups. I was standing less than a metre from them when he beckoned me to join them. Politely, I declined his offer. I wasn't sure I was ready to have my two best friends watch me fuck two total strangers. And I am sure Rob and Mel weren't ready for that either.

The three of us meandered back to the main cocktail lounge, and I leant against the bar. I sipped on my drink and watched with intrigue as a guy next to me expertly removed the dress of his partner. He proceeded to fuck her right there on the barstool next to me.

I casually turned my head to confer with Mel; however, she had moved off and was in deep conversation with the young woman we had just seen with her legs in stirrups fucking her boyfriend. When I noticed the young woman fondling my mate's voluminous breasts, I thought it was time I ordered another drink.

I shifted my attention to a woman working the pole on the dance floor.

Rob walked over to me. 'Rivers, you want to have a go on that pole, don't you? I can see it in your eyes. Don't tell me you don't want to.'

'Hm, maybe I do,' I replied.

'Come on then. Give me your dress. Go do your thing,' Rob said.

I didn't need a whole lot of encouragement as it happened. The three cosmopolitans I had consumed gave me all the confidence I needed.

I worked the pole for ten minutes and lost myself to the music. Sweat sprayed from my body, and my muscles screamed in ecstasy. Around and around I spun in my G-string, bra, and four-inch heels. In that moment, I didn't have a care in the world. It was exhilarating and liberating letting my inhibitions go. I attracted an audience and received applause when I was done.

Rob and Mel watched my every move. Rob turned his head to Mel and said, 'She's not bad. I didn't know Rivers could dance like that.'

'Yeah, well, that makes two of us.'

A month later I was back in Canterbury. Through some connections of Mel's, we were invited to another swinger party at a private residence in the middle of nowhere in rural South Canterbury. Mel arrived first so she was able to provide me with an escorted tour of the property.

I like to think I am open-minded but that place made me feel uncomfortable. The atmosphere was thick with a dark, sexual tension.

The three-car garage had been converted into a bondage and discipline dungeon. Everything was black, grey, and red. The interior appeared macabre and gothic in style. There were bondage beds, spreader bars, shackles, stocks, hoods, collars, and chastity belts on the walls and at various points on the floor around the room.

Ten people stood in various states of dress and undress, sipping on their drinks. They seemed to fidget with forced chatter. I felt anticipation claw the air.

'It's about to become a free-for-all in here. I think we should move back to the lounge,' I said to Mel.

As we rambled throughout the expansive home, I noticed all the doors had been removed from the bedrooms. Each bedroom contained a super king-size bed and a bedside table with disinfectant, wipes, and condoms. Plastic sheeting covered the bare mattresses. There were no pillows or bed dressings or curtains at the windows. There were cameras and television screens in every room.

I went in search of the kitchen for a glass of water, and found myself confronted by a young blond man standing naked and blocking my path in the middle of the living room. He had an unnerving, vacant look in his eyes and was wearing a silver-studded collar with a chain dangling from his neck. He had numerous nipple and lip piercings, and a sequin sheath covering his limp cock. I was fascinated by his whole demeanour.

A couple of guys were idly standing watching people as they moved through the rooms. They wore black leather underwear and silver chain jewellery. They held floggers and riding crops. One wore a mask.

As Mel and I moved outside, a couple sauntered past me and gave me a look which said, *Hey, hot stuff, come join us*. I kept on walking and sat outside with my friend.

I looked at one of the big-screen televisions through the window from my vantage point and saw the couple that had not long walked past me engaging in some very rough group sex with a few other people.

By midnight I asked Mel, 'Doll, have you seen enough?'

'Yep, I sure have,' she said.

And we left.

Over several cups of hot chocolate at an all-night café, Mel and I had a quiet debrief. We both agreed, as entertaining as it was to capture a glimpse of the swinger and deviant world, we both realised it wasn't for us.

As the months and years passed, and once I was able to get over the immediate shock of my separation, I slowly reclaimed some confidence. I discovered I was free to experience the world through fresh eyes. There were no controls and no limitations, apart from those I imposed on myself. My curious nature opened doors I had previously overlooked due to the constraints of my marriage.

I was blessed to be able to share good times with my friends. My experiences were generally positive with no damaging effects apart from giving me stomach aches from all the laughter.

PART THREE

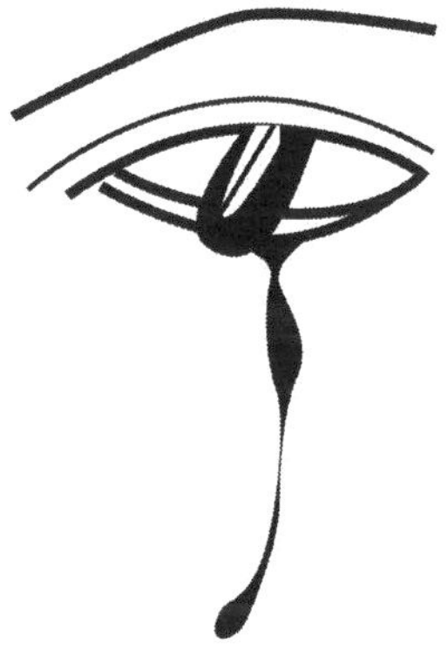

HEARTACHE AND ANGUISH

nineteen

Why marry Tim?

Advice to young writers

The thing you are most afraid to write.
Write that.

Salt, Nayyirah Waheed

Why did I decide to marry Tim? What characteristics did he possess that made him shine above every other man that crossed my path? Was it really about him being worthy? Or was it about something else altogether?

The answer to the riddle lies with me. It was *my* past that defined the decisions and the outcomes of the events I have described. I believe Tim was already a sexually confused narcissist when we met. At the time, I failed to see him for who he truly was, for reasons I will explain.

As a child growing up in the mid-1970s, my home life was basic. My father, mother, an older sister, and I lived on my father's family farm, along a gravel road, 10 kilometres from the nearest grocery store. Two vehicles drove past our home daily: the mailman, who delivered our newspaper and post, and a neighbour, who drove his rusty truck to check his cattle. You could always see the dust before you ever heard a vehicle.

The school bus dropped my sister and me off with another neighbour's three kids a kilometre from our farm gate. We scuffed our shoes, picked flowers, and sometimes sang as we wandered home. The other kids walked home in the opposite direction.

An old man with a kindly, unshaven face and the smell of despair lived along our route. Like his body, Stanley's home was wasting away. His garden was a maze of overgrown weeds and his front door was stiff to open. We brought light to his otherwise secluded life and he gave us jam-filled Shrewsbury biscuits in exchange for our time.

One afternoon, my sister and I arrived home with biscuits bulging from our pockets.

Our mother was surprised. 'Did Stanley give you all those biscuits?'

'Stanley wasn't home,' said my sister. 'We helped ourselves.'

In a world before mobile phones, the Internet, and instant gratification, we amused ourselves on the farm by making bows and arrows and building tree huts. There was an enormous weeping willow that grew sideways across the river. I remember spending endless hours nailing wooden fence battens in a horizontal fashion up the side of the slanting trunk. The battens became the ladder to my make-believe world. I'd lie flat on my stomach on the platform I had built between the boughs of the tree overlooking the water. Sleek, black eels appeared to hover effortlessly in the shallows below. I was mesmerised by them as they swam close to the riverbank looking for tadpoles, midges, and mice. New willow leaves grew along citrine tentacles. They waved in the wind and stroked my face. "There, there, child," they caressed and comforted me.

With gumboots on and my mother's kitchen sieve in my hand, I'd escape the confines of the farmhouse and head for the rolling hills and creeks that criss-crossed the paddocks. I spent hours standing knee-deep in water, trawling for tiny fish and tadpoles. It took Mum a while to work out why her sieve had turned to rust. She didn't seem to care.

I was desperate to take my prize catch home. I filled an empty plastic ice cream container with water and tiny fish from the creek and carefully placed it on the back of my bicycle carrier. It was a short ride home across uneven grassy ground, stony gateways, and through gullies with channels of mud baked as hard as bricks in the sun. I remember my dismay when I arrived home; the container was completely empty. It had been a bumpy ride that day!

Building dams to create swimming holes was always one of my favourite summer pastimes – until Dad worked out what I was doing and told me not to. 'Emma, how am I supposed to water the animals if you cut off the water supply?' he would say.

In winter, we'd make home-made skis from any old flotsam and jetsam we could lay our hands on. We used hay bale twine to tie our gumboots to random wooden planks of differing lengths. Our ski poles were made from discarded TV aerial rods. We were never going to win design awards with our creations, let alone ski down a slope. More often than not, we'd trudge to the top of the hill with our skis in tow and pretend we were snowballs and roll to the bottom.

I didn't see a lot of my dad when I was young. He was always busy on the farm. In summer, he would shear each and every one of our 3,000 sheep. He'd be drenching, dipping, drilling, docking, drafting, dagging, crutching, weaning, haymaking, harvesting crops, burning rubble, fencing, harvesting deer velvet, buying and selling animals, and taking them in our truck to the "works" (the abattoir). In winter, it was all about the care of the animals. I learnt to drive at a very young age as Dad needed my sister and me to drive the truck while he was on the back feeding out hay to the sheep and deer.

It wasn't an easy life on the farm. We were snowed in for an entire month one winter when snowdrifts reached the height of the windows. We had no electricity over that time; evenings were cut short and limited to candlelight. My mother cooked our meals on an open fire.

The farmhouse was almost a hundred years old when we took over the farm. A big wooden telephone hung high on the wall in the hallway. I could never reach it. It had a winding ringer at the side and operated via an exchange system on a "party line". There were no private telephone conversations – not with the neighbours potentially listening in.

Our home had cracked and creaking floorboards. The roof had sagging eaves. The wind whistled and the roofing iron rattled in the high winds of summer. In winter, I had ice-cold feet and painful chilblains. The morning air turned my breath to frozen fog. We filled in time waiting for the school bus by smashing ice-covered puddles with our hockey sticks. I wore so many woollen jerseys I could barely move and so many pairs of socks it was difficult getting my feet into my boots.

I peeled the generations of time from the walls of our family home as layer upon layer of tattered floral wallpaper beckoned nimble fingers. We had a black-and-white television that offered two channels. I remember the "clunk-clunk" sound of the dial as Mum changed the channels. Television transmission used to stop at around 10 pm in the "olden days".

Hot midsummer nor'west winds rasped my face and brought smells I recognised as home. I savoured the brush of long summer grass against my thighs. I picked a roadside dog daisy with elegant and slender white petals for my mother one day and presented it to her as a rare treasure.

'Oh, not one of those disgusting dog daisies,' she said. 'Take it outside. I can't stand the smell.'

I cried. How could she not see the smelly dog daisy I gave her was the only precious thing I had to offer? I was six years old at the time.

My sister and I played on the single bed frame squeezed into the corner of the spare room. There was no mattress on it but that didn't matter as we never had visitors to stay anyway. The bed consisted of a wooden frame with a wire-mesh base. The spare bed became our indoor trampoline.

I have happy memories of playing in the spare room with my sister; jumping up and down, shrieking with laughter. We'd land on our bottoms and bounce off the walls. We imagined we were circus acrobats.

One day my memories of the spare room changed. Happy recollections were swept aside and replaced with feelings of fear and uncertainty.

The room felt suddenly damp and cold. The brightly coloured wallpaper of our wondrous circus playroom now looked stained and faded. A thick mat of cobwebs crazed the blackened glass panes of the aged sash window. I saw my father's silhouette framed by the late-afternoon sun that peered in and hovered low in the sky behind him. He stood over me with his left hand stretched out towards me, luring me to come nearer with the promise of "sweets". I can still remember the taste and smell of the sickly silver ball cake decorations he held in his outstretched palm. From that moment on, I would always pick off and discard the glimmering silver balls from slices of iced birthday cake at my friends' birthday parties.

My memories of being in the spare bedroom with my father are fractured. I remember the confusion. Why was my father alone with me? Why was he offering me sweets? We weren't allowed sweets, and they weren't really sweets anyway. I heard the screaming silence of my fear. Where was my mother?

I was sexually abused by my father and emotionally abandoned by my mother. These two factors cemented deep-seated feelings of inadequacy, fear, and insecurity within me. I was to bear the brunt of my parents' poor decisions throughout my life with the choices I was to make, and the emotional responses I developed to the situations I faced.

I suffered repetitive urinary tract infections as a young child. I screamed in pain with the burning and itching sensation within my private parts. My mother never took me to the doctor despite my pain and discomfort. She must have known the cause of my distress, yet she chose to ignore it.

I was sent to boarding school at the age of twelve. My mother's family money paid for my education. I was never asked whether I wanted to go to boarding school, I was simply told what was happening.

As a child, there were many times when I felt my mother was disinterested in parenting. It seemed convenient for her to send my sister and me away from home for our secondary school education. Perhaps she wanted to keep us away from our father? I am aware my mother was suffering from depression over that time, as she had lost her father to a sudden, massive stroke when I was eleven. She struggled to find any motivation and often spent her afternoons in bed.

Boarding school filled me with fear. There were catty cliques and jealousies. I found it difficult to adjust to my surroundings. The environment was a complete contrast to the peace and solitude I had enjoyed living on the farm.

Strict hierarchical divisions separated year groups. As juniors, we were subjected to "initiations" and "fagging" rituals and were considered slaves to our senior masters. Juniors were forced to stand alone in front of senior girls and carry out demeaning acts. I got off lightly as I was told to sing a nursery rhyme of my choice. One poor persecuted child had to pretend to fuck a broomstick in front of 30 seniors.

There was "starvation day" where the juniors were force-fed at breakfast then not allowed to eat for the rest of the day. The seniors who lorded over us partied in the senior common room and had a food fight which the juniors were forced to clean up. Anger and disgust fuelled my contempt as I scraped trodden peas from the carpet with a knife.

I hated the bullying, the bitchiness, the rivalry, and the elitism the environment fostered. For a child who enjoyed nature, peaceful solitude, and escapism with art and imagination, there was no space for my mind and soul to wander within the confines of boarding school.

We lived by the bell and were severely punished with deprivation if we dared fall out of line. We were allowed to venture beyond the school gates once a week for two hours to walk or bike to the local shops. Playing sport allowed the captive's noose to be slackened. I joined teams and clubs with off-site games and practices.

Between regular dormitory inspections, laundry roster, breakfast and mealtime duties, school lessons, music and sports practices, and homework before and after dinner, we were allocated one hour of free time a day before lights out at 8.30 pm.

I was crammed like a sardine into a dormitory room with eleven other girls one term. As penguins, we stood in line and waited our turn to shower. If we took longer than our allocated three to five minutes, a cup of cold water came over the top.

I became accustomed to the threat of harsh discipline and a life dogged with constant low-lying levels of anxiety. Despite the persistent pulse of girls and activity all around, I felt completely isolated and alone.

Table manners were drilled into us all. We were told never to reach across the dining table or to ask for anything. 'Young women with manners must wait to be offered food or be invited to act,' bellowed the matron.

'Would you like some butter?' we'd say to the girl across the table as she buttered her toast quarters so elegantly. If she still didn't get the message, she was promptly given a jab in the shins with an errant foot. That usually worked.

We were taught to keep our elbows off the table, we were not to start eating until everyone had been served, we had to chew with our mouth closed, always use a napkin and under no circumstances were we ever to use it as a handkerchief. Butter and condiments were to be placed to the side of the plate, no fingers – with the exception of breaking your toast into quarters before buttering them individually as you went. Soup spoons to be drawn away from you in the bowl and, once you had finished, the spoon was to be placed on your side plate, not left sitting in the empty bowl. Cutlery was to be used in sequence from outside in, with the exception of the dessertspoon and fork, which were positioned at the top of your placemat. Once your main meal had been eaten, your knife and fork were to be placed side by side in the centre of your plate, at twelve o'clock, with the fork to the left and tines down, knife to the right and blade facing to the centre of the plate. Always thank your host and, even if you don't like it, eat it.

There was one lonely black dial phone on the wall in the locker bay at the bottom of the back stairs that all the girls had to share. We were allocated one five-minute collect call home to our parents each week. I remember the queue of broken hearts sitting on the stairs with their heads resting in their hands. Blank faces stared listlessly through vertical bars of the stair railings as they waited their turn.

We were allowed three "weekend leaves" and four "day leave" passes per term. If we had girlfriends who were day girls, we were rationed one additional day of freedom per term, to spend with them outside prison. Most of my friends were day girls.

At 6 am on a chilly autumn morning shortly after my thirteenth birthday, I packed a few essentials into my school backpack. I retrieved my pushbike from the shed outside and I pedalled away from the boarding hostel as quickly as my legs could move. The futility of my actions rapidly dawned on me. An hour into my break for freedom, I turned around and pedalled back to prison.

Flashbacks and memories I thought I had buried long ago still haunt me. I can still feel the horror of being physically dragged from the car and left on the hostel steps. Tears streamed down my face as I saw my parents' car tail lights disappear into the distance.

Abandonment breeds abandonment as hurt begets hurt. The isolation and emotional pain I was feeling spiralled into eating disorders through my teens. Food became my comforter and my enemy, as were the affections of my parents. I was screaming inside to a world that didn't care.

I remember gazing at one of my class photos thinking how fat and ugly I was. My mother had decided to cut my luscious, long blonde hair into a short, spiky style. My hair darkened overnight. I thought I looked like an unattractive boy.

I bought a calorie counter and a book called *Raw Energy*. I discovered an apple has 228 kilojoules and a slice of bread around 455 kilojoules. It didn't take long for me to lose seven kilograms on a daily diet limited to 2,000 kilojoules. The dieting and weight loss affected my menstrual cycle. I had one period at fourteen years of age and then they disappeared completely for the following five years. I always wondered whether I would have difficulty getting pregnant.

When I was sixteen, the anorexia evolved into bulimia. During some of the worst periods of the bulimia, I induced myself to vomit up to ten times a day. It worsened over periods of stress and loneliness. Bulimia is a self-perpetuating condition – the worse the bulimia got, the more isolation and shame I felt, which in turn just made the bulimia worse.

I became emotionally withdrawn. I remember turning down an offer to play hockey in Australia because I was so scared people would learn of my problem and judge me.

Outwardly, I appeared frail. My hair became dry and dull, my eyes lost their sparkle. I was slight but not emaciated. Due to the secrecy that goes hand in hand with bulimia, almost no one knew of the torment devouring my mind.

Eventually my parents saw the sense in excising me from the boarding school environment. Their solution was to put me out to private board in Christchurch. I was with one family for just over a year. I was then sent to live with an elderly couple who followed the Exclusive Brethren faith. I felt dislocated and alone living with "the unusual people". They didn't have a television. I was not allowed to use their telephone. I biked to school as early as I could each morning in an effort to get away from them. I filled in my time at school from 7.30 am through to 6 pm each day with piano and choir practice before school, lessons during the day, and always sport – lots and lots of sport, after school. I played tennis in the summer and hockey in the winter. I spent 30 minutes each evening having dinner with "the unusual people". I did my homework in my tiny bedroom upstairs in the evenings, and I often cried myself to sleep.

I was sent to live with a great-aunt for six months and then to live with another elderly woman whose husband had died.

After a few months, I refused to go back to live with the aging widow. I came to understand what foster children must go through. I felt nomadic and unwanted. I got used to relationships with people that were based on surface communication only. Pleasantries were exchanged, but I was aware no one gave a shit about what was going on inside my head or my heart.

When I was still at school, my parents sent me to a psychiatrist. I was required to ride my push-bike to her consulting rooms. My two-wheeled companion waited for me on the bleak, lonely pavement outside.

The psychiatrist was an austere woman with an oily complexion and chisel-like facial features. Her hair was shoulder length – straight, black, and parted down the middle. She wore black from head to toe. Her eyes cast down her slender nose towards me. She asked me questions about school, my interests and hobbies, and how I felt. I held my emotions under lock and key. Who was she to me? I wasn't about to share my secrets with a cold witch who was being paid to "care".

With a quick look at her watch, time was up, and I was escorted to her door.

I saw the witch twice. Apart from appeasing my parents' guilt, I believe the visits achieved nothing.

In a nutshell, my high school years were far from ideal. The anorexia, bulimia, and a bout of glandular fever prevented me from reaching my goals with my sport. Despite my physical challenges, I still achieved a level of success with my sporting pursuits and was selected for representative teams.

By some stroke of luck, I managed to get exceptionally good grades at school. I qualified to enroll in the "pre-med" course at university.

I recall a conversation with my mother many years ago when she asked, 'Do you feel your father and I let you down, Emma?'

'Well, yes,' I said. 'That would be a fair comment.'

'I'm sorry you feel that way,' she replied. My mother had just drawn me in to slap me harder.

She was always too quick to mount me as a trophy on her mantel. She took claim over my achievements. 'You do realise your father and I sacrificed a lot to provide you with your education,' she said, over and over again.

As an adult, I now understand her behaviour – she was turning the guilt and shame she should have felt because of her poor parenting, back towards me, in an attempt to make me grateful for her mistreatment. When I was young, I was never able to understand her manipulations.

I recall being home for the Christmas holidays of 1986–87. I was fifteen when my end-of-year national School Certificate exam marks arrived in the mail. I overheard my mother talking to her friend on the telephone. She was gloating about my average exam mark – well over 80% for the six subjects I took. She told her friend my average mark was only 1.3% lower than my sister's results from the previous year. To my face she would say, 'Oh, we never compare you and your sister.'

Six years later, I overheard my father telling his friend over the telephone all about my sister's thesis topic for her university honours law degree.

By that stage, I had switched from studying pre-medicine, had completed a genetic engineering degree (science) and had embarked on a postgraduate diploma in commerce. I was getting straight As. I hadn't studied commerce at undergraduate level, so my grades with third year, 300 level, economics, statistics, business management, and marketing papers were quite an accomplishment.

Once my father had finished his conversation, I decided I would test him. 'I just heard you talking to your friend, Dad. I'm curious. What do you think I'm studying at university this year?'

'Oh, you're doing some science thing, aren't you?' he said.

I felt crushed but I never let on.

Graduation ceremonies are a big deal for families, particularly when you have two daughters being "capped" on the same day at the Christchurch Town Hall.

I went to a grad party the night before. When my parents and my sister came to collect me from my boyfriend's flat the morning of the ceremony, I was so hung-over I couldn't get out of bed. My mother was furious. I couldn't have cared less.

As far as I could tell, my father had little interest in my achievements and ambitions. My mother would have used the occasion to put a feather in her own cap.

My parents watched my sister walk across the stage to receive her double degree that day. My name was called. I was not there to walk across the stage and accept mine.

Hurts sit and fester. An emotionally injured child searches for warmth and sanctuary. The child matures; however, the wounds are slow to heal. Inevitably, the long-term vulnerabilities and hurts I felt became invisible badges of failed relationships and poor decisions I wore on my sleeves.

I had so few memories of the sexual abuse I suffered at the hands of my father. The memories I did have were vague and felt almost like a dream. Nothing made sense until 1994, when my sister spelt it out to me in black and white. I was twenty-three at the time.

My sister is fifteen months older than me. Her memories of the events that happened when I was between three and six years old were more developed than mine. She was able to describe in detail how, at night, our father entered the bedroom we shared. She recounted how she lay in her own bed and watched him rape me in mine. She told me our father's abuse was predominantly directed at me. Because I was younger, perhaps he thought I wouldn't remember.

Later in 1994, my sister called a family meeting to discuss the sexual abuse. Watching my parents deny any knowledge of what had happened was paralysing.

'You're just a couple of bitches – you'll destroy everything I've worked for. I won't let you do this to me,' Dad ranted. He stormed from my sister's apartment and slammed the door as he went.

With a shallow breath and a sigh, my mother stood up from her comfortable chair and said, 'I had better go with your father.' She looked towards the door and left without saying another word. My parents' dance of power, position, and the influence of money flashed before my eyes.

My mother walked that day for fear of losing her life of privilege. She had not engaged in paid work since well before she was married. I am sure she was aware of the consequences should she decide to leave my father, even though a considerable portion of their wealth was derived from her family money.

My father stayed with my mother for his own reasons: access to my mother's family money and to perpetuate the façade and status of a stable marriage, I guess. He had been brought up in an abusive family environment with a physically violent and alcoholic father. His parents divorced when he was in his early twenties. Perhaps he wanted to save my sister and me from that trauma?

The actions of my parents that evening were pivotal in shaping my value system. I vowed I would never allow myself to be involved in a relationship like theirs. And I would never sacrifice the happiness of my child for my own selfish motivations.

For a period of eighteen months following that meeting, I struggled to concentrate on my work. I quit my well-paid university graduate position, moved away from Christchurch and engaged in a series of nonsense jobs that taught me nothing and took me nowhere instead. I was medicated on high doses of Prozac, and suicidal thoughts regularly became part of my everyday reality.

My sister released her burden of guilt when she chose to share her recovered memories of our childhood sexual abuse with me. She told me she felt regret for not defending me against our father when we were young. I struggled to come to terms with what my sister had offloaded onto me. It would have been easier to cope had she stayed to support me.

'I'm sorry I can't help you through this,' she said. 'I'm grappling with it myself.' And with that, she turned and left me to it.

My aunt was there for me. But no one else. I had never felt more alone in this world.

There is a particular sense of distaste that lingers with discussions of childhood sexual abuse and incest. People simply do not want to talk about it, let alone be associated with it. It's not a giant leap to conclude that the compounding layers of isolation act to exacerbate the burden and harm experienced by the sexual abuse survivor.

My defensive action of shutting down my emotions sent waves of influence across all aspects of my life. I subconsciously sent messages to men – back away, I'm nervous, I'm unsure of myself, I'm scared of letting you in. I was creating confusion. Men simply couldn't be bothered with that, or me.

The tsunami wave of destruction carried on unabated. I came to realise if I was honest about my past and spoke of my true heart and experiences, my act of transparency swiftly led to rejection.

At the age of twenty-four, I took my first steps along a path of consciously turning my thoughts around. The revelations of the sexual abuse and the verbalisation of my pain began to gently lift the heavy burden that weighed on me. At last my inner turmoil had a name. I was a "sexual abuse survivor".

My sister's revelations helped me understand why I had been self-harming with eating disorders, and why I lacked self-confidence. It still took me a long time to come to terms with what had happened, and my recovery from bulimia was incremental and slow. Day by day, I tried to eat sensibly. I wasn't always successful. If I had a bad day, I simply wiped the slate clean and started afresh the following day. It took me two years to control my bulimia, and four years to wean myself off Prozac.

Recovering from an eating disorder takes the sufferer on a long and arduous journey. With many addictions, the cure is centred upon the addict abstaining from their poison. When you are addicted to food or have a harmful relationship with food, you can't simply give up eating. I remember the psychological games I fought for years to control my eating and to change my relationship with food. At least three times a day, my inner demons surfaced and tested me. The evil elves lured me to eat and fill the empty void of pain I felt. I was aware they were leading me to a place of depression and isolation with my head in the toilet. I knew only too well the acrid, sandpaper aftertaste of vomit in my throat and the smell that lingered in my nose. I remembered my swollen tummy, the tremors and shakes as my blood sugar levels peaked and troughed – the shame that consumed me all the way down to my toes. I was done with that. I wanted to be healthy and free. I had no choice but to privately battle and conquer my addiction at least three times a day, every day, until the cravings began to subside.

For seventeen years, from the age of twenty-four through to forty-one, I rarely talked to my parents. Over that time, I felt it was impossible to have a relationship with them. My heart was torn between desperation for their love and acceptance, and my inability to rationalise my anger towards them. I felt shackled with shame as a consequence of their actions and denials in respect of the sexual abuse. I also feared their rejection.

My father told his brother's wife that he had in fact been sexually abused himself as a young child. It was my father's opinion that I should accept my situation and move on, as he had. He stopped short of admitting any responsibility in respect of my sister and me.

He never apologised for what he did and never explained his actions to me personally, but I was able to better understand him from the statement he had made to my aunt.

My mother later divulged to my aunt that she, too, had been sexually assaulted as a teenager.

Were my parents of the opinion that because they were sexually abused, that made it acceptable for me to suffer the same trauma? Well, it wasn't okay. It was their responsibility to protect me.

Interestingly, my sister sought solace with religion. She found God in 1994. By 2010, she had given God the slip.

The lingering, long-term impact of the childhood sexual abuse was to manifest itself in a deeply ingrained subconscious belief that I was simply not worthy of emotional care from a man. Time and time again, I saw patterns of behaviour repeat themselves. I settled for less from men: less affection, less honesty, less nurturing, less time, and less commitment. I came to expect rejection as an inevitable ending to any relationship I had with a man.

I was in a relationship for five years while at university. My young love and I grew up together in a time before the Internet and overt promiscuity. We were two young adults who laughed together, played sport together, and experienced many firsts together. Life was our wonderland.

In 1994, when I reached out to my boyfriend for support, he abandoned me. Looking back, I understand he was too young and inexperienced in life to have been able to offer me much in the way of guidance or assistance.

I craved his love and his embrace all the same. Adjusting to life without him, on the back of the difficulties I had with my family, crippled me. I never felt for Tim the way I felt for my first love. I named my treasured Bella after his niece.

When speaking to a lost love;
"What would you like to say?
All the things you want to say to someone who suddenly went away
How you miss them
How the air was sucked out of your lungs the moment they left
How you will never ever fully inhale again in the same way
How you miss them
How you miss them until your teeth ache."

River, British television drama, 2015.
Written by Abi Morgan. Episode 1.6

For a few years from 2000 to November 2002, I felt as though my life had turned a corner and I was finally heading in the right direction. I was engaged to a successful young barrister. I felt safe with him; his intelligence and capabilities inspired me. I had launched my architectural practice and opened a small retail store in central Auckland. My fiancé and I had renovated a home together, and we had purchased a holiday home on an island in the Hauraki Gulf. We owned a power boat and enjoyed weekends away fishing and exploring on the island. I thought we were laying the foundations for a future together.

When he ended our relationship in early November 2002, as he placed his crumb-covered breakfast plate in the kitchen sink, I felt my world implode. I asked him why he was leaving me. 'It's because of your family,' he said. 'It's fucked up. You'll be OK, Emma, if you get some help, but I can't be that man and stay for you.'

He walked towards the front door. He leant down and collected his briefcase before he opened the door and left. He was gone before I had a chance to respond.

A week later I phoned and asked him what I should do with the $36,000 engagement ring – a 2.1 carat brilliant-cut diamond solitaire with four oblong diamond baguettes set in platinum – he had custom designed and made for me. I offered to give the ring back. 'Keep the ring. You've probably earned it,' he said.

There was only a brief discussion over the division of our assets. I made no claim over our joint property assets. I knew not to go into battle with a talented barrister. I felt relieved to come out of the relationship with my fledgling architectural design practice and shop still in my own name.

In early December 2002, I discovered my ex-fiancé had been sleeping with another woman behind my back for quite some time. The pain of that discovery was unbearable. I fell apart.

The years of sexual abuse as a child, the abandonment of my parents, the hurts, the eating disorders, my failed relationships, my struggles to reach my professional goals, all began to drag me down into a black whirlpool of inescapable despair. I felt my hands reach out for support, yet there was no one around who could offer me any help. Mel had recently moved back to Christchurch and my aunt was overseas.

On 9 December 2002, I wrote a note to my nana. I thanked her for all she had done for me as a child and apologised for the pain my actions would bring. I swallowed eighty-four paracetamol tablets and went to bed.

I woke up five hours later. It wasn't my time to die.

My brush with death didn't feel that dramatic at the time. There was no pain and no fear. I woke in my own bed in a daze. I remember thinking, *Oh fuck, if I'm not going to die and I've swallowed that many pills, perhaps I've done some serious damage to myself?* So I called an ambulance. I didn't have any more pills to take. I thought eighty-four would do the job.

My decision to take my own life had nothing to do with wanting attention. I literally had nothing left and no one to turn to. I wasn't able to cope any longer. I had lost my will to fight and was too ashamed to reach out for help. I thought if I was to tell people about what had happened to me, I would be subjected to more pain and rejection. I wanted the pain to end, and I saw no other means of avoiding it.

I was taken to hospital and my stomach was pumped. I was put under 24-hour surveillance in a ward with a few other patients. I was assessed and discharged two days later.

I had three friends visit me while I was in hospital. My fiancé was not one of them.

I went back to work two days after I was discharged. My sister dropped in to see me at my store. She stayed for ten minutes.

Mel flew up from the South Island and stayed with me for a week. She helped me pack my belongings and move from the home I had shared with my fiancé to a one-bedroom flat.

I had no home visits from any health professionals. I was encouraged to attend a weekly, one-hour counselling session with a psychologist. I was charged $120 per hour for her services and was required to cover half the cost myself. I told her I did not want to be medicated. I understood why I had ended up in the situation I was in, and I hoped she would be able to assist me in adopting strategies for change. Antidepressants weren't going to do that. They just numbed my brain.

I laid a molestation complaint against my father with the police two months later, in February 2003. The police asked whether I wanted them to charge my mother as well, for willfully aiding and abetting the sexual abuse carried out by my father. The task of having to decide whether to charge my mother or not was one of the hardest decisions of my life. I was still so angry with her. I wanted to make her accountable with my father. From a place within my heart that I struggled to access, I drew on enough forgiveness to instruct the police to charge only my father, even though I believed my mother was equally responsible for the crimes. I just couldn't bring myself to have her charged.

My suicide attempt was the catalyst which, oddly enough, gave me the confidence to step forward and make a statement to the police about my childhood sexual abuse. At the time, I was at rock bottom. I had nothing left to lose.

They contacted my sister and requested an interview with her. She refused to meet with them or to make a statement. She told me I needed to forgive our father, as she had done. She suggested I seek solace in religion. We never discussed religion or the sexual abuse again.

The police spoke to my father. He denied the accusation. Without the support of my mother and sister, and with no historical medical information to support my statement, the police had to let the matter go. I was later told that the investigating officers who interviewed my father believed he was lying when he denied my accusation.

The complaint in respect of my father was my way of saying: "You have sexually abused me and abandoned me, physically, and emotionally. I am worth more than that. You need to answer for what you have done."

Involving the police further alienated my parents and my sister. That was one of the few times I took a stand against my family, and it had taken a brush with death to get me to that point.

Interestingly, my mother phoned me in April 2003, some four months after my suicide attempt. The purpose of her call was to let me know my nana had passed away. I had barely spoken to my mother in years. I casually asked her whether my sister had told her about what had happened to me in December 2002.

'No,' she responded.

I told her about my suicide attempt. 'So, Mum, you really had no idea I had been in hospital?' I asked her.

'No, your sister never said anything to us,' she replied.

That was the end of the conversation. There was no, "Oh, I am so shocked to hear that, darling. Are you OK? What can I do to help?" There was nothing more than a cordial, "Will you be coming to your nana's funeral? It's on Tuesday next week."

When I met Tim in February 2003, I was still in a distressed and vulnerable emotional state. I was honest with him and told him about my suicide attempt. I told him about my broken family and the sexual abuse. I thought I would get it all out in the open at an early stage so my imminent rejection would come sooner and be easier to handle.

Contrary to what I was expecting, he didn't appear to judge me. I was relieved beyond words. Little did I realise, as a narcissist, he would have seen my character flaws as a weakness through which he would be able to control me. He was able to provide me with security, which he knew I would cling to at all costs.

Tim wooed me with exquisite bunches of flowers and weekend trips away. He wined and dined me, and proposed to me within five months of our meeting. I felt so grateful to have him in my life. I loved him and felt loved in return.

When we married, in February 2004, I didn't invite my parents, my sister, or any other members of my family to our wedding.

Soon after, Tim's underlying and true nature began to reveal itself. He began to exert his control over me.

Our wedding and honeymoon cost $44,000, of which Tim contributed $7,000 and his parents $1,000. I paid the balance, some $36,000. My businesses were turning over good money at that time, so I was in a position to pay. The trend for the future was set from that moment. He successfully manipulated me into paying for the greater share of the renovation of our family home. I paid the bulk of our international airfares and accommodation when we travelled. I covered the full cost of the renovation of the Mill, and I serviced the mortgage as well.

My father rang me when my mother was hospitalised in 2009, but aside from those few telephone conversations regarding her health, I had nothing to do with my parents until I rang them in March 2012, when I invited them to Bella's fourth birthday party.

The subconscious mind works in mysterious ways. Perhaps it was having some space from my parents for all those years, or maybe it was my own personal growth and maturity, that brought me to the conclusion that my emotions would be better spent with acceptance of my parents as they were, rather than harbouring anger for them.

Had my subconscious detected an acceleration of trouble in my relationship with Tim when I rang my parents? Was I being guided along a path to bring me closer to my family?

Interestingly, my parents never discussed my father's conversation with the police or my accusation of molestation with me. My father never apologised for his actions and neither did my mother. And yet, when I asked him for help in mid-2012, after Tim left for Australia and demanded a divorce from me, he did so willingly. He never hesitated.

twenty

Next minute

One minute I was married and living a seemingly stable and respectable life. Next minute I was a solo mother from West Auckland carrying a distasteful social stigma.

One minute I thought my husband was straight. Next minute I was being told he was gay or bisexual.

One minute I was able to provide a stable home for my child. Next minute I didn't know how I was going to pay the mortgage. Would Bella and I end up homeless?

Within the blink of an eye, my life and my perceived reality had changed irrevocably. I felt blindsided and overwhelmed.

At the time, I was being told to be strong for Bella, that I must not cry or show emotion in front of her. I was told I must never speak badly of Tim in front of Bella. I wanted to scream: "You can all fuck off! You have no idea how this feels! Stop being so naïve and idealistic! Of course it hurts. Of course I'm angry. I'm not a robot! How dare people think they can stand on their pedestals passing comments and insinuate it's acceptable for him to treat Bella and me like this! Particularly when they've never faced a comparable situation."

Why are people no longer shocked when marriages end? When did it become okay for men to abandon their families with nonchalance? Why are caregivers being forced to struggle raising children on their own? How have adults become so selfish and their actions so fluid and destructive? What has happened to society's moral compass? Once upon a time, people valued marriage, honesty, and raising a family with values and integrity. Not any more it seems.

If only society and government would get a backbone and stop being so politically correct, then maybe men like my ex-husband would think twice about treating their families with such cruelty and contempt.

As long as women stay in destructive relationships, as long as society accepts substandard behaviour, and as long as abandoned families remain financially marginalised, the behaviours and attitudes will continue. Some women simply have no choice but to stay. Or do they? I see a complex tapestry of relationships coexisting in our communities. For every desperate situation, there are others where people must live with the compromises born from the choices they've made.

To some women, I metaphorically say, go on, go back to being smug in your marriages where you choose to work one day a week while you drink yourselves to oblivion and get middle-age spread.

You complain about your hard-working husbands, yet all the while you look down your noses at solo mothers like me. Your hand goes out for your weekly allowance as you siphon money from the grocery budget. Somehow you manage to justify theft and label it as your "escape fund for a rainy day".

You're happy to spend money on yourself and not your family because you believe you are entitled to your luxuries although you have not worked for them.

Or do you work for them? In the bedroom, doing what he wants, when he wants, how he wants, as often as he wants, just so you can live in your nice house and prolong the pretense of stability.

And when you all have your dinner parties and you no longer invite me, as you think I may be a threat, just you be mindful of the fact that what happened to me could also happen to you. Yes, you.

And for the record, I am not the least bit tempted by your husbands. I do not find their "Dad bods" attractive. I am not interested in the types of men who arrogantly stroke their own egos, with incessant talk of rugby, cars, boats, and property, all the while they belittle you in public and control you behind closed doors. Your husbands would never be able to handle a woman like me, so you're safe, for now.

I have been told around 40% of the married men who drink at the local rugby club are having affairs behind their wives' backs. That's a fairly confronting statistic. And you think your husband is different?

You told me your husband allowed you to spend $80,000 on a new kitchen because you caught him having an affair. The thing that amazed me the most is that you thought a kitchen was a justifiable trade for fidelity.

There are those of you out there who have seen your friends get left with nothing when their husband leaves.

Your husband is smart and he has a network of companies and trusts. He has had you sign so many legal documents over the years. Between mashing the potatoes and checking your sons' homework, all number of things were slid across the kitchen bench for you to sign. You wouldn't have the foggiest idea about what you do or do not own.

The reality is, if he left you, you wouldn't recognise your life any more. You would have to pack your bags and leave your home, and live your life in rental accommodation. You could never pay a mortgage, the school fees, the legal fees, and cover living expenses for you and your children all on your own, with your part-time job working reception at the local medical centre.

So you stay and sign whatever papers are passed your way. You're aware that to protest and refuse to sign would cause an argument – there would be hell to pay. Either way you are stuffed. Can you not see how your life hangs in the balance? All it would take is a slim, big-breasted plaything to catch his eye, and then you'd be cast aside. Unless he values the pretence of marriage, and then you're safe as long as you can keep your mouth shut and turn a blind eye.

You couldn't possibly sacrifice driving your Range Rover, your shopping trips to Melbourne, or your annual winter escape to Fiji. Some of you already ignore your husband's online dating profiles. You've been reading the sexting dialogue between him and a couple of chicks from God knows where. How does he find the time, you wonder? Have you confronted him over it? No, I didn't think so.

And what about when you walked in on your husband having sex with your so-called friend on the sofa in her lounge, and you stood there and watched them for a minute before you let them know you were there?

As you and I strode out side by side on the treadmills at the gym, you described to me in graphic detail how shocked your husband was when he realised you were there. You relayed to me how his cock reappeared from your so-called friend's pussy and flicked back and hit your husband on his fat stomach. You were venting, so I listened … but really?

To start with you said you were staying for the kids. After a while the constant lies took their toll on you and you left. As the months rolled by, I recognised the despair in your eyes and the effect your husband's legal attacks were taking on your health. No one deserves to be treated as you were.

I sat through hearing all about the ins and outs of tubal ligation surgery as one of you didn't want any more children. You qualified your decision by saying you only agreed to have the surgery because your husband said he would have a vasectomy at the same time. Now that story really did floor me. Did you really just admit to me that you condone your husband having affairs and are okay with it as long as he is not having children with his hookups, whores, and mistresses? Seriously? Can you even hear yourself speak?

And these are just a few of the stories I have heard over the years.

I believe there is often a gradual and yet quite dramatic change in attitudes of people in marriages and long-term relationships over time. I see power shifts happening more organically through circumstance rather than from intentional change. People fall into certain habits due to changing roles, particularly once children arrive.

I see young couples who are very much in love. They are predominantly in power-sharing, mutually dependent relationships. They confide in each other. They consult each other on major decisions regarding lifestyle and expenditure of joint "family" money. They reinforce their love with displays of trust and consideration. Young couples in love make plans together, they socialise together, they take time to consider the wants and needs of the other person. They relish celebrating special occasions, buying gifts for each other, and creating memories together.

Whether married or not, familiarity and lack of consideration within a relationship will create contempt for the other party. For example, if one party is continually late home from work and fails to call ahead, tensions build. Their relationship chills – just like dinner which has been left to go cold in the fridge.

Or maybe she continues with her penchant for buying handbags when they are desperately saving for a deposit on their first home. It's the little resentments and irritations at first.

They decide to have a baby.

Life changes dramatically for the couple. They're both exhausted, and they're struggling to make ends meet. Between living expenses and the baby, and with just one income, there's no money for a beer at the rugby club and certainly no money for new handbags.

She is stuck at home – lonely, irritable and constantly tired. What happened to the glamorous life she once led? Parties, concerts, and weekends away are all a distant memory.

He feels taken for granted. All he does is work hard for his family and the minute he steps through the door he gets snapped at. His once gorgeous girlfriend is now overweight, depressed, angry, and they're not making love as much as they used to. He thinks he deserves more and can do better.

One Saturday he gets so annoyed with her constant nagging and lists of jobs, he decides to disappear to the rugby club. He sees all his mates, turns his phone off and gets lost within beer oblivion.

There are a few tidy chicks down at the clubrooms tonight. He slips off his wedding ring and buys the hottie with the impressive rack a wine. The hottie isn't wearing sweatpants and an oversized, faded T-shirt covering a multitude of post-baby excuses. This chick looks mint – pert butt in her skinny jeans, low-cut top, OMG her rack. And those lips. I can't wait to feel those lips around my cock, he is thinking.

He crawls home at 4 am reeking of beer and bathroom sex. The wife is furious. How dare he do this to her. Next minute, what does she do about it? Nothing.

She can't leave. She has no job, a six-month-old baby, and another on the way.

The rest is history.

This and other similar scenarios play out every day in every suburb across every town in New Zealand.

Or have I got it all wrong? Am I a delusional idealist hoping for true love? Does true love even exist in today's world? Have people become so materialistic and preoccupied with status, sex, money, and their own selfish sense of entitlement that they willingly auction off their values to the highest bidder?

Where is the patience, the understanding, and the concept of joint sacrifice? It appears to me that as soon as the going gets a little tough, one or both parties simply decides to ditch the other and move on.

The proliferation of social media and online dating enables this behaviour. It's just too easy for people to hook-up.

And what about the children?

Do many parents consider the impact of their actions on their children? Or are parents these days happy with government agencies being the ambulance at the bottom of the cliff?

None of it sits right with me.

I thought of my hopes and dreams for my own marriage. I know, in my heart, I tried.

The Reasons "We" Chose To Be

Stay forever in my mind
As you so perfectly are today
Languishing in the wonder of our love

Let me see your eyes
Burn with desire
As you are
So alive and wanting
Of me

Laugh out loud
Cherish my smile
Kiss my lips and
Caress my pert breasts

Collar trivial daily grievances
Keep them at bay
Let them not seep in
And cloud our perfect memories;

Protect my heart
Keep it pure;
Free of nuances and infidelity

Remember today
For when we are old and grey
Our heads filled with a
Lifetime of minor maladies;
The reasons
"We"
Chose to be

twenty-one

Divorce by stealth

Tim's sister strode uninvited into my home on 28 February 2015 and threw divorce papers at my feet. I was so shocked to see her I was lost for words.

'They're dissolution of marriage papers. Consider yourself served,' she snarled at me with that hollow, lifeless gaze she had nailed to perfection. Her grey eyes and pale skin were as corpse-like and dead as her soul.

She turned and left.

As I closed the door behind her, my legs gave way. I fell to the ground in tears.

My barrister went on maternity leave two and a half months after I was served with the divorce papers. Neither she nor her replacement fully informed me of the dissolution of marriage process. I simply thought the divorce was in limbo as I had not signed the papers and had not heard anything to suggest it had been finalised.

On 3 November 2015, I met with my replacement solicitor and barrister in Auckland. I was due back in court two days later for the next hearing of the relationship property matter.

'Could you please explain something to me,' I said, pointing at the words on a page of Tim's affidavit. 'In this sentence here, his lawyer makes a reference to the dissolution of marriage having already taken place.' I leaned forward across the table, still pointing to the words. I pushed the page towards both women as they sat across from me. 'Am I divorced?' I asked, as I looked them both in the eye and waited for a response.

'Well, yes, you might be,' replied my solicitor.

'What do you mean I *might* be?' I said. 'Considering we are here today because of my relationship property matter and divorce, could you please contact his lawyer and find out what on earth is going on? If I am already divorced, don't you think I deserve to know?'

My solicitor promptly contacted Tim's lawyer.

I was not presented with the confirmation of divorce papers until 6 November 2015. They were "delivered" to me via email.

Tim had filed for divorce on his own at the end of February 2015. I was to later learn that because I did not oppose his application, the divorce went ahead and was granted on 17 March 2015.

I was informed of my divorce status exactly seven months and twenty days after it happened. In effect, Tim had divorced me behind my back, without my consent, or my knowledge. And yes, it is possible to do that.

I had been married to Tim for over eleven years. We had a daughter together. His act of not presenting me with the divorce papers was one of the lowest things he stooped to.

twenty-two

My father is dead

My sister telephoned me at 8 am on 10 November 2015. She told me our father had cooked himself some fried eggs for breakfast and placed them on the coffee table in front of the sofa where he liked to sit and watch sport on TV. He was mad about all sports, particularly golf and rugby.

As he sat down, my father had a massive heart attack. He fell. The impact of his head hitting the ground projected his false teeth a distance of three metres to the other side of the room. He was dead before his head hit the floor.

His fried eggs still sat on the table. I don't know why the image of the eggs sitting there waiting for my father to return bothers me so much. But it does.

Get up, Dad. Eat your eggs, I silently shouted to him.

Four days after I discovered Tim had divorced me behind my back, my father suddenly died. I was numb with grief. Paralysed with shock.

Mel stood beside me as I spoke to the five hundred people gathered within the local community church at my father's funeral. I needed her support that day; I was fearful I would collapse or have an asthma attack under the pressure.

After a number of false starts when I choked on my words and struggled to hold back tears, I spoke eloquently and from the heart about my father's kindness and his warm humour. I shared stories of the guidance and leadership he had shown my sister and me through our childhood years growing up on the farm.

How he was at times blunt but always fair. I relayed how he once screamed at us across the farmyard: "You girls are no more use to me than tits on a bull! Get moving! Do as you're told!"

I described my father's strong work ethic and his loyalty to our mother. I acknowledged his strength and how he challenged me, how he taught me to be adventurous, fearless, and brave.

Privately, I missed my father's steadfast solidarity – his calm and considered judgement, and advice on the end of the phone.

Sliding Tears Weep From My Eyes

Staring into blank space
Ringing in my ears
Shallow hollow breaths
As my heart
You are gone
Noise all around me
I hear nothing
I am numb
Screaming silence
Sliding tears
Weep from my eyes
Without your strength
I fear my legs
May give way
Your voice told me
I needn't fear
As you would be there for me
You gave your time so willingly
As if to say you valued me
The phone doesn't ring
You are tone deaf to my calls
Heaven beckoned
Calling your name
My father
You are gone

I enjoyed the communication I had with my father between 2012 and 2015. I discovered we were alike in many ways. We were both relaxed and easy-going by nature, open-minded, and curious. He had a sharp wit and a passion for learning. He was a brilliant sportsman and loved to see progress and "getting shit done".

My father had a direct and extremely effective way of encouraging me. "You know you can do this, Emma. What are you waiting for? Get on with it," he'd say. I still hear his voice. There was little indecision with my dad. It was never *could* I achieve a goal, for he assumed completeness – it was more about supporting me in making the decisions necessary to accomplish what I had set out to do. We understood each other, as we approached life with the same attitude. He was a straight shooter, and I respected him for that.

When I doubted myself, I thought of him. I dried my eyes, I took a deep breath and I strode ahead. I faced my fears with dignity, in part because of the challenges I had experienced in my past. Oddly enough, my father had, in part, made me the person I was.

Despite never discussing or resolving the root of our dissent, my father and I were able to forgive each other over our faults and failings. The tragedy of his death will forever live in the fact we had overcome so much in our relationship, and had such a small window of time together at the end of his life.

I had always imagined receiving a bedside confession from him. I wanted to hear his words of sorrow, of regret and sadness for what he did to me when I was young. I wanted to hear him take responsibility for the way his actions took a carving knife to my life. I felt I needed to hear his regret for all the time we both missed out on, and for the happiness and opportunities his actions took away from me. But that wasn't to be.

Instead, I came to appreciate and accept the concept of remorse without acknowledgment of the misdeed. I understood how my father had made a terrible mistake as a younger man and how he had lived with, and paid for, his poor decision for most of his adult life. My ability to forgive him had set us both free to genuinely love each other.

It took me close to forty years to come to terms with what he did, and then he died so suddenly. I was heartbroken and also very grateful for our shared forgiveness.

I always wanted Dad to be proud of me. I hoped he was.

twenty-three

Grief and resilience

Therapy

the hard season
will
split you through.
do not worry.
you will bleed water.
do not worry.
this is grief.
your face will fall out and down your skin
and
there will be scorching.
but do not worry.
keep speaking the years from their hiding places.
keep coughing up smoke from all the deaths you have died.
keep the rage tender.
because the soft season will come.
it will come.
loud.

ready.
gulping.
both hands in your chest.
up all night.
up all of the nights.
to drink all damage into love.

Salt, Nayyirah Waheed

Exactly how did I manage to navigate a path through the quagmire of grief, betrayal, abandonment, loss, and shame of divorce? How did I manage to find the strength to fight Tim when so many cannot, when presented with similar adversity?

Was it a case of mental fortitude? Was it due to my strong support networks? Was it about making the right decisions? How much is mental health related to physical health? Had my past provided me with the experience and coping skills to weather the storms? Or is resilience and the ability to cope a combination of all these factors?

My grief was centred around loss – loss of my marriage, loss of my family unit, loss of a secure future, loss of support from a husband who was supposed to be there for Bella and me, loss of social status, loss of my businesses, loss of trust and belief in humanity. I was also grieving the loss of my father.

I feared I wouldn't be able to cope. I thought I would fail, as I was *already* a failure (at marriage). What would the future hold now for Bella and me? There was a continual gnawing fear that I may not be able to pay the mortgage and other bills. Would I end up homeless and penniless with a child to care for?

After everything I had worked for, and all the sacrifices I had made throughout my life to ensure my financial security and self-determination, I was terrified of having to be reliant on a man. I wondered if the day would come when I would have to be with a man, not because I wanted him or because I was in love with him, but because I needed financial security. Would I one day end up having to pimp myself out to the highest bidder?

The gravity of that thought hung over me as a cloud. I understood the implication of such a decision – it would kill my spirit and place my daughter and me at risk. Making a decision to be with a male for financial security would be my absolute last resort. I thought about how so many women place themselves and their children at risk with similar decisions every day. I prayed my strength would save us from such a fate.

The journey of grief is an emotional roller coaster. Grief took me to highs as I mentally latched onto new relationships, certain events, and happenings planned for the future. I came to recognise I had unwittingly set myself up for failure and the disappointment that followed when my expectations were not realised. There were many times when I felt I was losing control.

As if from nowhere, grief paralysed me. It hit me like a wall and stopped me in my tracks. My ability to control my reactions simply disappeared as pain rolled over me in waves. I had no choice but to withdraw, breathe, cry, and let the emotion pass, however long it took. Fear, and feelings of loss and defeat, soon returned to haunt me.

Little things triggered my flashbacks and feelings of utter worthlessness – children's birthday parties, school gatherings, and Bella's sports events were the main culprits.

Thoughtless comments from strangers stabbed me through the heart. One day I had a woman describe to me how unhappy her brother was in his marriage. 'You could always be his bit on the side until his wife steps back into line.'

WTF! I was a solo parent. I wasn't a homewrecker, a whore, or someone's temporary fill-in. The prejudice I was subjected to as a solo mother was thick at times.

Attending children's birthday parties was a significant challenge. Naturally, husbands were in attendance with their wives and children. Seeing happy families confronted everything Bella and I had lost. I am sure she felt it too.

I once sat next to a woman at Friday afternoon school assembly in late 2014. She said, 'I haven't seen your husband at school events. Does he travel for work?'

'Well, I guess you could say he travels for work,' I said. 'He works in Australia.' I had to muster all my strength to stay calm and not cry. All she had to do was look and check for a wedding ring. Was I expecting too much?

There were always feelings of inadequacy. I was routinely confronted with a barrage of personal questions from near strangers. What does your husband do? Oh, so you don't have a husband? But how long have you been separated?

'What's a lovely woman like you doing on your own?' I was asked on the sideline of Bella's hockey game one Saturday morning. How do you answer a question like that? Was I now less of a woman because I had been hurt so deeply that I now feared men? The woman had no idea how her words cut me to the core. I guess she genuinely didn't understand.

There were innuendos – there must be something wrong with me as I was attractive and yet I did not have a partner. Clearly, I was damaged goods in people's eyes.

People commented about the age of my car. 'Isn't it time for an upgrade, Emma?' some would say.

I didn't really care that my car was so old, but I felt judged and put down by their comments. I wanted to scream, "I'd love to see how you'd cope in similar circumstances." But I didn't scream – a reaction like that would only make me look deranged – so I internalised my grief and pain some more.

I read a wonderful book *Stumbling Stones – A Path Through Grief, Love and Loss* by Dr Airdre Grant. This is what she had to say:

> *Anger, pain and fear are all part of the deal with grief.*
>
> *Whatever way you come to it, the journey through grief is long and unpredictable. The only way through it is through it. There are no shortcuts. The more you step into it, the better.*
>
> *Avoidance only brings it back more strongly later on.*
>
> *Better to lash yourself to the mast and sail into the storm. What choice do you have? And after others have tired of you and gone back to their lives, you still have to sail the sea. Things happen on that journey. Friendships are formed, and gifts arrive from unexpected sources.*

I came to appreciate my ability to experience happiness and love in the future was dependent on whether I was able to release the grief and sadness that weighed so heavily upon me. With time and self-reflection, I also recognised the emotions I was experiencing were more or less following a grief pathway with four distinct stages:

1) Catastrophe and Bewilderment – a period immediately following a loss where an individual experiences feelings of disbelief, and is dazed and confused. The loss is difficult to accept and emotions shut down for a time.

2) Chaos and Longing – seeking to fill the gaping hole that has been left, either by reflecting on the past and wanting the person that has left to return, or by replacing that person with someone else, or engaging in an activity in an attempt to fill the void. There is often anger and frustration as the future the person once imagined is no longer possible.

3) Heartache and Anguish – marked by a period of misery and despair. During this phase the sufferer may feel weak, as though there is no way out or through their pain.

4) Rehabilitation and Reformation – this phase is defined by clarity of thinking, setting goals and establishing new routines. Trust and positivity gradually return. Feelings of pain and loss shift from being at the forefront of everyday thoughts and move to a place where they can be managed.

I am not sure there is a magical remedy for dealing with grief or for overcoming it. Some people say it helps to talk and write about pain. That works to a degree, but there have been times when I have just wanted to put a lid on the pain and forget about it. Talking about it seemed to prolong the torture.

I have heard many people talk of the concept of "time being a healer". It's possible time allows the layering of happier memories over pain. The impact of past events and experiences is somehow diluted and softened as a result.

Maybe, with the passage of time, new healthier relationships or environments can act as a distraction from the past. These new experiences can aid in reprogramming behaviour and emotional responses. Confidence is gained from knowing you are capable of leaving the past where it belongs. In effect, you have given yourself permission to move on.

Talking things through with friends and professionals can assist in understanding causes of events and also triggers for responses and behaviours. Plans for fresh beginnings and new responses can be formulated and experimented with. Work must be done towards changing our own attitudes and behaviour. Without a change, why should we expect a different result?

When push comes to shove, time doesn't alter the original event. And yet time allows you the opportunity to accept the past. Life happens. Shit happens. To everyone in varying degrees. The past is the past. It's best to focus on looking to the future. Everyone has the ability to change their future, but it's impossible to change the past.

I'm a great believer in taking charge, if you can. It is incredibly empowering to say, 'No, you can't do that to me any longer. And no, I won't allow myself to feel this way. I deserve a happy future. I owe that to myself.' If you have the power to control your environment today, you can transform outcomes tomorrow.

I still became sad and down from time to time, but I understood that the emotions I was experiencing were often a result of exhaustion from working long hours and not getting sufficient rest. I always viewed a bad day as a bad day. It wasn't a bad week or a bad life, it was simply a bad day. I often said out loud to myself, 'I am going to be OK. It will all be OK. I will have a rest and when I wake, I will feel a lot better.' For the most part, my strategy really worked.

I told myself, *Tim chose the wrong woman to take on.* You simply cannot beat a person who is not prepared to roll over in defeat. And I was that person. Whatever abuse or threats he threw at me, I vowed I would take them. No matter what.

For the Sake of My Child

Finding energy
When I have none
My well is dry
I am blinded by the sun

A mirage
Of hope
I see it fade
What I thought once real
Is now gone

Not having a choice
But to carry on
All for the sake of my child
A parent understands

If I can keep my head
When all about me are losing theirs,
Says Mr Kipling, I will be fine

I do know one thing
He underestimated me
And he
Is about to see

twenty-four

The Lawyer

You would have thought I had seen enough of lawyers over the past few years. I wondered, at the time, why I had accepted an invitation for a drink and dinner from a lawyer. I had already been engaged to and discarded by one barrister. What was I thinking?

As a child playing with matches, I was mesmerised by flames. I just couldn't help myself.

The Lawyer and I clicked immediately. He said all the right things; he was charming, in fact. Lawyers are paid to be charming. I knew the drill, and still, I fell for him like a schoolgirl.

I was so desperate for love. Each time I met a new paramour, I believed he could be the one. I lost myself to the idea of love. It was pathetic really.

Adam the Lawyer was also an American. His upbringing in Hawaii fuelled his love of the sea and water sports. He was quietly confident, full of warmth and light, with a mature enthusiasm. At 185 centimetres, he was tall, handsome, and very sporty.

For eight years he was a machine gunner in the Marines and served two tours in Iraq. I saw tears well in his eyes as he told me of the friends he had lost in combat. He studied law once he was discharged from the Marines.

The man was an exotic wonderland of mystery. His energy and unique blend of charisma, intelligence, and physicality captivated my imagination. I was drawn to his quick wit and his able mind.

I saw in him a reflection of myself. He was the first to identify it; he told me so over our first date of pizza and wine. He reached across the table and gently held my hand. He ran the thumb of his left hand across the top of my right hand. With his fingertips beneath mine, he delicately teased my palm as he drew his hand away. It was a simple, gentle gesture, yet it was incredibly intimate. I knew I wanted him from that moment.

We had fantastic chemistry. His smouldering, smiling chestnut eyes were equally warm and knowing. I was a moth being drawn to his flame. He was incredibly polite, as most Americans seem to be, and I loved the juxtaposition of his polished manners and the raw energy of his lust. I relished the abrasion of his closely shaven beard against my face. I lost myself to his tender kisses and his hard, wanting body.

Adam told me he was learning Portuguese. I downloaded a translation application onto my mobile phone so I could message him in Portuguese. He was convinced I was fluent in the language for quite some time. When I finally let him in on my joke he laughed out loud. He thought I was hysterical.

We talked of travel and plans for the future. I told him of my admiration for the States and how I had wanted to expand my business there but my visa application had been turned down. 'Marry me,' he said. 'You won't need a visa then.'

Adam was, quite simply, everything I thought I was looking for.

In Time I Could Love You

With quiet anticipation; an inner purr
I inhale with trepidation
The corners of my mouth; they curl
I dip my head and blush

Firm knuckles on wood
With scrambling confidence
I scatter
To prise with shaking wrist the lever
And still
I slam it shut

Emma Rivers

With shortened breath
My back towards the door
I lift my eyes and dream
One last peak through the keyhole
My moistened lips, they part
I am aghast
As you stand afore me

You are a Christmas gift
Laid beneath my tree
I wish to peel away your shiny wrap;
Just a corner
Are you really as you appear to be?

You see my courage where others see weakness; a threat
You understand when it might seem easy to judge
You radiate a voice of reassurance; of light
Sharp wit and joy
You utter the very words
As the sentences form inside my head

You have shown bravery and honour
Serving in desert storms
Your beautiful soul simmers gently
Beyond two golden chestnut eyes

A divine intoxicating concoction
Excitement as sherbet on my tongue
A feeling of wanting
To talk and make love until dawn

The stars have aligned
With sliding doors
A chance meeting
I am within your sight

The air smells sweet
The day shines bright

With the thought
I will see you again

I must take a chance if I am to move on
With faltering voice, I whisper
In time
I could
Love
You

A few months later Adam broke it to me that he had started seeing another woman. He almost looked defeated as he admitted he had chosen her over me for convenience. She was not "the one" and no comparison to me, he explained.

I was desperate to hide the hurt that threatened to well within my eyes. I took a deep breath, elegantly pushed my coffee cup aside and crossed my arms. I leant forward and gently placed both my elbows and arms on the table. With a wry smile I said, 'Well, Adam, I know Christchurch. I'm a Cantabrian by birth, remember.'

Adam stared at me and nodded. I could tell he was wondering what was coming next.

'Look, unless this chick's an import, she'll have an ass twice the size of mine and half my personality. Humpf. She doesn't bother me at all,' I said. I put my nose in the air and let out a barely audible snort.

He threw back his head and laughed as he said, 'And with those words, gorgeous, that's why you are so special.'

I was surprised he bought my lie. I was completely cut to pieces.

It may have been the prospect of a long-distance relationship that deterred Adam from pursuing me, or the fact I had a young child. Maybe it was my lengthy court case. He was a lawyer, after all, and he had been through a divorce himself. Maybe he didn't want the drama? I asked him whether my court issue bothered him. He told me it didn't. Rather, he said he saw me as a bright star full of life and love, despite my current obstacles. He told me of his admiration for me. If anything, he said my obstacles had given me the chance to show the world how truly wonderful I was. 'Emma, if only you lived in Christchurch,' he said.

Maybe he just wanted a convenient fuck?

Adam walked me to my car that afternoon. He gripped my shoulders firmly and kissed me longingly, several times. I felt he did not want to let me go.

And yet, he already had.

Letting Go

If I could
Find the strength
I would tell you
How I picture us
Together

Making dinner
Making love
Making memories

But I don't
And I won't

Instead

I write your name in the clouds
And I watch
You drift away

As the weeks rolled on, I came to understand that meeting Adam and developing feelings for him was as much about distracting myself from the torture of the pain of the court case and my father's death as it was about us. I allowed him to open a door to my heart. I felt a brief period of joy, a taste of what might be for the future.

Adam gave me hope that there would be someone like him out there for me one day.

twenty-five

What about love?

to be only
loved skin deep
is a double edged
sword

for we leave too
many pieces behind
and continue to love
the idea of what
could be

e corona

As the months and years dragged on, fatigue laid down her weary bones beside me. I couldn't shake her. There were some days where I felt okay, but for the most part I felt drained, fragile, and weak. I was being smothered by a blanket of sadness.

Every now and again I woke in the morning with a hint of hope only to have Tim hurl another defamatory and obstructive legal action at me. I began to lose strength. Each time I fell down, it took a little longer to gather myself and regroup. His attacks slowly but surely ate away at my soul.

I was heartbroken with the breakdown of my marriage and the death of my father. In an attempt to dull the pain, I sought solace in grasping at relationships with men that were never built to last.

I was aware my childhood experiences with sexual abuse and the abandonment I had endured throughout my life had contributed to some of my poor decisions. I couldn't carry on living like that. A change of attitude was required; I needed to make different choices and conserve my energy.

I became more considered with prospective love interests and I went on fewer dates. When I did venture out, my brief excursions for a coffee, lunch or dinner, typically ended with a blunt evaluation to my friends, 'Oh, he was nice enough, but he wasn't my type.'

Was I losing my sense of humour? Yes, probably. Was I tired of the let-downs? Yep, definitely. Was I struggling with the realisation the guy for me was a fantasy I had created in my own mind? Absolutely. Did the guy actually exist? I began to doubt it.

We trust to our peril
But to not is to be alone
And then oh, the silence

River, British television mini-series, 2015.
Written by Abi Morgan. Episode 1.3.

Loneliness had become my friend. Somehow I'd taken a ride on a carousel to an abyss called nowhere. I felt lost.

I had no idea how I was to move forward with a romantic relationship. How was I supposed to trust again? I lacked the confidence required to take a risk with my heart. I knew I would be unable to cope with another major emotional upset should I open my heart to a man and have it not work out. I realised I was resilient, but I was also well aware I was not entirely indestructible.

The worry of having a mental or physical breakdown clawed at my back and followed me as a shadow. I was powerless to escape my fear.

I felt trapped, in some type of warped relationship no man's land. As a self-protection mechanism, I shut down my emotions. I refused to commit – to anyone, or anything. Having a man in my life seemed like another burden, another pressure putting demands on my time. I was torn; I came to fear the very thing I longed for – love.

As Janet Fitch wrote in *White Oleander*, I too felt myself detach from life and love. My focus shifted in my attempt to block out the pain.

> *'So what about love?' I asked.*
>
> *'So what about it …?'*
>
> *'Don't you believe in it?'*
>
> *'I don't believe in it the way people believe in God or the tooth fairy. It's more like the National Enquirer. A big headline and a very dull story.'*
>
> *'So what do you believe in?' I asked her.*
>
> *'I believe in living as I like. I see a Stickley lamp, a cashmere sweater, and I know I can have it. I own two houses besides this. When the ashtrays are full in my car, I'll sell it.'*

By the beginning of 2016, my lack of confidence with men began to show. I tried to participate in mixed gender group activities but I found socialising difficult. I always felt so small and unsure of my surroundings. I forced myself to go on two separate party bus trips with a group of lovely, genuine people. For the most part I felt entirely overwhelmed.

I continued to receive attention from men, regardless of the insecurities I was shielding. I guess I was too attractive to go unnoticed yet too hesitant to take things any further than a flirtatious dalliance.

On one of the bus trips, I was asked by an attractive, educated man how it was possible I had no idea of how beautiful and desirable I was to men. I could sense my eyes fall and I looked away. I was acutely aware my heart was crying.

Sharp-toothed Lambs

After a while the
Knocks and scrapes;
The scars
Of a well-worn life,

Begin to show

The veneer of vanity
Hiding hurts
That are
Not always on the surface
For beauty is merely a commodity
We pay for in time and cost

It's the concept of being numb
To the advances
Of a handsome stranger
The fear of not knowing
Whether his affections
Are genuine or
Extended in deceit
I cannot tell

Frightened as a child
I see an invisible prison
Sharp-toothed lambs
Lure me to slaughter

I have almost lost hope
In the honour of a good man
How to believe?
And yet protect myself

It is time to retreat
I must let my heart heal
And be content
To wait
And watch
The grey skies pass

Oh, how I missed the companionship and conversation of a confident, educated man. I yearned for the reassurance and calming sense of security that comes with a relationship. The human touch, the intimacy, his smell. I longed for the power of strong thighs, the urgency of his want. The feel of warm, wanting breath, and a rasp-like tongue on my neck. I missed the hunger of his eyes.

A part of my soul lay dormant without a man in my life, and yet I had to accept things as they were. I reminded myself the legal assault would end at some stage. I was conscious of my need for clear mental space to complete this manuscript. I felt it would be impossible to write freely and honestly about the very personal details of my life if I had a man offering his opinions and judgements over what I should or should not write. I had to be free to close one door before I opened another.

twenty-six

The law is an ass

Over time, Tim became more threatening with his correspondence to my lawyers and also within his affidavits. He tried anything he could think of to cause me problems and irritations.

He claimed Bella and I were living at the Mill property illegally as we weren't personally paying rent. He said I owed our trust $105,000 in lieu of unpaid rent, even though one of my father's companies was meeting the trust's mortgage obligations to the bank by paying commercial rent to the trust for the use of the Mill.

Several property valuation reports I paid for provided evidence confirming the company was paying twice the expected market rental for the Mill. Tim refused to agree to have the monthly mortgage repayments brought back to a more realistic level, and because he refused to contribute to the mortgage, the companies had no alternative but to pay the bank.

He wouldn't sign off on our trust tax returns, resulting in them being filed late, which in turn caused problems for me with the IRD. Tim refused to contribute to the income tax, the GST, and the accounting costs associated with the financial reporting of the trust. I was left to cover these costs, which totalled around $48,000 per annum. This was on top of the legal, accounting, and valuation fees I was paying to defend myself against him in court.

Tim denied me access to funds from the sale of our family home until he was cautioned about his behaviour by the judge. Even then I was only able to access less than a quarter of the funds.

His unwillingness to be reasonable and his refusal to settle was a tactic he used for nearly five years. Over that time I believe he hoped I would crack – emotionally, physically, or financially – under the pressure.

His strategy almost worked. There were countless times when I couldn't pay my bills. The water pump stopped working. I couldn't afford to replace it, so for two years I had to walk outside, down the side of the Mill, sometimes in the dark and often in the rain, to turn the pump on every time I wanted to use the water.

The radiator of my dilapidated car blew up in the middle of five lanes of evening rush-hour traffic on the North-Western Motorway. The force of the explosion blew a dinner-plate-sized hole in the radiator. The experience was terrifying and if I had been travelling at speed, I would probably have been seriously injured in an accident.

With no warning, the bank froze all my accounts in early 2015. I had fallen behind in paying back the business loan, so they decided to freeze everything – my personal account as well. I couldn't even access money for petrol or groceries.

I lived in fear that I would not be able to pay the professionals I relied on. At one point, my accountant refused to release the financial reports for the company until I settled my outstanding debt to him of $10,000. I needed the reports for my legal defence. I was robbing Peter to pay Paul, out of pure desperation.

In early November 2016, one of the law firm's partners walked unannounced into a meeting I was having with my solicitor, my sister, and Mel. He asked which one of us was Emma and immediately launched into his ultimatum without shaking my hand.

All I was able to focus on was the man's sweaty forehead and the flushed, bulbous underside of his double chin as he stood over me with his arms folded. I remained seated. He told me it would be in my best interest to settle with Tim sooner rather than later. Should the matter not settle at the Judicial Settlement Conference, and go on to a four- to six-day court hearing the following year, the firm would require me to pay all outstanding fees, plus a sum of $100,000 cash up front for their fees in relation to the hearing before they would consider continuing to represent me.

With the death of my father and their knowledge of my finite access to funds, had the law firm simply decided they wanted the matter over and done with? It was obvious they were no longer interested in acting for me. I was being intimidated and pressured by my own lawyers to accept whatever deal came my way, irrespective of whether it was a fair settlement or in my best interests.

The partner did not check on the identities of my sister and Mel. They could have been my bank representatives for all he knew.

I was twice let down by my highly paid barrister.

Three working days before the spousal maintenance hearing in early May 2015, she rang and informed me she was unable to represent me in court the following week due to her heavy workload. Her replacement was a less-experienced staff solicitor who happened to be seven and a half months pregnant at the time. My legal professionals cornered me into accepting a less-than-ideal situation for my defence.

And then again, in early 2016, my original barrister abruptly withdrew her services, this time permanently, as she was appointed to the bar as a judge.

So much for the $27,000 in fees I had already paid her. I was told I was going to receive a comprehensive document (without charge) outlining the issues and the actions taken to date as a means of assisting handover to the next barrister. Did the document ever materialise? No, it didn't. Was I surprised? Not at all.

It was incredibly frustrating to see my hard-earned money being siphoned off to legal and accounting professionals, valuers, banks, and the tax department. At times my situation felt utterly hopeless; no matter how hard I worked, no matter what I was earning, I was haemorrhaging money and there seemed no end in sight. With every court appearance, with every invoice from the professionals, and with the months and years that dragged on, my strength weakened.

The true cost was not only felt with the financial pressure I was forced to bear. Tim's legal action stripped me of time with my daughter. It took away much of my energy. I would never recapture the time lost in defending myself, or the time I spent earning money to line the pockets of so many others.

And what exactly did Tim think was going to happen to Bella if he was successful in destroying me? Did he even care?

How was any of that fair when the action Tim brought to court was based on a lie? In 2013, he claimed the collective value of my businesses was $745,000, yet his own professional business valuer could only come up with a valuation figure of $200,000 at best.

Why hadn't my lawyers pressured Tim to prove his case from the beginning, or at least support his case with evidence? Tim was able to attack me through the courts with next-to-no supporting documentation. It cost me hundreds of thousands of dollars to prove he lied and even then there were no financial or legal repercussions for Tim once his lie was proven.

Surely the actions of the barrister and law firm were in breach of the Lawyers and Conveyancers Act (Lawyers: Conduct and Client Care Rules 2008)? And surely Tim should have to answer for his abuse of the legal system?

What if I couldn't earn enough money for my defence, or if I didn't have access to money through my parents? Then what? I lose? And Tim wins because he lied and he got away with it?

Where are the rights for the victims of injustice? Where are the rights for the financially marginalised mother and child? What sort of world are we living in where this sort of rodent behaviour is allowable? How the hell was any of it fair?

The Law is an ass.

twenty-seven

To the naysayers

I was devastated by the loss of my father. I missed his company, his humour, and his calming influence. Without his patient and considered advice, I felt adrift and very alone.

In the absence of his steadfast support and reassurance, I was scared for my future. I knew my mother would choose to stand back and watch me flounder rather than offer financial and emotional support.

To my father, I verbally implored, 'What would you do, Dad? Please help me find the answers and the strength to carry on.' My chats to my father became a meditation of sorts.

The relationship I had with my mother had never been easy. I always chose my words carefully with her. Her sense of entitlement made her opinionated and quick to judge.

Our conversations typically involved her saying, 'Well at any rate,' several times, as she dismissed my viewpoint or changed the subject from issues she was neither interested nor schooled in. There were so many layers of rejection and measured levels of empathy between us. She grew to become the antithesis of my father in her later years; she was as closed as he was open.

My waking hours were spent working and worrying. My sleeping hours were spent in night sweats and nightmares. I regularly woke to wet sheets and feelings of fear and panic. I dreamt I was being attacked. I spent hours lying awake in bed trying to avoid the very thing my mind and body needed – sleep.

Fear was a physical entity for me. It looked and felt like a heavy white blanket. It was hot and then cold, and it suffocated me. Fear appeared as a blinding white light in my dreams.

One evening in August 2016, I phoned my mother. I described my desperation to her. How I was physically exhausted and mentally drained from working long hours, looking after Bella, and trying to cope with the enormous financial pressure I was under. My accountant was refusing to release my accounts because I owed him $10,000. Without the accounts, my legal defence would be suspended and fall over. If I couldn't pay the accountant, I would lose the court case. I would lose everything.

Deep down I was still the same little girl offering my mother the smelly, white-petalled dog daisy. I needed her to see me, to help me, and to comfort me.

'Other solo mothers seem to manage. And I hear the businesses aren't doing that well,' she said.

I was in tears as I told her I was on the verge of suicide.

'You've felt that way before,' she responded.

Her words cut me as razors. How could she be so unkind? Had she forgotten about my suicide attempt thirteen years previously? Did she care so little for my welfare that she wasn't taking my plea for help seriously? It's not as if I was crying wolf. What did she think would happen to Bella if I was unable to find the strength to carry on?

Her response should have come as no surprise to me. This was not the first time she had shown me her harsh, judgemental side. The sands of time had done little to elicit an empathetic response from her.

'The businesses haven't been reporting great results, Mum, that's true. But the companies are paying all the legal fees, the forensic accounting fees, and the valuation reports for the court case. You do realise the businesses are also paying the mortgage, the council rates, insurance, maintenance on the property, and all the tax and GST for the trust, don't you? I'm not totally useless, Mum. I do actually have assets,' I tried to explain to her.

'Well, we don't know what assets you do or do not have at this stage, though, do we?' was her response.

Nothing I could have said would have made any difference. She was unwavering in her condemnation. I felt she was punishing me for the breakdown of my marriage and the shame it brought to her doorstep. She thought she was better than me.

'Look, I'm just not in a position to help you. All my money is accounted for,' she informed me.

My mother is a woman of significant financial means.

'Dad would have helped me, Mum. He wouldn't have hung me out to dry.' My challenge fuelled her fury.

'Don't you dare speak to me like that!' she screamed down the telephone and abruptly hung up.

I waited for her apology for five long days.

Within a few weeks of our phone conversation, I discovered my mother had only just settled on the purchase of a sizeable commercial property, paying with cash.

Six months later she purchased another property.

She eventually gave me $10,000 towards my legal defence. She offered no further assistance apart from childcare.

The dismissive and judgemental attitudes of my mother and sister drove me to fight on. Despite what they both thought, I wasn't worthless or useless! To myself, I quietly thanked them. They had just provided me with an incentive to prove them both wrong. I was able to dig a little deeper. And I would do it on my own.

I woke at 3 am. Tim was physically assaulting me in my sleep. I literally screamed and wailed out of fear for ten minutes. Vomit lay on my pillow and I was having a severe asthma attack. I was on the verge of calling an ambulance for myself.

The following day I had to collect Bella from Tim. It happened to be one of the rare weekends they spent together. As he stood leaning against his sister's car in the supermarket car park, he looked particularly smug and noticeably more conceited than normal. I was curious about his demeanour and wondered why he seemed so pleased with himself.

As the years progressed, I was able to observe him at a less-involved distance. I came to recognise the subtle "tells" of his behaviour – the way he sometimes minced across the car park, the effeminate lisp in his voice, his fastidious grooming, the overindulgence in his application of cologne, and the questionable clothing. And yet, at other times, he was able to display a more masculine authority over a situation. A new partner and one more child later made no difference; he wasn't fooling me. I could still see the vile deception he flaunted. But then again, I knew his secrets. He hated me for it.

I buckled Bella into my car and we drove off.

'Mummy, I have something exciting arriving in December,' said Bella as we merged onto the motorway.

'Oh, how cool. What is it?' I asked, thinking she might be getting a new toy.

'I'm getting a baby brother,' she continued.

I thought I was going to be sick, again. My arms trembled as I drove home. I was experiencing shock.

I had to question Tim's sanity with respect to having another child in his mid-forties. In April 2016, he claimed he was seeing a psychologist because of stress. Seriously now, was he looking for sympathy? Surely another child would only add to his stress?

He also disclosed that he had been in hospital for two and a half weeks, as he had once again developed prostatitis. He went on to explain he was being treated with a lengthy course of strong oral antibiotics around that time. Was he up to his old tricks? Was he having sex with men again?

He claimed his partner's historic home was being levelled according to council orders. Tim explained there were structural concerns and the home was to be completely rebuilt. That simply defied logic to me. Rather than demolishing historic homes, don't they repair and restore them instead?

He wrote of how he was struggling financially, how he was having to provide rental accommodation for his family in Sydney while the rebuild was taking place.

I was now being told a son would be born in December 2016. So that's what the house rebuild was all about. They were rebuilding to accommodate a growing family, not because of structural concerns, as he claimed.

To hear he was having another child made me feel sad for Bella, as I knew she would become even less of a priority for him.

I was curious to see how Tim would cope with the compounding stress of his health issues, moving a young family into rental accommodation, the financial cost and stress that goes hand in hand with a substantial renovation, a newborn baby, and the pressures of an ongoing court case?

From my own experience of living with him, I understood that he had zero tolerance for stress of any kind. How he thought he would fly through the turmoil he had created for himself was anyone's guess.

My friends picked his demise. 'You're only as sick as your secrets,' Mel reminded me. 'Tim is riddled with secrets. They'll be eating him alive.'

'This new baby will be his undoing,' said Skye. 'His partner will put an end to it all. Hang in there, Emma. You haven't got long to go now.'

twenty-eight

Suicide lay in wait

In general, days were easier than nights. My ability to cope became dependent on how tired I was and how much emotional and financial pressure I was under. I felt as though I was lying permanently on a torture rack. Some days the screws were tightened, other days I was just left lying alone and imprisoned with my own fear.

I contemplated suicide a lot through the months of 2016. I had lost faith in love and fairness. The assistance I received from my mother and sister was measured and came with condemnation. I believed that aside from a few friends and my aunt, who stood by me, no one could be trusted. People were either lying to me or they were capable of lying to me. And if they weren't, then they probably just wanted to fuck me financially or physically.

I feared I would have a breakdown. I wondered whether I was being a good mother to Bella. Most nights I lay awake and fretted over how I was supposed to pay the mortgage and cover the day-to-day bills. Could I afford food for the week? Was my car going to break down again? It had travelled over 460,000 kilometres, and was on borrowed time.

I prayed for good health. If I lost my ability to work, I would be unable to pay the lawyers and the accountants. Would Tim then win by default?

I was resilient. I had proven that, but what kind of shell of my former self was really left?

My mother suggested I go to the doctor and get medicated for depression. It took all my strength to stop myself from screaming down the phone to her, '*Fuck you, Mum!*' I wanted to berate her for being so judgemental. But I didn't. There was no point.

Was she so ignorant she was unable to understand that someone with depression would never be able to withstand the pressure I was under? Did I have to be fucking perfect all the fucking time? Did anyone stop to think that perhaps I was struggling with the constant attacks, the lies, the accusations, the deceit, the exhaustion of solo parenting and running businesses, the financial pressure, loneliness, and maybe – just maybe – I was missing my dad?

From Beyond the Brink

Despair swirls all around me
Suicide pulls up her chair
She taps me on my shoulder
I turn and face the other cheek

I have screamed out loud
These lungs have bled
My dissolving heart a putrid mess
No one sees this private, ugly world
Save for my beautiful face

A vacant gaze towards nothingness
My life left hanging in mid-air
A labyrinth of choices, crossroads, futile paths
Wobegone, I am shackled
To this harrowing ordeal

I wake today to a light room
Pure and calm
I find my peace
Clean and fresh white cotton sheets
A feather duvet
Comforts, cocoons, and protects

Air billows
My feet swing to the edge
Grasping life with both hands
I draw back the curtains
And lever open the new day

With cheek pressed to the pane
My finger carves "hope" through condensation
Fresh-cut grass wafts by
A ladybird lands on my nose
And so,
I start again

Another day back
From beyond the brink
Where near all has been lost
And not

For I am still here
And there is light and love
Left for me in this world
I "hope"

Insecurities have invariably been woven into the fabric of my life. They simmer gently beneath the surface and have gone undetected by all except my closest friends.

There has always been the immense capability of my public professional work, with just a hint of apprehension to my demeanour.

To the outside world I strode ahead. Some would say they saw a person full of energy and light. And yet my warm smile and eyes held a world of private pain. Most people never saw the struggling, wounded child at my core, slaying demons in my sleep. She was full of doubt and fear. She never felt quite good enough.

I have become more at ease with my insecurities as I have aged. I now openly speak of this with my friends. Being honest about it has helped me make decisions and set boundaries for myself.

Perhaps the shame and "weight" people carry with emotional trauma may explain why and how people fall through the cracks. Suicide seems to come from nowhere. And yet, she has always been there, hovering.

Suicide lay in wait. She gently picked people off the ledge.

'I never knew she was suicidal. She always seemed so on top of things,' people said. But those people never saw the private face.

How do you know to reach out for help when you feel shame and have a fear of showing weakness as a person suffering from trauma? I was fearful of being judged and rejected. Pride can be a very self-limiting word.

I reached out to my mother in vain. I should have known better.

My friends saved me: Laura, Mel, Skye, Kate, Rob, Tayla and my aunt.

I got to the stage where I struggled to recognise a lie from the truth. It became easier to be on my own where no one could harm me.

I lost my confidence with men. There had been too many hurts, too many lost loves, and so many layers of betrayal. I seemed to have tripped and fallen down some type of relationship rabbit hole. I looked up to the sky. There was no ladder, no path to guide my way back.

Tim stole my heart. He tore it up into a million pieces and threw them in my face. I didn't know how to heal my heart. How was I to find my way back? Would I ever make sense of the world again?

I considered my lack of judgement. What type of person unwittingly marries a homosexual or bisexual man? Why couldn't a decent, honest man find me? What was so wrong with me that I looked past the honest men and fell prey to him?

So many self-deprecating thoughts slushed from side to side in my brain. I always found myself at the same end point – I simply felt unworthy of love.

Pennies to the Well

I gather pennies;
Remnants of my soul
A life in tatters
Strewn about
Slipping through cracks in the ground
I rummage
With fraught desperation
On my knees
Fingers to the quick
Losing grip
Scratching dirt
The pieces don't fit

I am deeply injured
And I know it
My limp wrist
Throws pennies
To the well

I feared I would succumb to suicide. I gave all the energy I could to getting through each day. I had to really focus on *not* taking my own life. Not for my sake, but for Bella's. I couldn't bear the thought of her being raised by her father. She needed my love so I had to stay alive for her.

I leant on my friends. They talked to me for hours on the phone and calmed my fears. Not once did they ever judge me or speak harshly to me. They encouraged me to carry on, to fight, and to remain strong for Bella.

Isabella

The responsibility
Can almost crush me at times
Yet I rise and rise to your needs
You are my daughter
I gave you life
Isabella
You are the air that I breathe

PART FOUR

REHABILITATION AND REFORMATION

twenty-nine

On the road

Exactly how did I manage to earn enough money to cover the costs of the lawyers, accountants, mortgage repayments, day-to-day personal living expenses, and business overheads between 2012 and 2017?

I worked hard and made sensible business decisions, I guess. I knew the market the businesses operated in very well; I knew what stock to buy, where to buy it, when to buy it, how much it would cost, how much I should pay, and how much I needed to sell it for to make a profit and still remain competitive. I knew how to negotiate a deal. Experience had taught me how to manage my cash flow to accommodate fluctuations in sales throughout the year. I understood my competitors and the buying behaviour of my customers. I knew when and how to time my sales to beat my competitors to the market. Service and flexibility as a supplier is important, and I never made the process unnecessarily difficult for my customers. I was always as flexible as I could be with credit terms, and that bought me loyalty.

Being on the road selling to my wholesale customers had its benefits and its challenges. The biggest challenge was being away from Bella. We missed each other and she needed me.

My mother, Laura, Mel, Skye, Kate, and my aunt were very generous with their time. They cared for Bella while I was away. They got her off to school, checked she had completed her homework, read her stories and made sure she was eating properly. They took over the constant nagging of telling her to wash her hair, and go to the toilet and clean her teeth before she went to bed. The generous help I received from my friends and my mother enabled me to focus on sales.

Travelling the country selling homeware to retailers was exhausting work. But it wasn't all bad. I considered myself lucky to have the freedom to enjoy the stunning landscapes of our amazing country.

If I was driving the Kaikōura coastline during the day, I'd pull over and wander along the shoreline, jump across boulders, and sit and gaze in wonder at the seal colonies. I'd draw the bite of the cold sea air in through my lungs, and let the wind dance with my hair.

I've sat and watched mist hover over Lake Tūtira and gazed at pink sunrises over Mount Taranaki. I have seen sunlight glisten and dance from the waters of the southern lakes and admired the barren beauty of views from the Crown Range and Lindis Pass.

The trips to the South Island were always the toughest physically. The driving distances were huge. Unpacking my car in yet another small town when I was far from home after a fourteen-hour day was tough going. Scrambling to find something to eat when it was getting late, with small-town restaurants closing their kitchens at 7.30 pm, always meant resorting to a deserted supermarket. If the supermarket was closed, I went hungry.

I got tired of the constant packing and unpacking. Little things irritated me – motel soap typically smelt like caustic oven cleaner, and I refused to drink their disgusting budget powdered coffee. I regularly woke in the middle of the night disorientated, with no clue in the world as to where I was.

I had a few very special clients that I was fortunate to get to know over the many years I called on them. They invited me to stay with them at their homes. One particular kind treasure (Stormi) put hot-water bottles in the bed she always made so beautifully for me. I loved her spare room – it had yellow floral wallpaper that covered the walls and the ceiling. I pulled the sheets right up beneath my chin and savoured the simple pleasure of lying in bed gazing at the crystal chandelier above my head.

Stormi went to considerable effort and cooked nutritious meals for me. She bought fresh and local produce; always Southland seafood – mussels or blue cod. I didn't have the heart to tell her I wasn't a fan of seafood, and never left a crumb on my plate.

As well as home décor items and furniture, Stormi sold elegant after-five and occasion wear fashions in her store. I helped her out by modelling dresses for her.

She put my photos up on her Facebook page and her website. I always enjoyed spending time with Stormi, and I was able to amass an enviable wardrobe through many years calling on her and the generous discounts she gave me.

When I travelled, my station wagon was literally full to the brim with samples. I had two 20-kilogram sample cases plus various random items of sampling and my personal luggage crammed into every available space in my car. I needed to take several trips back and forth to unload and I was never guaranteed a park nearby. Heaven forbid if it was raining.

I had my car towed one day in Wellington as my park turned into a bus stop after 3 pm. My customer was late, and then she took her time viewing the range, only to tell me she had already spent her entire budget for the month. By the time I had finished with her, I had no order to show for my labours and my car had disappeared. In desperation, I wandered down the street to seek assistance from another of my customers. I dragged my two heavy sample cases behind me down the pavement of one of the busiest streets in the country. I told my customer of my predicament. She kindly gave me $80 cash so I could take a cab and retrieve my car. The 130-kilogram female cab driver spent ten minutes lecturing me about how irresponsible I was to have left my mobile phone and wallet in my car when I had a dependent child at home. 'What if something had happened to your daughter and you couldn't be contacted?' she scolded me. I had no option but to bite my tongue and take her lashing. If she had decided to stop the car and put me out, I would have been in a seriously compromised position. That was not one of my better days.

I sat through a 5.6 magnitude earthquake in Wellington six months later. I gave up on the city after that. I'd had enough.

Exhaustion got the better of me one night. I was staying at another kind and generous customer's home in Gisborne. At 2 am I woke and ran to the bathroom with vomiting and diarrhoea. I ended up making a bed for myself on the bathroom floor. My customer stroked my hair and held my hand off and on throughout the night.

The following day I had to drive back to Auckland and visit a customer along the way. Despite having to stop several times due to my discomfort, I made a $2,500 sale, and I arrived back in time to collect Bella from school.

Days like that revealed the raw underbelly of the impact of Tim's prolonged attack; I was exhausted and my health was suffering. There was no allowance for a sick day with the bear and its claws planted firmly in my back.

Most of my customers were lovely. I'd chat to them about their lives, their businesses, and their children. We'd talk about challenges happening in the marketplace and discussed strategies for dealing with their issues. I had eighteen years' experience as a retailer, and they all knew that. I told them what was happening in retail in other areas of New Zealand, what trends I saw coming through, and so on.

I had one special man say to me, 'Emma have you ever thought about why you do so well with sales?' It was a fairly direct question. The smile and look of warmth on his face let me know his question was coming from a kind place.

'I'm not sure really. But I guess you're gonna tell me, right?' I replied with a grin.

'It's because you turn up, Emma, when so many others don't. You give me a call, you arrive on time looking great, and I basically buy whatever you have to show me. Did you realise most of your competitors phone or email and ask *me* to travel to Auckland to see *them*?'

Clearly there was more to it than the simple act of "turning up". The lesson was: If you want something out of life, you must get off your ass and work for it. You can't botox your ass. There is no quick fix in life.

I have always taken great pride in my work. From my early twenties, when I chose to throw away my career in the pharmaceutical industry to pursue my creative dream with architectural studies in London, I have lived by this philosophy: Follow your passion, pursue a career you enjoy and never "work" another day of your life.

thirty

Chasing moonbeams

The demands on my time were relentless throughout 2016. My reserves of energy were desperately low, yet I still managed to continue to haul myself from the abyss of despair. I completed my work and my daily tasks to the best of my ability.

I mentally put my problems into a box and parked them off to the side – in a place that would allow me to carry on, regardless of the negativity that threatened. The realisation that I was in control of my emotions was empowering. I was determined to make the most of every opportunity that came my way. I even created a few for Bella and me.

In April 2016, I took Bella down to the local hockey club for the season muster. She had a brand-new bright-pink hockey stick my mother had given her for Christmas. She looked so cute with her matching bright-pink top, a pink hockey ball, and pink running shoes. I hoped her involvement with a hockey team would help build her confidence, teach her about commitment and grow her circle of friends.

She was hesitant to begin with, but it didn't take long before she was running effortlessly around the turf, laughing, and enjoying time with her new friends. She always looked forward to hockey practice and to the interclub games on Saturday mornings. I enjoyed the quality time we had together.

Being back on the hockey turf stirred something inside me. I approached Dave, the club captain, and asked whether the club had a senior women's team.

Dave's eyes lit up. 'Do you play?' he asked enthusiastically.

'Ah, well, I used to play,' I replied.

Little did Dave realise, but it had been twenty-seven years since I had played a game of hockey.

I joined the senior women's team that night and never looked back. Within a few weeks, I was confidently controlling the ball, brushing up on rule changes and learning a new position on the field. The majority of the other women in my team were much younger, but no one seemed to care how old I was. We were just a bunch of ladies with a shared passion and a whole lot of energy.

Our team won some games. We lost a few. We played in the rain, heat, hail, and at night under lights. We got together as a team for fitness training and also for team-building outings such as paintball, pizza, and quiz nights. It was so wonderful to be part of a larger family that didn't involve work. I thrived on the experience.

Towards the end of the 2016 hockey season, Dave emailed all club members and asked us for our nominations for Most Valuable Player, Most Improved Player, Sportsmanship Award, and so on, for our individual teams. There were also a number of club awards as well.

Once I finished emailing Dave with my nominations, I continued: *Dave, I'd like to suggest a new category for club awards this year. How about one for Comeback of the Year? And you know what, Dave, I'd like to nominate myself for that. You may not know this, but it's been twenty-seven years since I played hockey, and my team won the senior women's championship.*

I was just having a laugh with him – I didn't expect him to do anything more with my suggestion. Two weeks later he texted me: *Hey Emma, how would you like to donate a cup for Comeback of the Year?*

I bought a smart-looking silver-plated cup. It was about 30 centimetres tall and it shone brighter than the Eiffel Tower. Dave had the trophy engraved "The Emma Rivers Cup for Comeback of the Year" and he presented me with it in front of 120 senior members at the awards ceremony. Despite the fact I had paid for the cup myself and the whole thing had been my idea, I felt so proud. I had once again proven to myself that if I could find the strength to stand with confidence and set some goals, I would achieve my dreams. If I could think it, I could do it.

Bella and I entered the 2016 Auckland KIDs marathon. We ran the 2.2-kilometre course together, wearing matching outfits – orange shorts, mint-coloured singlet tops, and white caps. Bella's face beamed with delight as she was awarded her participation medal by the Mayor of Auckland. It was another highlight of our year.

I enrolled in contemporary dance lessons with my friend Skye. All the women in the class had danced before. I was very much a beginner compared to everyone else.

Bella had the annoying task of watching her mother struggle through the lessons. At one point I asked her, 'Darling, how's Mum doing with her dancing?'

'You're crap at dancing, Mum,' she replied. She was being blunt but fair. That's something my dad would have said. I had to laugh.

I was trying to teach my daughter about perseverance and tenacity. I wanted her to understand how it's normal to struggle when learning something new. With time and practice, your skill level and sense of enjoyment grows.

A few months later, with restrained optimism, I asked Bella again. 'So darling, how's Mum doing with her dancing now?'

'Oh, Mum. You're worse than crap. You're so much better at hockey. Stick with that,' she said.

My theory was clearly flawed.

Chasing Moonbeams

To feel and see and live
And breathe in
And exhale

To leap and crash
And dream and die
And sometimes all at once

And for it to all be okay
I am blessed and cursed
Within a single heartbeat

It's like living on Mars

Life gets lonely
Chasing moonbeams

Bella and I attended "Seasons" grief and loss counselling which was being coordinated by the local church. While the children went off with their therapist to discuss how their individual loss had affected them, we mothers were able to chat amongst ourselves and process our pain in a supportive and understanding environment.

I met with two of the mothers outside of the arranged weekly meetings. We created a Facebook chat group and vented to each other in confidence about issues we could relate to.

Our network of three soon grew to five as yet two more of our friends found themselves deceived and discarded. While other separated women spoke of the "day their husbands left", we referred to it as our "Liberation Day".

With time, the focus of our bimonthly get-togethers shifted to chats about changing careers, buying and selling homes, sharing the joys of our growing children, dating escapades, and appreciation of our freedom and growing confidence. We laughed hysterically and celebrated our friendship.

Unofficially, we called ourselves the Parakai Ex Wives Club, or PEWC for short.

I suggested we should all be "co-leaders" of PEWC; however, the response I got was this: 'Don't be a dick, Emma. We're not the bloody Green Party.' It was unanimously decided that I was to be referred to as the "Esteemed Leader". I put together a brief club constitution as follows:

1) New PEWC members must be nominated by existing members. New PEWC members are to be approved by all members. No skanks or homewreckers will be allowed to infiltrate our ranks.
2) Each new PEWC member to be issued with a PEWC initialled wine glass. The "Esteemed Leader" makes these with love and nail polish so please don't put them in the dishwasher. PEWC wine glasses to be brought to all meetings.
3) Support to all members, day and night, no questions asked. Offers of assistance with childcare, gifts, food parcels, paying bills, or whatever, to be accepted, with no expectation of reciprocity.
4) Naming and shaming at meetings to be encouraged. Get it off your chest, as that's what we're here for. Crying is fine. We've all been there.
5) Interjections, re-enactments, photos, videos, and activities are all acceptable at meetings. As are male strippers, as they're always a nice distraction.

6) No taking the moral high ground on anything, and no judgy bullshit, 'cos deep down we're all capable of anything when they take our kids, our money, our careers, and they fuck around on us.
7) Membership to PEWC is for life, even if you pair up. Good luck with that. LOL.
8) There will never be any membership fees. Only love and friendship given freely.
9) PEWC meetings to be attended strictly by members only. Unless you invite a friend to boost numbers – for sex toy parties, for instance.
10) Always remember they did us a favour by setting us free. And no matter how bad it feels, it's only a bad day, not a bad life. We have our children and wonderful friends to guide us through.

As a young child I yearned to draw and paint. My drive to create never left me

I always wanted to be an artist; however, I was swayed with a heavy hand by my parents and the school I attended, to pursue a more academic path. As I persevered with organic chemistry, genetic engineering, and business management papers at university, I always knew in my heart something was missing.

I consider myself lucky to have found an equilibrium where I can combine the intellectual stimulation of running businesses within the design industry. I have created a life which allows me the freedom to be involved in sport, travel, manage my time as I see fit, and pursue artistic hobbies such as writing and painting.

It had been some twelve years since I had been in the right creative headspace to paint. As I developed some concepts and sketched my ideas, I thought of Bella and the loss she had suffered when my dad and our elderly friend Gray had passed away. Gray's wife Laura told Bella that he had come back as a tūī. When Dad passed away in November 2015, I told Bella her grandad had come back as a pīwakawaka (fantail). It was wonderful to see these native birds in our garden at home. Bella and I sat outside and talked to them as we would have talked to Gray and Grandad. I painted a portrait of Bella with a tūī looking down on her from above and a pīwakawaka sitting on her shoulder. They were her "Guardians to Watch over Me".

I entered three acrylic paintings into the local area arts festival in 2016. I was shocked to learn that out of a class of 126 entries, I was awarded second place for my portrait of Bella. I hope she will always remember the evening when she watched her mother walk across the stage to receive a prize for the painting that was all about her, and will remember how much she is loved.

I continued with my poetry writing through 2016 and received some positive feedback from my friends. Every now and again, when I had a spare moment, I wrote a chapter or two for my developing manuscript.

Despite the gnawing agony of the court case, 2016 proved to be one of the most successful and fulfilling years I had experienced in a very long time. Perhaps I was settling into a life of independence? I was enjoying the freedom I was afforded without a man in my life. It was liberating. I was quietly capturing the essence of who I really was.

To Be Free

To be able to show restraint
And
Stop.
And
Wait.
Such blessings appear to have passed me by
A body and mind with no "off" switch – on fire
I struggle to find my peace
A young bitch – on heat
Vying for my freedom
I ache to live life fast
And run and hold it all at once
In my grasp
It's too much for most
They don't understand
So I must wait and be tethered
Lead straining at my neck
Some say I should breathe
Just "be"
More "grounded"
But they are just labels
For those who have never known
What it means to fly
And
To be free

The closer I came to the end of the legal battle, it become apparent the outcome of the court case was in fact secondary to the inspirational journey I had been on. I had grown spiritually, I had matured, and I had "found myself" along the way. I discovered I had huge reserves of inner strength and amazing support networks. I realised the skills, gifts, and talents I drew upon to help me deal with my trauma were already within me. The outcome of the court case was going to make very little difference to my day-to-day life, as I was already content with who I was. In effect, I had already won.

It filled me with pride to see my daughter thrive, despite the abandonment by her father. Bella was a well-adjusted child. She was reaching all her milestones at school and she was gaining confidence with her sport. She was kind natured with an infectious sense of humour. She made friends easily and was polite and courteous. I was incredibly proud of her.

For so long, I felt as though I was living in the shadow of an impenetrable brick wall. There was no way over that wall, or around it. Instead, I felt myself chipping at it with a needle.

And then, miraculously, without notice, I began to see fine cracks appearing at the base of the wall. For the first time in four years, I felt glimmers of light and hope reach me from the other side.

My mood lifted ever so slightly. My close friends noticed the subtle changes in my demeanour. I began to talk of plans for the future, places I wanted to visit, things I would do with Bella. I saw fun and laughter on the horizon. I saw myself finishing my manuscript.

I knew I was edging closer to the end of my nightmare with Tim, even though I had no concept of how "The End" would present itself.

thirty-one

The rumble in the jungle

The devil whispered in my ear,
'You're not strong enough to withstand the storm.'
Today, I whispered in the devil's ear,
'I am the storm.'

Anonymous

So many skills and life lessons are learned on the sports field. As a child, I unwittingly engaged in strategic role plays with my hockey and tennis teammates. Participation in sport strengthened me and prepared me for the challenges that lay ahead. Through sweat, disappointments, tears, and joy, I was to learn the art of perseverance, to weather physical and mental hardship, to work within a team, to strategise an attack, to defend against adversaries, to play by the rules, and to still think for myself.

There is no better example of how the art of strategy can turn an underdog into a victor than with the legendary boxing match between the then-undefeated heavyweight champion George Foreman and the challenger Muhammad Ali. The "Rumble in the Jungle" of 30 October 1974 has been called the greatest sporting event of the twentieth century – and with good reason.

At 25 years of age, the younger and stronger Foreman was favoured to win over the older and well-worn 32-year-old Ali. Foreman was feared for his size and the power of his explosive punches. He was unbeaten in 34 pro fights, and all but two had ended in knockouts.

There were genuine fears for Ali's safety. Ali was older, and although he was light on his feet and famed for his speed and technical skills, Foreman was the more formidable boxer.

Ali adopted a "rope-a-dope" tactic. He lured Foreman into attacking him on the ropes. Ali conserved his energy and outwrestled Foreman by hugging him and pushing on his neck. He taunted Foreman in their clinches by saying, 'They told me you could punch, George!'

About the seventh round, Foreman punched Ali hard in the jaw. Ali held Foreman and whispered in his ear, 'That all you got, George?'

By the eighth round, Foreman had worn himself out taking countless wild shots at Ali. His punches and defence became ineffective. Ali pounced and landed several right hooks over Foreman's jab, followed by a five-punch combination, culminating in a left hook and a hard-right punch straight to the face. Foreman fell to the floor and never got up.

Ali did not win through superior physical force; he won through toughness, durability and strategy. He let Foreman attack him for seven rounds and in the process had to bear a serious amount of pain. But Foreman simply didn't have the conditioning to go the full distance. Ali was able to lure his opponent into a weakened position. Only then did he go in for the kill and sucker-punched him.

I was the underdog going into battle against Tim. He had the edge over me with his ability in, and experience of, accounting and finance. His earning capacity outstripped mine by a country mile. He had adequate rest and time to recharge, as he was awarded paid holidays through his job, and for his first two and a half years in Australia he had almost no childcare responsibilities. He had planned for my financial destruction well before he abandoned Bella and me for his new life in Sydney – he had the element of surprise. Tim lied repeatedly in court and in affidavits. He dragged out the settlement process to burden me with oppressive and debilitating professional fees. He was scrupulous in his drive to destroy me.

To survive the pressure, I had to think and act like Ali. I had to remain calm, conserve my energy, and wait for my chance to retaliate. I devised a strategy that relied upon carefully considered decision-making. I showed restraint and concentrated on my health. I was meticulous with my preparation of information for the court. My delivery of facts was sharp and accurate.

Tim underestimated my determination and my ability to work tirelessly with no rest. He thought I would break, and although my health wavered and there were times when I struggled mentally, I refused to give up. I always rose to the occasion. I was unbreakable.

I clung to the ropes of the boxing ring just as Ali did. I took blow after blow from Tim. I had no choice. I had to suck it up, tough it out, and keep going back for more. I couldn't intimidate him. I couldn't outearn him, and I couldn't outspend him with lawyers. I had to hold my position as best I could and wait and pray for the noose of his lies to tighten around his neck.

If I had given in, I would have lost everything. I was sure of that. To keep my head clear and my resolve centred on success, I simply eliminated defeat or surrender as an option. What Tim got to witness was true grit.

My test was always going to be whether I would be strong enough to hang in there to the last round. I ached for my moment in the ring to set the record straight once and for all.

thirty-two

Financial asphyxiation

Restraint

I am lost at the point
Of trying not to hate you
And wishing
You were dead

In January 2016, as per judge's orders of November 2015, Tim was required to release specific information relating to the financial position, banking history, employment status, property ownership and evidence of any mortgages against any property owned by himself and/or his partner. When I discovered critical documents were deliberately not supplied in the discovery bundle, I emailed my lawyer several times to request she contact Tim's lawyer to demand access to the missing information. My emails were ignored.

I believe the missing information would have strengthened my spousal maintenance and s182 applications. It would have provided proof that Tim lied under oath at the spousal maintenance hearing and shown Tim and his partner were in a very strong financial position compared to my much weaker position.

I spent at least fifty hours combing Tim's bank and Visa statements looking for irregularities. I cross-referenced his expenditure with his passport to track his movements and compared his claims for expenditure on Bella to actual dates when he was with her.

As part of Tim's plea of poverty, and justification for why he should not be expected to pay spousal maintenance, he claimed to have spent $16,900 on Bella, over and above the money he spent on child support in the 12 months to July 2014.

He presented comprehensive tables of expense claims and declared he had spent money strawberry picking with Bella in Sydney when she was in New Zealand with me. He claimed to have spent $200 on toys for her at a company called Station Red, also in Sydney. After a ten-second Google search I discovered Station Red was a fine dining restaurant, not a toy store. And again, Bella was in New Zealand with me at the time.

Tim claimed to have spent $2,900 on toys and gifts for Bella at the airport duty free. I checked the transaction dates and discovered he had spent that amount as he was *leaving* New Zealand, not as he was on his way to see his daughter.

Tim claimed to have spent $5,600 on airfares, accommodation and taxis for Bella over one month in 2014. I checked his passport and Visa statements and discovered he had spent the money on a trip to Fiji. Bella never travelled to Fiji with her father.

I was able to ascertain Tim had not in fact spent anywhere near $16,900 on Bella. The figure was closer to $2,000, but even that was being generous.

I discovered $43,000 had disappeared from our joint cash funds immediately prior to Tim leaving New Zealand in 2012. There was also the $82,000 of superannuation funds he took with him when our marriage ended.

Tim operated a foreign exchange account throughout our marriage. He did not tell me about this account while we were married. The only statement I was allowed access to was dated the month he left for Sydney in March 2012. The account had a zero balance. My lawyers did not request further discovery of transaction history for that foreign exchange account or other hidden accounts in Australia and New Zealand, despite my many requests for them to do so.

There was a deposit of $5,700 into his Australian bank account in 2013 with a Forex notation. I suspected he was receiving income from foreign exchange trades or income from other sources.

There were other mysterious deposits of $30,000 and $20,000 which were not related to his salaried job. I had to assume these were interest or dividend payments from his investments.

Whatever money Tim was sitting on in Australia, I was certain he had amassed it through the years of our marriage. Half of that money was mine.

On 31 March 2016, I received an invoice for $ 30,800 from my lawyers for work they did between 1 December 2015 and 18 March 2016 in relation to the preparation of an affidavit for my spousal maintenance, s182 application and relationship property matters. Despite the affidavit being filed well over a month late, it was clear from their charges that the law firm were still pursuing my case.

And then with no warning and no direction or instruction from me, my lawyers decided in May 2016 that they were going to direct their energy on formulating an offer for settlement.

When my lawyer informed me she intended to disregard all the evidence I had unearthed in respect of Tim's hidden money and she was not going to enforce the release of missing discovery as per the judge's orders of November 2015, I was angry and disappointed.

'But why do you continue to let him away with it? Are you seriously going to allow him to walk all over me and steal relationship assets? What about my spousal maintenance and s182 applications? Will he never be held accountable for what he has done?' I asked.

'Settlements are all about compromise and concessions,' she said. 'We can't put an offer on the table that is loaded with further accusations. It would simply inflame the situation and be counterproductive,' she replied.

'For God's sake. I need a moment. I'm going to the ladies,' I said, as I got up and left the room.

I suspected my lawyer's instruction to ignore the financial information I had uncovered came from higher up. Was the partner pulling the strings? Had he decided to seek a quick settlement, regardless of whether it was in my best interest?

As far as I was concerned, they were in breach of the Lawyers and Conveyancers Act (Lawyers: Conduct and Client Care) Rules 2008 for not acting on my instructions and for putting their own motivations ahead of mine. I considered whether I would need to consult the Law Society. But what exactly could I do about it at that time? Nothing. The law firm representing me had me cornered. I could barely contain my outrage.

I was told by my lawyer that my offer for settlement would also leave out all monies Tim potentially owed me for spousal maintenance. Despite my objections to their decisions and directions, my lawyers also withdrew my application for a greater share of the trust assets. As per section 182 of the Property (Relationships)

Act, I was potentially entitled to a greater share of the trust assets because of my diminished earnings and my role as primary caregiver to our only daughter. My lawyers also told me that I should mentally prepare myself to move on my expectations and make additional financial concessions over and above the ones we had just discussed, if I wanted to reach a settlement end point.

My offer for settlement was filed in June 2016 with the expectation that Tim's counter-offer would quickly follow in reply.

In August 2016, Tim's solicitor was contacted and questioned about his position in respect of our settlement offer as they had failed to respond. We received a one-paragraph reply to our 200-page offer document. In summation, he rejected my offer for settlement because he thought it was just a regurgitation of previous information already submitted. He argued I had not provided any documentation in support of my position.

What a lot of bullshit. But after dealing with his lies and manipulations for four years, I would have been naive to expect anything more from him. Again, his was a tactical move.

I found the situation incredibly frustrating. He was stonewalling me, *again*. He had lured me into a position of spending another $35,000 with lawyers and accountants, with the preparation of the offer document. He had offered nothing in response and spent very little money on his own legal representation.

I felt the months of 2016 drag on. It was excruciating. I was travelling a lot with work. I was missing Bella, and I was tired. I had the continual pressure of paying the legal and accounting fees. Tim was again refusing to set the mortgage for the Mill property at interest only, so I was required to pay $5,400 in interest and capital mortgage payments to the bank each month without a single cent from him. There were additional outgoings and overheads associated with the running of our trust and costs for maintaining the property, which he refused to contribute to. And yet he had the audacity to claim half the value of our assets.

I was being financially asphyxiated by stealth.

In September 2016, my lawyer informed me I would be participating in a one-day Judicial Settlement Conference scheduled for 8 November 2016. Both the applicant and respondent to the matter were required to attend and they had to be accompanied by their respective lawyers. A judge would preside over the mediation and direct proceedings.

By the beginning of November, I was in full despair. All I could see was more emotional pain and enormous cost on the horizon with a four- to six-day court hearing sometime in 2017. Given Tim's behaviour, I doubted we would be successful in reaching a settlement on 8 November.

I had no idea how I would be able to sustain an escalation of pressure through the next year. I feared my fragile physical state would deteriorate further and I would finally succumb to a breakdown or worse. I knew I would find it almost impossible to cope financially with the additional $100,000 in legal fees for the 2017 hearing, on top of the fees I had already been invoiced.

I received further invoices of $40,000 from my lawyers in relation to the work they did immediately before and after the settlement conference. That took the professional fees (legal, accounting and valuation) I was charged to over $400,000 since separation date.

As 8 November 2016 approached, I was constantly tearful. I wasn't sleeping. I wasn't really eating.

I was aware of the severity of my situation. If I was unable to reach a settlement with Tim on 8 November, and without access to additional funds to continue with my defence, I would lose my life's work, my home, and my livelihood in one clean sweep.

At that stage, I was unaware $100,000 had been set aside for me from my father's estate. I was not informed of this or the release date of the money until later in November 2016. As I have already said, timing is everything.

thirty-three

Let's finish this

she
has
been through
hell
so believe me when
I say
fear her when she looks
into a fire and smiles

e corona

The ending to the legal nightmare crept silently up behind me. It took me by the throat with both hands, kicked me in the kidneys, and released me in the blink of an eye.

Tim arrived at court with not one, but two legal representatives. He had a solicitor and a barrister. I had one solicitor, who had been working with me on my case for three and a half years. Tim's solicitor had been working on his case for eighteen months. His barrister had joined his legal team within the past few months.

I was given permission to have Mel accompany me as a support person in the courtroom for the duration of the day-long ordeal.

The settlement conference started at 10 am sharp. The judge smiled and appeared relaxed. His knowing eyes were sharp, and I could tell he was astute.

He started the day by confirming everyone's identity and advising us he had only received the file that morning. He explained he'd had minimal time to read over historical affidavits and past documentation over and above the latest affidavits.

The judge addressed me. 'So, Emma, I take it you are the Applicant and Tim is the Respondent?'

'No, sir. I am the Respondent in this matter,' I replied.

'Oh, I see,' said the judge, raising his left eyebrow. He would have known that from reading the affidavits. That was the first hint I had of his underlying opinions, and I believed he was making a point of the fact the situation was very unusual. It is not common for men to pursue their ex-wives in court over relationship assets.

Tim and his lawyers were allowed to speak first. They spent twenty minutes declaring their position. All I heard were lies and distorted truths. I was angry yet I remained calm.

From across the large, round table I observed Tim's every move. I saw the same body language from him that I had seen in earlier court appearances – that hangdog look that said, "take pity on me".

My lawyer spoke for me and presented my case.

As noon approached, Tim attempted to describe to the judge how reasonable and conciliatory he had been, that he had tried to settle with me but I had refused to negotiate. He described his generous concession of accepting a lower valuation of $200,000 for my businesses.

With that comment I saw red and could no longer contain myself. I interrupted him and from my seat across the table, I let him have it.

'I'm tired of your lies and mistruths, Tim. I'm not going to sit here and listen to your manufactured nonsense any longer. You were the company accountant from 2003 to 2012, and over that time you never once recorded a profit for the companies. I made a very reasonable settlement offer to you in 2012 and we were $117,000 apart in what we were both seeking. It was *you* who refused to negotiate, Tim, not me. Rather than negotiate with me, you threatened me. You told me that unless I accepted your offer you would destroy me. You then fabricated a valuation of $745,000 for my businesses with no supporting documentation or financial proof of that valuation. You took me to court on that basis. Your valuation was not based on actual figures. As my company accountant, you knew the businesses were basically worthless. You simply made the valuation up. You never thought I'd be able to defend myself against your lies in court, and you assumed you would be able to walk away with everything as a result. But, unluckily for you, Tim, I do actually have a backbone, and I am not about to have you take everything we had and everything I worked for. And that is why we are here today. It's not about you being conciliatory; it's about your threats and your lies. It's as simple as that.'

And with that, I shut my mouth and waited for the response.

Tim's lawyers immediately and abruptly turned and looked at Tim. I could see emotions of surprise and concern on their faces. The judge raised his left eyebrow again.

I believe neither Tim's solicitor or his barrister had read his original affidavit from early 2013. They were both unaware of his original lie. The judge was similarly in the dark until I set the record straight.

When we broke for lunch I felt despondent. Tim and his legal team were still playing hardball. They were making it clear they were only interested in settling if the figures were to be based on *his* valuations for the businesses and for the Mill property. They were ignoring the valuation reports from the professionals I had employed. He and his lawyers were refusing to take into consideration any adjustments for the money I had spent on the mortgage, accounting fees, income tax, GST, council rates, insurance, and maintenance for the Mill. I was doubtful an agreement could be reached.

The mood changed within the courtroom after lunch. His lawyers appeared to be more receptive to talking of average valuations for the Mill, rather than claiming Tim's inflated valuation as the basis for their calculations. Perhaps they had come to realise there was additional information and evidence he had withheld from them? Maybe they had talked some sense into him over lunch?

The judge carefully controlled the afternoon's proceedings. 'So, Tim, what's this about you taking a 20-foot container of chattels with you to Australia?' he asked.

'Well, the container wasn't full,' Tim responded.

I silently laughed as he had just confirmed information I had suspected all along.

I had a copy of a receipt for $5,165 from a removal company, that Tim had submitted as evidence in 2013. At the time, he was arguing how the move to Australia had cost him a lot of money. Some months later, he claimed to have taken very little with him to Australia. And despite stating in a lawyers letter dated June 2012 that all the household chattels had been evenly divided, Tim now claimed I was in possession of all our $182,000 worth of chattels.

I dealt with freight companies all the time with the importing business. I had emailed my freight consultant and asked him to tell me what volume of goods could be moved to Australia for $5,165. He informed me you could move a 20-foot container for that.

So when Tim responded to the judge saying the container wasn't full, I didn't actually know for sure if he had taken a 20-foot container until he admitted it to the judge.

I brought to the attention of the judge and Tim's legal team the existence of an affidavit that had been presented to the court in 2013 whereby he had claimed I was in possession of a painting and four light fittings. He claimed the collective value of these items was $35,000.

'I am more than happy to have the painting and the light fittings delivered to Tim's lawyers' office tomorrow if it pleases Your Honour. In that way we could wipe $35,000 off my side of the ledger and transfer it to Tim's side,' I suggested.

'That's a ridiculous idea. Those chattels have no value to my client,' responded Tim's barrister.

She fell right into my trap. I dangled that carrot knowing full well Tim didn't want the lights or the painting. I was just surprised it was the barrister, not Tim, who bit the carrot and confirmed that fact.

'Well, isn't that interesting,' I said to the barrister. 'If the chattels are of no value to Tim, as you say, then why don't we just wipe the entire value of the chattels off the board and be done with it.'

His barrister sat with pursed lips and glared at me. I had just outsmarted her and there was nothing she could say in response.

Despite the evidence we had, my solicitor did not argue that the chattels had already been divided evenly and fairly. I was required to compensate Tim $182,000, as I not only lost $91,000 in paying Tim for overvalued goods he already had in his possession, but I also lost the difference in value between the "book value" of goods I had in my possession. In hindsight, I wonder whether this was all part of the deal I now suspect my lawyer had arranged behind closed doors with Tim's lawyer, prior to the settlement conference.

At one point the judge asked me how the court action had affected Bella and me emotionally, and also how our day-to-day lives had been impacted. I explained that we had not been on holiday together in well over four years and that I had not been able to form a new relationship due to the pressures of the court case and because I had very little and irregular assistance with childcare. I told him I drove a very old car with over 460,000 kilometres on the clock and I couldn't afford to upgrade it.

The judge said, 'So, Emma, you have been suffering then?'

'Yes, sir. Both Bella and I have been suffering.'

At that, Tim interjected with considerable sarcasm. He leaned across the table and snarled, 'Oh really, Emma. You have suffered? Have you *really* suffered, though, Emma?'

His outburst was vulgar and distasteful. He showed bitter resentment, spite, and jealousy. It was plain to see. He almost spat at me across the table. And he did it in front of the judge.

Over and above the financial pressure, the personal cost of Tim's actions was expressed in missed opportunities – how little quality time I was able to share with Bella, and the trauma we both felt with Tim's abandonment and attacks. There was also the lack of time Bella had with her father and her realisation that he chose not to prioritise his time for her.

By 4 pm, we were edging closer to a settlement point. The smirk that had been plastered all over Tim's face during the morning had disappeared. He was scowling with bitter hatred. If he could have reached across the table and strangled me, he would have.

Tim lacked credibility, and his barrister, in particular, didn't know her facts. She became emotional and loud. At one point, she interrupted me as I described events that had occurred in early 2012. I rebuked her. 'You're commenting about events you know nothing of. You weren't there. You have no place to offer an opinion. Please keep your opinions to yourself,' I exclaimed.

Basically I was sick of the bullshit. I wasn't going to be bullied and manipulated any longer. And I didn't give a damn whether she was a high court barrister being paid $800 per hour or not. She didn't know what she was talking about, so I called her on it.

Tim argued he believed I was carrying more stock in the businesses than the accounts recorded. And yet he could hardly say, 'Well, Your Honour, when I was doing the accounts for Emma, I undervalued the stock, therefore I believe she is still doing it.'

Tim protested that some of the legal and accounting costs for my defence were being paid for by the companies. He was angry that I had the ability to distort the valuations of the businesses by assimilating costs through the companies and adjusting stock levels. Well, he should have thought of that before he deceived me, abandoned Bella and me, took me to court, tried to destroy me, and before he tried to take all our money.

As the day dragged on, the judge pulled us closer towards a mediated middle ground. Tim is all about control so he dug his toes in and refused to concede to the negotiation of $4,000 so we could settle, with me paying Tim $86,000 on top of other cash he would receive from one of our trusts. Tim wanted me to pay him $90,000, not $86,000.

The judge said, 'So, Tim, for the sake of $4,000 you are prepared to risk a four- to six-day court hearing that will happen eighteen months from now. That will cost you a minimum of $100,000 on top of the money you have already spent. A significant emotional cost will come with that. There is also litigation risk, Tim – you could lose to Emma. You could lose a whole lot more. So for the sake of $4,000, you are prepared to take that chance?'

'All right then. I'll take the $86,000,' snapped Tim.

Within a heartbeat I slapped the palm of my right hand forcefully on the table. I said, 'Excellent. I'll pay you $86,000. It's a deal. I'm tired. I want to go home.'

'I was only thinking about it,' replied Tim.

Typical. He just had to draw it out as long as he could.

The judge was getting annoyed. 'I see.' He raised his left eyebrow and inhaled.

'All right, I'll accept it. But I'll need time to think about it,' continued Tim.

Tim was trying to find an angle to come back at a later stage and demand more money, but the judge could see that and was having none of it.

'If you need to consider your position, Tim, you are welcome to talk to counsel in a meeting room. However, I strongly suggest it would be in both your best interests to settle this matter today,' instructed the judge. 'I'm in no hurry, I will stay until a settlement is agreed upon,' he said.

The words, 'OK then,' wheezed from Tim's pursed lips.

My lawyer came to court on 8 November 2016 with the settlement documents prepared. Financial sums and a few conditions were recorded, Tim and I signed the documents, and it was over.

I strode out of that meeting room at 6.15 pm in a bit of a daze. I breathed for the first time in four years and eight months.

We had just reached an agreement which would see Tim take all the remaining cash ($235,000) that was still being held in trust from the sale of our family home, back in 2012. I also had to give Tim a further $86,000 cash. He got to keep the $125,000 cash he took with him to Australia and another $100,000 that had already been released to him from one of our trusts. In exchange, I was assigned the full ownership of the Mill property and the businesses, including the remaining debt. Interestingly, the court completely disregarded the capital my father invested to relaunch the businesses and the fact the businesses were owned by my father's estate. I was forced to concede defeat over the distribution of household chattels.

I was experiencing a level of shock and mixed emotions of relief and defeat. Was the nightmare really over?

As we left the building, my lawyer apologised to me. She said the settlement was not a fair reflection of what I should have received.

Mel and I drove into Auckland and had a casual bite to eat at a restaurant on the harbour. I sat and sipped a glass of champagne in complete disbelief of my freedom. It was the first glass of alcohol I had consumed in months. My smile and bright eyes lit the night sky.

I rang my mother and told her my news. I rang Laura. I rang my friend Rob and my aunt. I spoke to Skye. I sent a personal text to Kate. I sent a group text to all my other close friends letting them know a settlement had been reached. Then Mel and I drove home.

thirty-four

The lingering white room

The completion of the courtroom drama came out of nowhere. I liken what followed next to being thrown into a white room with no map or doorway in sight. I wasn't prepared for how I might feel at the end. With no time to have scenarios play out as role plays inside my mind, fear still clung to my bones.

I was to learn the agreement that was reached at the Judicial Settlement Conference had very little to do with the previous four years of communication between the lawyers. Our past appearances in court stood for very little as well. The agreement was thrashed out on averages, not technicalities. Tim lied in affidavits and court evidence. Having proof of his lies appeared to be irrelevant.

My lawyers and the court didn't seem to care about the truth. The fact our household chattels would have been worth a maximum of $50,000, given fifteen years' wear and tear, made no difference. Having a legal document from Tim's lawyer, which stated Tim had taken half the chattels with him to Australia, seemed to be immaterial. I could beat my head against a wall only so many times. I was made to take the hit and move on.

Same thing with the businesses – I lost a considerable sum when I was forced to pay Tim for a half share in businesses that were actually owned by my father's estate. There was no acknowledgement of my father's significant financial investment in setting up the new companies. Again, was I seeing the fruit of a back-room deal struck between two opposing lawyers?

The issue of Tim siphoning marital funds prior to his departure was never mentioned. For all I knew, there could have been a $300,000 nest egg earning him interest in carefully hidden accounts in Australia.

Tim received no punishment for his lies, over and above the fact he was not successful in his goal of destroying me. I was unable to apply for a costs award against Tim because the matter was settled in a mediated conference.

My representation in court didn't exactly provide me with a level playing field; I had to pay forensic accountants to assist me. As a chartered accountant, Tim did not have the same professional fees to pay, as he was doing 95% of the accounting work himself. I spent in excess of $100,000 on accountants and a further $45,000 on business and property valuations in respect of the relationship property matter. In comparison, Tim would have paid no more than $20,000 in total to business and property valuers.

I believe my lawyers could have done a better job for me.

As time went on, it became obvious the law firm who represented me was firstly motivated by fee generation, and secondly, by fee collection. The partner of the firm who oversaw my case played a very clever game of determining a path which I believe inflated my fees and exhausted my financial resources. I was quite sure the fees escalated the moment he worked out my parents had money. Twice, he suggested my mother or my deceased father's estate should step in and settle my account for outstanding fees. I had concerns over the huge sums of money I was being charged. My requests to have copies of time sheets relating to the work they were doing for me were either ignored or denied.

Providing me with the best representation and pursuing the most favourable outcome for me was not the firm's primary focus. My emails and phone calls were often ignored. My affidavits were filed late. Despite judges' orders requesting discovery of Tim and his partner's personal financial information, these important documents were not provided. My repeated reminders to my lawyers to follow up and demand the missing information were ignored.

Why didn't my legal team go hard up against Tim's initial claim that the businesses were worth $745,000? Why didn't they force him to prove his claim at the beginning? If he had been forced to prove it, I believe considerable economies in time and cost would have been seen. It was obvious securing a resolution with efficiency was not the primary goal of the law firm.

The conversation in the 2015 British television crime drama *Broadchurch* (Season 2, Episode 8) between two barristers at the completion of a courtroom tussle, sums it up: "I don't see the nobility in this job. I see a loaded, lopsided game, full of people justifying their cynicism as a higher calling. It's street fighting in wigs, that's all."

I considered the justice system and whether I had received a fair settlement. Was there a difference between an outcome that was considered just as opposed to fair? A fair settlement typically occurs when all parties are satisfied with the outcome. A just settlement adheres to the laws of the land and the outcome is decided by a third party or a judge in a court of law. Fairness is subjective, while justice is objective.

After five years of harrowing, emotional wrangling through the court system that brought me close to financial ruin and almost claimed my life through suicide, I felt the system had failed me. I did not consider I was treated with respect, nor was I awarded a fair settlement. The outcome was unjust. Had the matter been dealt with over a five-day court hearing in front of a judge with a legal team that had my best interests at heart, then I do believe I would have had a better chance at a just outcome. But that situation never eventuated. Life is never served in a vacuum of best-laid-out circumstances. We live in a grey world filled with imperfection and compromise at every turn. I had no choice but to accept the outcome as it was if I wanted to move on with my life and leave pain in the past.

The settlement did, however, allow me to keep my home. I lost my marriage, my father, my confidence, priceless experiences with my daughter, and, for a time, I lost my career. I had prayed all along to hold on to my home. The court had allowed for that, at least.

I didn't wake up the morning following the Judicial Settlement Conference feeling light or happy. The night sweats stopped immediately; however, I was tired, dazed and *still* fearful. I realised psychological freedom from Tim was not going to be achieved overnight.

My high-conflict divorce had left me with post-traumatic stress disorder. I was experiencing the following:

1) flashbacks and nightmares
2) living with fear
3) high levels of anxiety, asthma, insomnia, difficulty in focusing and extreme vigilance
4) hesitation and abnormal levels of risk assessment before action
5) avoidance of people and situations that triggered memories of the trauma, or situations involving conflict.

I wished I could have sat with my father and been able to describe in detail how I thrashed it out with Tim across the courtroom. In spite of my fear, I was brave and unflappable as I faced his anger. Dad would have been so proud of me.

I whispered to my father, 'I did it, Dad. I really did it. I so wish you were here to see my smile.'

Tears of relief streamed from my eyes.

I still had financial responsibilities. That's just a fact of life. I had a daughter to provide for and a mortgage to service. But I knew I could handle that. As my Dad once said to me, "Your mother and I have helped you, Emma, because you have proven to us that you get up and you work. We believe in you. We know you will achieve your goal once you set your mind to it, and we know you will do everything and anything you can to assist yourself."

Four days after the Judicial Settlement Conference, I reopened the retail store in the Mill. I set about clearing older stock. With the revenue from the store, the wholesale business and some architectural work, I knew the businesses would be able to continue paying my weekly wage and the business overheads. I would be able to survive financially and start rebuilding my life.

In early 2017, my mother facilitated the release of the $100,000 I was due to inherit from my father's estate and I was able to pay Tim the $86,000 as per the settlement agreement. I was grateful for my parents' support.

All I had left to do was to set up a new trust and secure a mortgage for the Mill with the bank. Negotiating with the banks proved to be a challenging exercise. In the eyes of any bank, I was a solo mother from West Auckland with a part-time job. My chances of securing finance were not great.

I am not one to run from my fears or a challenge. So with the support of a dear friend, who now acts as a corporate trustee for my trust, I set about negotiating interest rates and terms with two banks with the aim of playing one off against the other.

After a few stressful months where nothing seemed to be happening and the settlement date loomed closer and closer, my plan worked; I was offered mortgage finance for the Mill property by two banks. By the time I had finished, I had a sharp interest rate and favourable terms. Bella and I were safe and secure in our home. I was relieved beyond words.

Going through a separation, divorce, and court battle has been one of the hardest, most gut-wrenching, tiring, and emotionally painful experiences of my life. And yet it has been the most liberating and rewarding experience at the same time. I rediscovered myself and grew intellectually, creatively, and spiritually through the process.

It was time to breathe again; to release my fear, and focus on love and happiness. I understood I still needed professional help to process my trauma. That time had come.

There is no future in hate and wanting to destroy someone. I wish Tim had realised that, for it would have saved us all so much pain and sadness.

thirty-five

Forgiveness

I was desperate to make sense of my situation – to understand, to forgive, and to move on. I knew my ability to one day emerge from the grief surrounding the breakdown of my marriage was connected to my ability to forgive Tim for what he did to Bella and me. Forgiveness would release the burden of sadness and anger I felt. Whether that journey would take me two or twenty years, I knew I had to persevere and continue working towards my goal.

Dr Airdre Grant wrote in her book *Stumbling Stones, A Path Through Grief, Love and Loss*:

> *We are issued a challenge, one that can feel unbearable, unreasonable and hateful. Yet the challenge is that we must survive and, even more if possible, survive to be richer and stronger. Our loss never leaves and maybe, just maybe, we gain in ways we never knew would nourish our wounded hearts.*

I considered how I was able to forgive my father for what he did to me as a child. Despite how his actions had changed me, and despite all the pain I endured, with time, I was able to move past my anger. Even though he never apologised to me, in his own way he was able to right some wrongs by helping me when I reached out to him. His acts of kindness were olive branches that he extended to me in exchange for mine. I was able to forgive him and genuinely love him.

I considered the depth of my determination and my ability to control my attitudes and responses to stressful situations. Had I developed those skills as a direct result of the sexual abuse I had suffered in my childhood? Was I stronger as a consequence of that suffering?

I am grateful for my strength, as without it, I would never have been able to withstand the pressure of the discovery and/or suspicion of my ex-husband sleeping with men. Nor would I ever have been able to cope with the trauma of being dragged through court for almost five years. And yet I believe the decision I made to marry Tim came about because of the fragility I felt because of the abuse I had suffered at the hands of my father.

I thanked my father and cursed him in the same breath, as I did to my ex. Even for the hardships I endured through my marriage and the five years since, I was served a challenge: What did I want from life? How much did I want it? What was I prepared to do to achieve my dreams? What type of mother was I?

I likened my life experiences to a carousel of cause and effect, where outcomes fed off each other. I had acquired skills and knowledge that have helped me achieve my goals. For example, the self-control I had to harness to overcome my eating disorders in my earlier years and the knowledge of nutrition I learned along the way actually helped me achieve my bodybuilding goals.

I never told my ex-husband about my years battling eating disorders. He never knew the true depth of my inner strength. When I was forced to defend myself in court under a cloud of almost certain failure, I am sure my levels of dogged determination came as quite a surprise to him.

My journey to forgiving Tim would follow its own path. For a start, I could see the intent to harm was expressed very differently between Tim and my father. Tim deceived me from the beginning. He denied me the right of informed choice. He used me to breed and he wallowed in the spoils of my labour. I was manoeuvred into a position of vulnerability so he could have control over me and our joint finances. Tim plotted to destroy me with no regard to the welfare of our child.

If he had been open and honest about his sexuality, he would have had no choice but to step back and accept that he was wrong to have dragged me into marriage without full disclosure of his lifestyle. But he wasn't honest.

My father, on the other hand, may not have had any understanding of the long-term impact of his actions on my life when he chose to sexually abuse me. He probably thought I wouldn't remember what happened. I believe my father paid dearly for his mistake, and I do believe he tried to make amends for his actions in the final years of his life.

I wondered how my life would have turned out if my father hadn't abused me. I believe I would have made different choices. Whether or not they would have been good ones is impossible to know.

As opposed to my father, Tim showed no remorse or willingness to right any wrongdoing. He continued to attack me at every opportunity.

It is not easy to forgive, particularly when a betrayal has been deliberate and methodical.

When considering how I might forgive Tim, I realised that no two situations or individuals are the same, therefore the path to forgiveness will similarly be different and occur over a variable time frame. I don't think it's as simple as one day saying: "From this point on, I forgive that person for what they have done" because saying and feeling are two different things.

I considered what I stood to lose by holding on to my anger and pain. I also imagined how my life would be if I was able to let go of the past.

I made lists of the things I wanted to do, places I wanted to visit, and the qualities I sought in relationships. I wrote of what I needed to change in my life to allow me to achieve my dreams. I was determined to look ahead to the future with positivity.

thirty-six

Psithurism

Psithurism *(n.)* the sound of the wind in the trees and rustling leaves.

Sometime in 2015, I made a promise to myself: If I was able to survive Tim's legal attack and emerge with a thread of my financial shirt on my back and my sanity intact, I would allow myself to travel somewhere exotic, to take time out to reflect, to recharge, and to breathe. I had nowhere specific in mind at first. Just somewhere far away from my everyday life. A place where I was unreachable. Somewhere to find peace and tranquillity with the sights, sounds, feels, and smells of nature.

In late May 2017, I stood on the porch of a little log cabin in the woods of the Colorado Rocky Mountains and I held on to the wooden rail in front of my body with both hands. All I could hear was the low, humming rustle of a light breeze through the tall pines that enveloped me. I inhaled the crisp, mountain air and felt tears gently roll down my cheeks. I heard myself quietly say, 'Thank You, Lord, for bringing me to this place. Thank You for giving me the strength and courage to fight. Words will never truly convey how grateful I am to be here in this place.'

Part of my decision to come to the ranch was to complete the final few chapters of my manuscript. I wanted to close the chapter of my old life before I could wipe the slate clean and start afresh. The rugged beauty of the wilderness gave me the peace and freedom I needed to complete my story.

Four years earlier, when I began journaling and scribbling poems onto scraps of paper and receipts retrieved from my handbag, I had no idea I would write a book.

At first, my musings were outpourings of grief as I struggled to process the pain I was experiencing with the discovery of my husband's bisexuality, and his abandonment.

My story lay hidden within a coarse slab of clay. I savoured the writing journey and likened it to working at a potter's wheel; I cut back the crude layers of clay and the pretence of face; I let mud ooze through my fingers to reveal the hurts and stories I had buried so long ago. The memory of bitter betrayals made me spit with despair; countless times I felt the writing process take its brutal toll. Reliving pain over and over again, as I read and rewrote chapters, was by far the most difficult part of the writing journey. Still, I forced myself to see my task through to the end.

Writing gave me the freedom to purge pain onto paper. I was able to analyse my thoughts – was that how I truly felt or was I just having a bad day? Was I damaging myself with my behaviour? Could I do better?

There is never a single truth when writing of the past. Every act and thought is subjective as each party to the experience retains a different memory. Recollections of events and the emotions attached to those memories also change over time. Memories fade and are sometimes forgotten. Anyone's story is only ever how *they* remember it. Others may remember things differently.

Writing brought my memories back to life. They were no longer idle musings running rampant as a confusing labyrinth inside my head. They were all of a sudden real and they meant something. Perhaps my experiences and the decisions I made along the way might be of benefit to others as a means of insight and guidance moving forward.

I could have been consumed by bitterness and anger. I could have been swallowed by the enormity of day-to-day struggles. It would have been easy to have given in to the pressures that swirled all around me. But life happens, shit happens – to us all. Why should I have been spared?

Despite my past, or perhaps because of it, I have chosen acceptance and love over anger.

I discovered the true test of my humanity was not held within the cards I was dealt. My story became less about how others had treated me and more about how I responded in return. That was my lesson.

I will be judged for the decisions I have made, for my vulgarities, and for my opinions I have chosen to share. I have faults and failings, as does the next person.

I am happy to own them. These experiences have grounded me and made me appreciative of the life I have been gifted.

My story is about the truth. It is not about being pretty or compliant. It is a story of survival, of trying my best, protecting my child, and never giving up.

I will continue to be grateful for Bella, for our health, our family, and our friends. I have been blessed with resilience and an ability to cope. Even through some of my darkest days, I realised things could have been a lot worse. I didn't have cancer, for example, and Bella was well and happy. I had skills and abilities and a future to look forward to, whatever path I chose, or was forced to take.

Waking up in my log cabin, surrounded by the beauty of the Colorado Rocky Mountains, I felt I had arrived home. Countless times, in periods of stress and pain, I escaped to this place of calm through dreams, art and verse. Childhood memories were awakened: walking through thigh-high grass, wading through creeks and rivers, the smell of country air.

Adventurous by nature, I thrive on the challenge of "what if", "I can't wait", and "let's see". We weren't put on this earth to clock in and check out.

A woman who served me in a roadside diner, not far from my log cabin, warned me of bears and mountain lions. 'Probably best not to venture out alone,' she said. 'Two joggers were taken by mountain lions in our town in the past few years. Be very careful.'

I craved to inhale the mountain air and listen to the chorus of wind in aspen trees. I longed to drink water from babbling brooks, hear birdsong, and buzzing bees. Into a small backpack I bundled supplies for the day. I slid a sizeable knife from the cutlery drawer through my belt, and off I went.

The terrain was damp and boggy; it had snowed the previous day. I was being careful how I placed my feet for fear of injury.

Across grassy fields, through pine and conifer trees I wandered. Up steep inclines and rocky terrain I climbed.

The air grew thin; I struggled to breathe. I saw persistent snow flurries cower in the shade of trees. There were moose tracks aplenty, but their companions chose not to be seen. I watched an elk graze upon sweet spring grass. A fox looked up before he quickly ran past. I was able to capture a snapshot of his luscious and bushy, rust-coloured tail. I wanted to reach out and touch him.

As I perched on a large rock within a grove of aspens, I savoured the beautiful vista as far as my eyes could see. I sat for an hour and felt the wind dance. My eyes trailed butterflies, and I listened to a woodpecker hammer among the trees.

I heard my heart gently sing.

thirty-seven

But love …

Sex is an itch you just scratch,
But love …
It's the itch so far down your back,
You can't ever reach it with your own hand

River, British television drama, 2015.
Written by Abi Morgan. Episode 1.4

As the days came and went, and I was afforded the mental space to breathe and think, I came to realise I had not only fought for a secure future for Bella and me, but I had also fought for a chance to find true love.

I understood that without financial freedom, I would be denied the luxury of choice. To wake and now live unfettered, free from the fear of losing our home, and also without the distraction of legal proceedings, I discovered I had more time to focus on Bella and my career.

And with love … I decided I would stay single until I was sufficiently healed, enough to make the right choice for the right reasons.

I thought of, and compared, the differences between romantic lust and lasting true love. I could clearly see I had experienced the sweat and burn of romantic lust, but had I ever felt true love?

Was I being realistic to yearn for a heartfelt, honest love that is filled with passion?

Are our relationships merely reflections of our own fantasies?

Would I need to be more realistic and temper my expectations, to "let go" of myself and compromise, if I was to settle down with a man?

Perhaps I needed to shed my independence in part and expose my vulnerabilities to allow a man to care for me?

But how could I deny myself my own true heart and step away from who I was at my core?

To make space for love, I understood I had to open my heart, take risks and be brave in spite of my fear.

Everyone's needs in a loving and committed relationship are different. To me, love must walk hand in hand with freedom. I am wired to seek out new experiences, to challenge myself, and to strive for goals. I hope to be able to continue upon this pathway without the fear of jealousy.

> *I heard what you said. I'm not the silly romantic you think. I don't want the heavens or the shooting stars. I don't want gemstones or gold. I have those things already. I want … a steady hand. A kind soul. I want to fall asleep, and wake, knowing my heart is safe. I want to love, and be loved.*
>
> *The Dream Thief*, Shana Abé

I believe love is living with the security of knowing my partner will do the things he says he will do. Our daily interactions will centre around laughter, kind words, and gestures of encouragement with no expectation of return. He will challenge me and inspire me to become a better person.

Admiration, pride, and respect are words I will naturally think of as I describe him to my peers. I will be able to depend on my partner and trust him with my heart. With time, I will forget how it ever felt to hear the words, "I'm sorry". The man I love will be at his best when I am at my worst. He will know I would never hesitate to do the same for him.

I daydreamed of how it might feel to meet my true love. I imagined the warmth in my heart, my beaming smile, and the sparkle of excitement in my eyes.

Welcome us home

Where do you hide
With your scorching eyes?
And your stories of mirth
To ache my belly?

Captivate me with your intelligence
Let your warmth smoulder
And gently chisel my frost-caked
Broken heart

Walk with presence
To confidently claim all you own
And with humility
To respect
All who have nothing and no one

Accept me for who I am
Allow me the freedom
To adore you
Wildly
Without reservation

Love my daughter
Shelter us
Welcome us home

My heart was finally free.

Epilogue

Time heals in slow motion, and fears are not relinquished easily. Communication with Tim remains sporadic and unsettling for me. Despite his considerable income, Tim continues to thwart the system. He pays $78 per month in child support and defies the terms of the parenting order. He rarely sees Bella.

In mid-2018, an investigation was launched into the actions of my lawyers over the manner in which my case was managed and represented. Where most would tremble beneath the shadow and might of a law firm, I bravely brought them to account. The matter was settled at mediation in December 2019.

My friends remain steadfast and loyal with their unconditional love and support of Bella and me. To my friends, I love you all and will be forever in your debt for the kindness I have been shown.

Sadly, my courageous and brave friend Mia passed away in January 2019. Watching her once-vibrant spirit fade and witnessing her suffering was heartbreaking. Through all her pain she was never angry, bitter or jealous. She taught me to love unconditionally, to be patient, grateful and kind. Beautiful souls like Mia's are rare. Rest in peace, my treasured friend; you will be remembered.

The importing business will be sold and I have plans to move. I am ready for change; a fresh start. In mid-2019, I realised a lifelong ambition and attended a month-long fine arts summer school programme at the École des Beaux-Arts in the Latin Quarter of Paris. For a brief few weeks I was able to step through the looking glass and live the life I had always dreamed of. My days were filled with colour, light, painting, drawing, sculpture, gallery visits, walking, sunshine, space, parks, culture, sophistication, philosophy and inspiration at every turn.

Back home I continue to work and provide for my daughter. I attend the gym as often as I can; however, it is unlikely I will have the time and mental focus required for competition-level bodybuilding this year. I have not ruled out participation in the future.

PEWC has grown and now has a membership of eight dynamic and hilarious women. We continue to support and encourage each other in the challenges we all face as solo mothers. Raucous laughter, anger, tears and joy all come along for the wild ride that is our friendship. In February 2020, PEWC took part in the Great Lake Relay – a 155-kilometre relay around Lake Taupō. Our team dressed as 1980s aerobics instructors. We had a wonderful time together although many of us could barely move for days afterwards.

Bella continues to thrive and has blossomed into a vibrant, kind and considerate pre-teen. She brings me joy every day and I am so proud to be her mother. She radiates warmth and has a charming, quick wit about her. I can't wait to see what her future will bring.

Life has a curious habit of leading us along a winding path back to our beginning.

I have happy memories of being five years old and waiting for the school bus with the neighbour's kids. We threw stones, teased each other and scuffed our shoes on the dusty ground. I remember being intrigued by the attractive and cheeky elder brother of my oldest friend who stood next to me. At the time I had no idea my childhood curiosity for him would lead me to love.

I lost touch with him when he joined the army at the age of eighteen. In 2018, as I paid for my groceries at the local supermarket, he walked over to me and back into my life.

He is … the Soldier.

List of Poems by Emma Rivers

Reference List

Abé, Shana, 2007. "I heard what you said …", from *The Dream Thief*. Published by Bantam and Random House Publishing Group.

Chibnall, Chris, 2015. *Broadchurch*, British television drama. Directed by Mike Barker. Episode 8.

Congreve, William, 1693. *The Old Bachelor*.

Cope, Wendy, 2002. "Two Cures For Love", from *Serious Concerns*. Published by Faber & Faber.

Corona, E. Various quotes.

Fitch, Janet, 2001. *White Oleander*. Published by Little, Brown and Company.

Grant, Airdre, 2016. *Stumbling Stones – A Path Through Grief, Love and Loss*. Published by Hardie Grant.

Morgan, Abi, 2015. *River*, British television drama. Directed by Richard Laxton. Made by Kudos. Distributed globally by Shine International. Episodes 1.3, 1.4 and 1.6.

Waheed, Nayyirah. "Advice for young writers", from *Salt*. Published by CreateSpace Independent Publishing Platform, 2013.

Waheed, Nayyirah. "Therapy", from *Salt*. Published by CreateSpace Independent Publishing Platform, 2013.

Made in the USA
Columbia, SC
22 July 2021

42228320R00137